Breaking Bread

Every loaf of bread starts with a good lievito madre, this book is dedicated to mine. A woman who has taught me it is possible to move through life with positivity and love in the face of endless challenges.

Also for my bread and butter –
Billie, Annie, Lorien and Wilfred.

Breaking Bread

How Baking Shaped Our World

David Wright

Aurum

Quarto

First published in 2025 by Aurum
an imprint of The Quarto Group.
One Triptych Place, London, SE1 9SH
United Kingdom
T (0)20 7700 9000
www.Quarto.com

EEA Representation, WTS Tax d.o.o., Žanova ulica 3, 4000 Kranj, Slovenia

Text © 2025 David Wright
Design © 2025 Quarto Publishing Plc

David Wright has asserted his moral right to be identified as the Author of this Work in accordance with the Copyright Designs and Patents Act 1988.

All rights reserved. No part of this book may be reproduced or utilised in any form or by any means, electronic or mechanical, including photocopying, recording or by any information storage and retrieval system, without permission in writing from Aurum.

Every effort has been made to trace the copyright holders of material quoted in this book. If an application is made in writing to the publisher, any omissions will be included in future editions.

A catalogue record for this book is available from the British Library.

ISBN 978-0-71129-488-2
EBOOK ISBN 978-0-71129-490-5

10 9 8 7 6 5 4 3 2 1

Art Director: Paileen Currie
Cover Design and Illustration: Lisa Maltby
Editorial Director: Jenny Barr
Publisher: Richard Green
Senior Editor: Charlotte Frost
Senior Production Controller: Rohana Yusof

Typeset in Garamond Premier Pro by SX Composing DTP, Rayleigh, Essex SS6 9HQ

Printed by CPI Group (UK) Ltd, Croydon, CR0 4YY

Contents

	Foreword	1
	Introduction	5
1:	**Why Bread?**	21
	Creating, making, baking	
2:	**The Wheel of Life**	53
	A loaf's cycle	
3:	**Frankenloaf**	77
	Science and the perfect bread	
4:	**Sicker by the Slice**	101
	A marriage not made in heaven	
5:	**Big Bread**	131
	Industrial vs artisan bakeries	
6:	**The Breadline**	161
	The economics of a crust	
7:	**Flour Power**	183
	The politics of bread	
8:	**Bloody Bread**	203
	The costs of conquest	
9:	**Our Daily Bread**	227
	What the gods want	
10:	**Breaking bread**	243
	A once ropey baker looks to the future	
	Acknowledgements	261

Foreword

For the past thirty odd years, baking bread has been my place on the bookshelf of life. And though I started and worked in bakeries during that time, and have written about it at length, there have been many aspects of earning that crust that I've never discussed publicly – only privately with other bakers. Not that these discussions have been especially hushed and secretive: simply that some things are just easier to talk about with a baker who knows what you mean, gets the complication and feels a similar way to you. Sharing thoughts, complaints, contradictions about baking life and how that bread you're eating came to exist.

That's what I respond to most in David Wright's book. He steps right in there, taking you through the labyrinth of daily choices that face the baker who's trying to do their best while making a buck to survive until tomorrow.

As the third generation to take the helm of his family's bakery in Suffolk, where they'd been baking for seventy-five years, David has seen changes in customers' habits. He's witnessed the shift from people simply buying their everyday bread, sold in pound weights each morning, to today's customer, worried if it's 'authentic sourdough' and quizzing the shop assistant on how sustainable and rare grain the flour used is. From a time when women were expected to stay at home and bought their bread from the high street each morning, to today, where bakeries stay open all weekend but close for the first few days in the week instead. Where bakeries now stay open late into the evening to try and catch customers lured by the extended opening hours of supermarkets.

David sees, as I and hopefully you do, too, the inherent beauty in these hand-crafted loaves, the time and effort they represent. The way the seam of the dough runs neatly under the bottom crust (have a look next time), the sharpness of the blade that cuts that dashing sail-like fin that tears the loaf open, the flecks from the bran of different flour types that almost imperceptibly appear in the crumb, the level of shine and blistering that appears on the crust telling you the temperature it was matured at, and the steam that was formed when it baked.

Each loaf of bread is a co-operative venture involving hundreds of people, from the farm to the table, who rely on each other to make those connections smooth. When the world broke down during the pandemic, we all experienced firsthand how flour and bread availability suffered first. And it was arguably weird things that caused problems: breakdowns in the bagging equipment millers used to pack flour, something we customers never think about, caused supply problems under the strain. Truck drivers were reportedly unwilling to deliver into cities when the first fears about the virus were announced. While customers started panic-stockpiling flour and yeast, wondering if they would have to home bake for evermore.

We see in times of war, like now, where the bombing of bakeries and the severing of bread supplies is a tactical move to break citizens and starve them into submission. Russia's invasion of Ukraine caused blockades that stopped wheat from flowing easily to market, and sharply increased its cost, as David discusses in the book. And that means the price of flour increases, the price of bread skyrockets and, suddenly, life at a small bakery thousands of miles away becomes much harder. Same for rising fuel costs, which has caused many bakeries to shut when the economics of staying open stopped making sense.

Then there's the physical toll on the baker in working through the night on often little food and sleep to bake those beautiful breads for the morning. The excitement about baking right now, driven by books and TV shows, has called siren-like to avid home bakers to give up their day jobs and open a bakery, to risk everything to follow their dream. Going from making a loaf for friends to praise every time – *'you should bake for a living you know'* – to setting up on the high street at huge expense servicing daily customers who wonder why your bread is so much more expensive compared to the supermarket's, and stales so quickly compared to those much cheaper loaves.

David's book arrives at a crucial moment, as we grapple with questions about food security, sustainability and the true cost of what we eat. Through his deeply personal story of family legacy and loss, we gain insight into larger truths about our relationship with bread, that most basic yet profound of foods. His journey from inheriting a family bakery to its eventual closure, and then finding renewal in the craft he thought had broken him, mirrors the broader story of bread itself: how it must be broken to give life, how it can be reformed and made new.

This isn't just a book about bread though – it's about community, craft and the choices we make about how to feed ourselves and each other. David brings both practical wisdom and philosophical depth to questions that affect us all. What makes good bread? Who should make it? How do we balance tradition with progress?

At a time when industrial food systems are being questioned and artisan skills are being rediscovered, *Breaking Bread* offers a clear-eyed view of where we've been and where we might go next. It's essential reading for anyone who cares about the future of food, craft and community.

– Dan Lepard, London, 2024

Introduction

*Bread is a generous gift of nature, a food that can be
replaced by no other ... It is so perfectly adapted to men
that we turn our hearts to it almost as soon as we are born
and never tire of it to the hour of our death.*

Antoine-Augustin Parmentier, (1772)

Flour, water and salt. In its simplest form that's all bread is. Three
ingredients. That's all you need. This staple of life, this foodstuff
that has been around since civilisation began, has existed in different forms, in different peoples, and is that simple. Water and salt
provided by nature, wheat cultivated, harvested, threshed and
milled. If alchemy is the art of taking base materials and turning
them into gold, or an eternal elixir, then baking *is* alchemy.

Bread is more than its ingredients. While it can be a simple
combination of flour, water and salt, it rarely is. For me, the
most important added ingredient in breadmaking is the baker.
I have grown up around artisan or craft bakeries, places that have
accentuated the human interaction with dough. The character of
the artisan baker and their bread is entwined. That's what 'artisan'

6 | BREAKING BREAD

means to me, it is an indication of the way in which the quality can be measured. By calling a loaf 'artisan' it doesn't make it somehow better or more valuable; for me it is simply an admission that its quality is defined by the person who made it.

I have shared dough-shaping tables with beautiful, skilful and honest people and the bread we made reflected those qualities. I have also made bread with people whom I knew to be deceitful, duplicitous and mean – again the loaves were marked with these indelible character notes. Every baker's bread tells you something about their character. I am unable to escape my own and when I speak of bread in this book, despite my best efforts at impartiality, I will be tethered to my perspective.

I'm from a small village in rural Suffolk in the UK. It's the bottom half of the arse-like herniation that protrudes into the North Sea and forms the coast of East Anglia. Often described as flat with huge skies, this does it a disservice. Suffolk is a magical place, a living larder – with sea, rivers, forests and fertile flood plains. My childhood was spent in barns, in fields and by ponds. To temper how romantic that sounds, the activities were usually less innocent – throwing cans of deodorant onto bonfires or using agricultural marker spray to graffiti on the walls in the local farmyards were as likely pastimes as collecting frogspawn or hatching ducklings.

My appreciation for anything is enhanced if it's a bit broken. I love old shoes, trousers with holes in and people who have had to overcome great personal challenges. My love for bread is not based on it being perfect but for all its imperfections, and although I will suggest in this book that the baking industry is broken, it doesn't stop me from loving it. The proof is that I managed to find the energy to write this book at all, sandwiched between nightshifts

INTRODUCTION | 7

and childcare, I have found this process supremely challenging and restorative. When I began the book I felt like a broken baker but now having come to terms with my own personal challenges and the challenges faced by my industry, I am ready to go again.

Growing up in the sticks taught me to be curious, for better or worse, and how to occupy my mind in the absence of any age-appropriate stimulation. It could have been a very ordinary and sheltered upbringing but my mother and four older sisters brought a global influence into the house. My Mama, who is a master in the Japanese healing practice of Reiki has always been connected to a worldwide network of friends and while I was growing up our house always felt very open to guests.

Hospitality is at the heart of baking, and bread is a wonderful conduit for care. This is what has kept my passion alive, the love language of baking and the belief that its heart is pure. It is from this place of love that I write this book. A love for the place I'm from and the food that has defined me.

I have been a baker for most of my life. My ancestors were bakers. I smelled bread, played with the dough, tasted it even before I have memory. And through my career, I've seen the best and worst of the industry. I have worked in bakeries supplying the most prestigious food halls in Britain, Selfridges and Harrods, pristine operations that have the highest of standards. And I have worked in places infested with rodents popping their heads through gas burners, and all manner of insects crawling the walls. I've baked in the muddy fields of music festivals, in royal woodlands and on campfires. I've pretty much done it all. And that's what I'm sharing here. *Breaking Bread* is a mix of my life experience and that of my parents and grandparents, along with the many authors and people I listened to while in the bakery, on

8 | BREAKING BREAD

my own, while I created bread. It's knowledge learnt, knowledge lived and knowledge borrowed.

At the forefront of this book is bread. It has its own voice, its own life, for once the ingredients combine, many processes take place of their own accord. Transmutation of starches into sugars, formation of complex protein bonds, cell reproduction, gases expelled and encapsulated. The cold fire of fermentation breathing life into the inert clay and the hot fire of the oven forging this precious edible treasure into its own unique form.

Bread is simple. Or is it? The three ingredients at its core certainly appear to make it so at first glance. Yet it fulfils so many functions. It is central to our world. It serves our needs, fuels us, frees us from hunger. It has the power to do so many things: to civilise, unite, mend old feuds. It can be shared, stockpiled, withheld to punish or debase. It is a currency in itself, a gift and a curse. Bread can be elitist, common, and everything in-between. It can be pure and adulterated. Honest and nefarious.

Imagine the archetypal loaf of bread. Maybe it's a replica of a loaf you ate as a child, the one you made yourself as an adult or one you bought in the store. Just take some time to visualise it, the detail. Here is mine.

It has a glassine-blistered crust, bronzed but not evenly so, the recipient of a thousand fiery kisses. Where the belly of the loaf has rested on the hearth, the flanks arch upwards. The base is a dusty caramel, a thick sole but of the finest leather – deep, dark and complex.

The body has been frozen by fire, yet you can sense its vitality in every tiny, ruptured shard of varnished starch. When freshly peeled from the oven, the wafer-thin crust cracks as it meets the cold air of the bakery, the sounds punctuating the quiet. This percussion is accompanied by an intoxicating perfume.

Sweet. Earthy. It unlocks some deep carnal attraction, bypassing all the superficial layers of human existence, hitting a bass note that sends shivers through every synapse.

Once cool and cut, the honeycomb crumb inside is open to the world, soft white and flecked with bran. The sweet crust yields, when pushed, releasing a riff of robust flavours. It just has to be tasted. The texture is strong, with enough resilience to withstand a strong stroke of a knife loaded with not-yet-soft butter. Toasted grains, yogurt notes, creaminess in abundance and the warm blanket-like texture enriches the mouth, the body and mind, with every bite. That's the bread of my imagination.

Yet my loaf is not the one most of us encounter on a daily basis. The store-bought loaf, wrapped in plastic. A standard emoji – white, sliced, the very essence of homogeneity. I've eaten this loaf more than my imagined one – and about 80 per cent of the loaves available to us, in the West, conform to this type. The slices have the texture of roof insulation and will break if handled too roughly. They are tasteless, even odourless.

The crumb of the homogenous loaf can take only the softest of butters or margarine – even the lightest downward pressure breaks the aerated centre from the pallid, enfeebled crust. Yet this flyweight dominates the bakery market. Champion of Champions, the Great White Hope.

There is such a deep connection between humans and our trusty, crusty companion. A white farmhouse loaf, a dark rye brick, freshly baked baguette or soft buttery brioche, a tortilla, pitta, chapati – each of us has a different idea of what constitutes bread. And our relationship with it is personal. For some it is a staple, part of every meal, for others it is a poison to be avoided, its very ingredients making us unwell.

10 | BREAKING BREAD

Bread, made from a mix of flour, water and (sometimes) yeast, which is then baked, is an essential part of our history, every civilisation, every nation in the world, having a variant of it, something we can now experience firsthand through globalisation, migration, the internet. Bread is not just the white loaf I've described. Your ideal bread may, in fact, be different.

And yet isn't that the point?

Bread is a connecting piece of the human experience. It brings people together. We 'break bread' with each other and get to know each other better through doing so. The big three grains of wheat, rice and maize are undoubtedly ubiquitous but the products that come from them are wonderfully diverse. To me, it seems that bread is the most universal of products. If asked to cater a meal for the population of the globe, I would start with a basket of bread. A mix of flatbreads and fluffy rolls – made using whole grain flour. Simple and unpretentious, accessible to all, a perfect place to start a conversation. A relationship.

This is a book about bread, written by me, a baker. My qualification to speak on the subject has not been earned through academic study but through experience, hard graft and a love for what I do. I began working in the family bakery, aged eleven, sweeping floors and cleaning fridges, coming in at the scrag-end of the shift. I went on to work in other bakeries, such as Lily Vanilli, Pump Street Bakery and even did a voluntary stint at E5 Bakehouse, times I'll refer to later in this book. Bread has informed everything about me, my birth announced in the window display of the family bakery, festooned with blue balloons and teddy bears. I repeated that tradition when my daughter was born, displaying her birthweight as a pile of bread. So, bread really is part of the fabric of my being, central to my life, my history, upbringing. It has shaped me. My life story. And I'm not the only one.

Everything about me was tied to the bakery shop. Three storeys of Suffolk red brick, built in 1860, between a fire station and The White Hart Pub. After that first year as a barber's shop, there has been a bakery on this site, for over 150 years. The ghosts of bakers from three families – the Burkitts, Daniels, Wrights – watch over the centre of the small town of Woodbridge. Both of my children came straight to that building from the hospital. My ghost was supposed to remain there, but now, evicted, it must find another resting place. For various and many reasons, it was through *my* fingers that the end came. That the realities of the modern-baking world, poor decision-making and family legacy brought the bricks crashing down and the doors to close. After the bakery business folded, the site became a retail outlet for a semi-industrial bakery from out of town.

Before that, flour came to the back door via an alleyway and flowed through the rooms of the somewhat haphazard, antiquated building. Once the bread, rolls, cakes and biscuits were finished, they made their way onto the shop floor and out into the community in white paper bags stowed carefully in the hands and then bags of our loyal customers. It was a local bakery, yes, but the kind of bakery that is universal. I've connected with bakers all over the world who have been part of a similar family operation, some multi-generational, like mine. The pressures, the expectations, the way that identities are shaped from the same mould.

As an adult, I have worked countless night shifts, tipping bags of flour lovingly, tiredly, into mixers, cutting dough into fermentation tubs, scaling, shaping and baking loaves in a rhythm dictated by a soup of microscopic conductors. A nightly meditation on the purpose of all this arguably energy-rich food, punctuated by long periods of alone time, listening to the graveyard slot on BBC Radio 2, my channel of choice.

After attempting to follow my self-seeded passion of theatre, I had resigned myself to a life as a baker, something in my blood, attempting to find peace in the monotony and cycle of time, each tomorrow baked with yesterday's dough. A vampiric existence, lived under moonlight, with snatched naps during the day. Sometimes lonely, often sleep deprived and unsatisfied, I have, at times, questioned whether bread is a good thing. And certainly, over the years, that's a question that others have asked me, too.

It makes you fat, bloats you, binds you up. It's too expensive, too cheap, too soft, too hard ... We've heard it all when it comes to bread and its validity.

Celebrities tell us of its evils. An example – in 2021, actor and GOOP founder Gwyneth Paltrow was mocked in the media for saying on the SmartLess podcast that she went '*totally off the rails*' during the Covid Lockdowns, drinking alcohol and eating bread. *Gasp.* Yet Ms Paltrow's words are not uncommon. At food markets, I have watched people gaze lasciviously at the baked produce temptingly displayed on my stall, only to announce, 'I can't, it's not good for me. I *must* be good.' At moments like these, it feels like I'm selling food laced with asbestos. But why is that the case? When did bread become a measure of good and evil? Of madness and sanity?

This all got me thinking on the subject, pondering on whether there's some truth to what's being said not just to me in person, but reported in the media, in magazines, on the TV, Instagram,

TikTok. Is bread really that bad? It's a question important to me. It's my heritage and possibly my legacy.

I am the son of a baker, himself the son of a baker. Three unbroken generations, with skills passed down, hand to hand, father to son. A primogenital fantasy, allowing only the balding, white men access to the font of knowledge. A trail of breadcrumbs that stretches from the present day in 2024 all the way back to 1946. Each crusty little nugget, a signifier of a punishing shift, staring bleary-eyed into the mouth of an oven. And I was lucky to draw inspiration from the wonderful women in my family too: a food-obsessed mother and grandmothers who gave me some of my earliest, most precious gastronomic memories, many associated with spoon licking and pilfering from the biscuit tin. My family has, over generations, witnessed an explosion of change in the baking world – and the world at large. The gleaming edge of progress has scythed its course through the post-war age, moving so fast at times that there's still a lot to catch up on.

All of this accumulated knowledge is a hoard of treasure. The only truly valuable thing my family possessed, and the only thing the bailiffs and money lenders had no interest in collecting. I now teach at the Pump Street Workshop in the village of Orford, where I can share this legacy and knowledge with bakers who can, in turn, pass what is, I feel, precious cargo down through their own families and baking teams, too.

In *Breaking Bread*, my personal narrative is central to the more universal questions about bread and baking. About the people who make and shape the bread we buy and the difficulties that social and cultural change, food fads and health directives have had, and are having, on our industry. Our family bakery sadly closed its doors after seventy-five years, the bread we created had

14 | BREAKING BREAD

fed generations, people who stayed in the area and who moved away, changing communities which, in turn, fed into the way we operated as people, bakers and as a business. And yet does the closure of the bakery underline the very idea that bread is a dying foodstuff? Is it good or bad? And what does that even mean? If I want to make some value judgements on something so important to me, and to millions of other people, it makes sense to understand what those values are. So, I called on an old friend to get some perspective.

Chris Cowie is Professor in Philosophy at the University of Durham and specialises in how we think, right and wrong, good and bad. I first met Chris at King's College, in London where I was studying English with Film at the height of my efforts to create a career for myself outside of a bakery. We were in the same halls of residence and on the first morning there, I set the toaster on fire by putting a croissant into it. There was a cautionary sign above it, instructing me to refrain from doing this, but I assumed *that* was for non-bakers. Chris is a Northern Irishman who couldn't resist the opportunity to see the stupid Englishman who'd done that, up close and personal. So, you could say bread brought us together.

'There are a lot of different kinds of "good" and "bad", probably not as many as there are bread, but still plenty of kinds,' Chris tells me, before schooling me on the difference between 'attributive good', 'good for' and 'just good'. You can have a loaf of bread that is made well and is attributively good but made with ingredients that are 'bad' for people. Equally, a loaf could be made that is a boon for the health of the eater – so 'good for' them – yet is considered disgustingly bad tastewise by the eater.

It's hard to argue that bread is 'just good' though. Something that has required such a restructuring of the world can easily be

INTRODUCTION | 15

denigrated by those systems and people who have been displaced by it. Those impacted by the destruction of the underground forest of the chernozem in southern Ukraine, for example, or the indigenous populations of Australia, New Zealand and the Americas, would all have a thing to say about bread and bread-eaters. And not good things.

The conclusions I draw in this book are personal ones, informed by my life experiences, based on information gleaned from conversations with people like Chris and people in the industry. For most, the starting point was a question I'd asked of myself: what do you think of when you think of bread? The answers have been interesting, each differing according to the person, what they did, their particular circumstances at the time or in the past, their relationship to bread. Some appear in the book. For a surprising number, that question conjured up answers relating to *home*, a memory, often moving, of things past, of a way of life not necessarily still available to them now.

The title *Breaking Bread* seeks to portray some of the complexity of the subject. We break bread to share it, but we have broken bread in a more destructive sense too. Through adulteration, exploitation, colonisation and industrialisation, the bread that is part of my history and culture has been severed from its origins, becoming an accelerator to disease when it professes to be a sustainer of good health. I'm reminded of a line from Shakespeare's *Hamlet*: 'There is nothing either good or bad but thinking makes it so.'

In this book, I approach bread's validity from ten perspectives in ten chapters. Each will reveal something different about bread's relationship with me, the world and humanity. I won't be telling you what to eat. I don't have the answers, yet I know enough to ask the questions. I've also been lucky enough to bounce my musings off a host of wonderful bakers, writers, experts and friends like Chris, and bread enthusiasts from all over the world.

In the course of *Breaking Bread*, we will investigate how bread shapes identity. How it makes us who we are on a molecular level, how we are viewed by others and how we see ourselves. We will dig into the identity of the bread eater, the breadmaker and those who live outside the realm of bread. I will also attempt to shine a light on the kinds of bakers and bakeries that make the breads we eat.

We will see how the cycle of bread can produce a whole meal from a holistic system, where our bread originates and how great it can be when each stage is managed with care, compassion and skill. This may seem an idealised perspective but my examples are drawn from the real world, from my own experiences and from the inspiring people I have met. In doing this, I hope to show you the beauty in bread. That you'll share its joys with me.

The science of bread will unlock some of the knowledge that lies within each slice. This is partnered with the story of Frankenstein, both because of the use of 'Frankenloaf' to describe the bread that scientists have interfered with and the more subtle story of Promethean characters who have intended to do good, only to see their creations used for evil.

The health impacts of bread are one of the most widely discussed topics and I will try to shed some light on the reasons for increased symptoms and concerns caused by and surrounding our daily loaf. To do this, I have been assisted by some experts, such as Dr Seb Ambrozie and Dr Vanessa Kimbell, in the more technical aspects of gut health and how our bodies process it. I will also look at the health impact on bakers due to their working conditions, and the impact COVID-19 had on baking.

The strained dichotomy between industrialised bakeries and artisan bakeries provides a good insight into how both are viewed and view themselves. I'll attempt to build bridges between the factions in order to imagine a future with better bread at a scale to feed everyone. Are these two foes fighting from entrenched positions? Or do they have more in common than you might think?

I'll run the numbers on a loaf of artisan sourdough with one of the best bakeries in the UK. There will be discussions around the impact of bread as a symbol of value, as currency. We speak of 'earning a crust' and 'putting bread on the table', and 'breadwinners', responsible for the financial security of the home. These loaded terms need some attention.

Bread has been a political tool throughout history, and I'm interested in the ways it has exerted its power and where this power comes from. Why is wheat the top dog when it comes to cereal grains? And why is bread the number one product made from it? Has our love of bread been used as a form of social control?

Conflict and colonisation have a deep-seated relationship with bread, and I will attempt to explore this in a general sense but with special attention to conflicts in Ukraine throughout history. The ways in which bread has been weaponised during conflicts are testament to populations' reliance on it. Maybe bread is a weak spot in our defences? Are nations that rely too heavily on bread susceptible to attack?

Bread has long had close ties with religious ceremony, popping up in many of the major sacred books. The journey of bread – from grain to grist, porridge to parchment, starches to sugars, dough to delight – is one of continuous shapeshifting. Chameleon-esque, it suits many tables, religions, climates and occasions. Bread, a possible peacemaker that can bring togetherness through sharing in its commonality after all spiritual differences are brushed aside. But how do different religions view bread? Does it really feed the soul as well as the body? These are subjects I touch on but are far too huge and weighty for me, a layman, to deal with in any detail. And any opinions expressed are my own.

Finally, a key question of importance to me is – what is the future for bread? Is there one? Are its days, in fact, numbered? Is it a plague or nutritional salvation for an ever-expanding global population? Does the world need bread at all? Can bread be made with care and quality without sacrificing the baker who makes it? All these are important questions I hope to address to some degree.

The journey to this book, my journey through it, has not been an easy one. My personal relationship with bread is contentious. When it is bad, it can be evil, that I know, yet when it's good, the taste, the flavour, the impact on our senses, the joy it brings, can rival the most exotic foods on earth. This, more than anything, proves to me the power of bread. Yet, if I'm being honest, I never wanted to be a baker. It was never my dream. I saw what it could do to a person firsthand, its physical and mental impact, and I didn't want to follow in the footsteps of my parents, even though I love bread and love them. Their scars – literal and hidden – were visible to me, their son, as I grew up, the pain and suffering caused, not just from a job with incredibly long hours, involving great physical and mental endurance, palpable. I knew it was a job that asked everything from them, one that at the end of the day – or beginning – the customer might not appreciate, might not understand that quality should trump price, instead complaining to my parents that they could buy a loaf for a fraction of the price at the supermarket. I didn't want that for me. Not initially. And yet, despite this, circumstances have meant, I've dedicated most of my life to it. To bread. And I do find happiness in every smooth-skinned dough ball. Still get excited when loaves come out of the oven. Their smell, texture, taste.

Bread is an essential part of my story. And in all probability, it's part of yours, too, no matter what your background. Every civilisation has a form of bread, and how we create, make and bake it, how we sell it and buy it, our food security, our access to it, impacts on everything. Our health, our very being.

Bread affects our physical and mental well-being, and the way we make it, the ingredients, the seeds, the very earth we grow our grains in, the water we use and how we treat and sustain these natural resources, impact on the very health and future of our planet.

Bread is *that* important.

1

Why bread?

Creating, making, baking

This is the tale of a loaf of bread,
From the day that it was born,
In a baker's oven, baking hot,
On a cold and frosty morn.
This is the tale, I'll tell it now,
No need to ask me twice,
It's full of fun and flavour,
And I'll tell it . . . slice by slice.

– Allan Ahlberg, *Hooray for Bread (2013)*

It was Christmas Eve, and the bakers were starting early to get through the pile of orders. I was thirteen and this would be my first night shift. I had to be ready for three in the morning. To some of you, this probably sounds horrendous, a young boy starting work so early, but I was beyond excited. This was my family business. My heritage. My dad had worked here, my granddad and I'd been working here on Saturday and Sunday mornings for the last couple of years. But now? Now, I was going to be in the real thick of it. I'd tried to go to bed early, but couldn't sleep. Of course, I couldn't. I couldn't wait.

22 | BREAKING BREAD

Lying there, listening to the familiar sounds of the house – the chatter of family downstairs, laughter, the heavy thud of footsteps – how could I sleep? Everything was about to change. Even after the house had fallen silent, my thoughts were in overdrive. What would happen next? Would the bakery look, feel different, in the early hours? Would I be good enough? What if I let my dad down? As the hands on my sister's Disney alarm clock wheeled round and the time approached for me to get up, I became ever more restless. Finally, at two, I gave in to instinct, quickly washing and dressing in my pristine bakery whites.

Stealing down the stairs, I became aware of new sounds: the creak of the stairs under my feet, the stiffness of the door handle, hinges that needed oiling, cupboards that thumped back into place, even the rattle of my breakfast bowl on the table top. I've never eaten cereal so self-consciously. Then Dad appeared. He was early, as he usually was for anything. I could tell immediately he was pleased at my appearance, the fact I was ready. At my obvious excitement.

We left the house in the almost syrupy darkness, and I'll never forget that drive. I haven't been a passenger in a rally car, but the ride from the house to bakery must have been something like it. My dad's driving was usually pretty careful, but this drive was a revelation. He was mid-shift and the dough needed mixing, so he chucked our little Volkswagen Caddy into corners, double declutching through chicanes and reducing what was a fifteen-minute drive into a fraction of the time. When we arrived at the bakery, my eyes were on stalks and I was fully awake, adrenaline pumping through me, certainly ready to start the day.

My dad had disappeared inside by the time I got out, so I scuttled towards the bakery, down a dark passage between the old public toilets where I'd once seen a baker corner a river rat and bludgeon it to death using the handle of a broom. The Victorian brick walls were covered in a fine frost that was gilded by the sulphur street lights from the Woolworth's car park. The building had taken on a new personality in the early hours. The orchestra of machinery resonating through the skeleton of the structure was magnetic.

Tap-tap bang ... tap-tap bang. Tap-tap bang ... tap-tap bang—

Clutching my rolled-up apron tightly, I followed the familiar sound of the bread tins being knocked against the lip of the oven. The tea-stained light leaked from the back entrance to the downstairs bakery, creating a path to the instruments making this night music.

You reached the space via two rough concrete steps on which my dad would sharpen his dough knife on occasion. It was a contorted space, with bowed ceilings bespeckled with crust-coloured condensation. Everything was patched, repurposed or in need of renovation. The smell was like nothing I've smelled before or since – that of gas from a corroding pipe mixed with raw flour, beery fermentation and baked bread. This was a dangerous space, some might say the sounds and smells repellent, yet this was my family business and I was hooked.

The four bakers were seemingly oblivious to my presence. Their awkward movements over the flour-polished floor tiles invited catastrophe at every turn. But like well-rehearsed clowns, any possible collisions were avoided with half-turns and fortuitous, it seemed, ducks and swerves. Their faces were neutral, seemingly hard to read, but to me, as a boy, there was malice behind their mill-pond eyes. My dad stood in the corner watching the slapstick play out with a stern gaze, muttering disparagingly to himself but offering no instruction.

24 | BREAKING BREAD

The mixers that I'd previously seen as dormant pieces of furniture were full of life. To my left was a stack of Marriage's Flour sacks slightly masking the Artofex twin arm mixer in the corner, the metallic limbs diving into the dough with all the rhythm of a jazz band. My grandfather had bought the mixer second-hand. It was ancient, from the 1920s or 30s, so old the parts weren't made anymore. The green enamel paint was pitted with dinks and scratches. On the only occasion it broke down, a local farm engineer repurposed a combine harvester belt to get it back in motion. It was capable of mixing nearly two hundred kilos of dough and would get patched up after every shift with thick engine grease and a wet sponge – like a punch-drunk boxer about to be sent in for another round.

The large bowl turned slowly, the crooked fingers reaching in, pulling and stretching the dough in a way that mimicked the bakers of old who'd hunched over wooden troughs, forearms encased in dough. Once it had finished mixing, the Stop button was pushed and the whirring of the motor ceased, the greased-up cogs slowed and the machine slumped. In order for the arms to retract, you had to turn wheel-like knobs on the side. Then the bowl was removed and the dough covered with a giant linen cloth.

My attention was captured by the flickering fluorescent lights that bathed the cramped space in a dull sepia tone. The tiles on the wall reminded me of the tobacco-stained teeth of the barflies that haunted local pubs. They were covered in aged posters that called out for 'care and hygiene', signed off by the Association of Master Bakers. A calendar showcasing topless women, a present from one of the flour millers we dealt with, hung carelessly next to it. I'd watch the bakers mould a doughball in each hand while staring up at these women, imagining they were massaging breasts. Perhaps it got them through the shift, but even then I was ashamed for them and that my dad – father to my four sisters – didn't rip it down.

The light fell on the 'L'-shaped baker's bench, a smooth white polycarbonate surface that had cracked in places. The fractures had been filled with silicone and a questionable cement of old dough. My grandfather had installed solid beech work surfaces originally, but the local authority had deemed these a health hazard, so they were ripped out and replaced. The irony is that today most bakeries have hardwood surfaces, the plastic ones infinitely more capable of harbouring microbial nasties.

At home, I had been worried about making too much noise, yet here the bakers seemed to be happy making as much as possible. Every action was accentuated by a sound effect. To my young mind, it was so loud as almost to be unreal, like watching a Foley artist recreating sound for a film track, but this was living sound created by living people. A few years later, when some flats were built at the back of the bakery, they conducted some nighttime sound tests – and found the bakers made as much noise as a jumbo jet taking off. Luckily, there have been bakers banging their way through shifts since the 1860s, so the noise was seen as a fixture of the town, for most, an accepted part of its natural noise.

The workbench had a pile of dough at one end, a flabby, gelatinous flour-dusted hillock. Next to that stood a baker, chopping pieces off the belly which were then tossed onto a scale pan, the metal so pitted it looked as if it had recently returned from a rifle range. The dough was then thrown down in front of another baker to shape by hand, all origami-like folds and creases, which ratcheted the tension in the dough before it was immediately dipped in

26 | BREAKING BREAD

seeds and placed on trays before the outer skin of the dough lost its tackiness.

To the right of the workbench, another wall of flour sacks was surrounded by open bags, with pre-weighed additions of salt and fresh yeast waiting in line for their turn in the mixer. Dad had already taken up his position beside the cast iron body of the eighty-quart John Hunt mixer, the painted outside had been rubbed raw from where his hand had rested, over the years, as he watched the dough being wrestled by the planetary motion of the dough hook. This was where the speciality doughs were mixed, jobs that my dad kept to himself. A metal bucket of water stood next to him on the floor, and on the table behind him was a plastic jug, old enough that all the original measurements had worn off. The bucket was used at the beginning of the mix and the jug was then used to make finer adjustments. My dad would determine the water based on the sound the mixer made and, as the gears became stressed, he would dribble a little more water into the bowl, allowing some respite. Eventually the dough itself would start to slap against the stainless steel as the gluten developed, a round of applause for a batch well done. 'You mix with your ears,' my dad would tell me, something I've carried around with me since.

He never weighed the water. Hell, he never weighed the yeast or salt. I questioned him just once about this, a few years later, when I thought I knew a thing or two. (Spoiler alert, I didn't.) *You should really weigh the salt at least. That needs to be accurate,* I told him with all the faux authority I could muster. Dad said nothing, just walked away to the scales. Actions speak louder than words. He poured some salt onto the scale pan from his knotted fist. '*Two ounces,*' he muttered, as he dropped a two-ounce weight onto the platform. The scale sat in perfect balance. Two ounces, indeed. I said nothing. What was there to say? The man had been weighing out the same recipe for fifty years. It was in his blood – so much so he *was* the scales.

There was a stack of plastic tubs holding fermenting batches of dough and as the bakers finished processing one batch, they would ask Dad for the next one. He would walk to the mismatch of yellow and white tubs and tap one to indicate that it was next. Occasionally nothing would be ready, and the bakers would quickly disperse to take up prep jobs elsewhere in the bakery while they waited. All of the bread was yeasted at this time, with shorter windows for processing than sourdough, so the organisation had to be on point. The position my dad held was similar to a quarterback, dictating the plays to his offensive line, occasionally calling out if one of the doughs seemed to be ripening too fast.

All the bakers wore white like me, but their cotton uniforms were matted with flour. The exception was the oven man, his whites stained black from the carbonised flour that stuck to tins and trays. He bounded towards me from the hearth with a stack of tins, tucked into the crease where his belly had been pinched by his apron strings, and deposited them, with a crash, on the step beside me to cool.

Startled, I hopped down into the scrum, having to twist and turn through the crowded space like a commuter attempting to pass across the concourse at a busy metropolitan train station. Once through, I knew I'd be working upstairs. I would only get in the way if I stayed in the bread section.

The heat of the oven blasted me as I scuttled past. To my left, a prover door sat open. I could see the trays of bread inside the metal cabinet, a gas ring at the bottom heating a metal bowl filled with water that looked like it had been sourced from a local coven of witches. The steam had the ripe fragrance of a locker room and kept the dough flexible as it inflated with the gases of fermentation, before it was loaded into the wide decks of the oven.

The oven is the hardest position to work in. It's like being on the grill at a busy restaurant and you have to maintain a clear head in a self-inflicted chaos. It is the position that has the biggest impact on how the bread looks but because it's also physically torturous, it's a job often given to the least-skilled team member.

I love the oven and will usually take that job if there's a choice. The mental tetris that is required to make sure the bread goes in at the right time and is baked before the next batch is ready suits my personality. The scoring of the loaves, signing each one with the stroke of a blade is fun, even after you've done it several thousand times. All the heavy lifting can take its toll though and the most common ailment is an injured back, each tray weighing up to twenty kilos. Loading and then unloading for hours is a real sickener.

Any bakery has positions that are fairly common, much like the brigade system utilised by most kitchens across the world. In a bakery there's a 'mixer', who will – yep – mix the batches of dough and manage the fermentation. 'Table hands' are people who process the dough, cutting, scaling and shaping it ready for the oven. Then the oven person has to determine the readiness of the bread and bake it. The oven person and the mixer stay in communication to regulate the flow of bread. If the mixer processes too much dough, it will back up and overproof, which results in it having to be remoulded. If the oven person has empty decks, then the cost of heating the oven is wasted. *That* is

WHY BREAD? | 29

a cardinal sin. If the oven has space, you might hear the call to '*chuck it through*' or '*hold up!*', if there's a backlog.

Bakery shifts are like restaurant shifts in reverse. In a kitchen, the day starts with prep. It's the time when the pressure is off, and everything culminates in the final performance of service. In a bakery, it starts with service and finishes with the prep for the next day, especially in a sourdough bakery or one that makes a lot of viennoiserie like croissants.

That first night is etched into my memory. I experienced an addictive rush, like nothing I had felt before. The time flew by and, before I knew it, it was over. For that day. My identity had always been tied to the bakery through Dad and the family, but having an intimate knowledge of how it worked, and what my part in it could be, made it all the more special. I *felt* like a baker. It was in my blood.

It also brought home just how difficult the work was. And other factors: how sloppy the hygiene could be, how differently people worked, how not all bakers were the same. And there was the culture. Some thought it was OK to be rude, sexist, racist or disparaging towards each other. Would I be the same? I made a commitment to resist what I saw as a generational complacency towards such unacceptable behaviours.

My father handed out bottles of liquor from a cardboard box to each of the bakers, Tia Maria, Disaronno, Southern Comfort and saccharin spirits – he wished them a gruff 'Merry Christmas', then we were back in the car and on our way home, tired but satisfied. This time well within the speed limit.

A baker's day is a strange one, and yet I was to learn it was not without its pleasures. A piping hot roll straight from the oven, butter dripping from it, with a mug of strong tea. The comradery of your fellow workers. The strangeness mixed with joy at ending the day when most other peoples were just starting. Dawn, the sun rising to illuminate the fresh morning dew, the changing light soundtracked by birdsong. Blissful.

This first bakery was unique, a place unto its own and unlike any of the subsequent places where I plied my trade, mainly because no two bakeries are alike. In fact, no two *bakers* are alike.

Many of us start off as home bakers, producing enough bread for the household. This is probably the most joyous kind of baker to be. A home baker can produce incredible bread at a fraction of the cost of a bakery. A little knowledge, a lot of patience and an understanding that it won't be perfect are the main tools – and access to an oven or some form of heat. Over the years I've taught hundreds of home bakers, most of whom felt happy to bake at home, others who were tempted to do it as a job, cajoled by their friends and family, and images of popular shows like *The Great British Bake Off* and the success of some of its winners.

Then there are micro-bakeries, run from a garage or any small space that'll hold a mini bread oven. The micro-bakery has come into its own since the global financial crash of 2008 when a stream of redundant ex-office workers pinned their payouts on market stall operations, like those found in east London's Broadway Market, and with every existential crisis there seems to be a new wave. Of course it's not as simple as it sounds. You need to get your kitchen registered with the health inspector and front up some cash for a small mixer, a fridge and an oven. And yet you can go from baking twenty to fifty loaves a day in an operation like this and many places have stretched that even further.

These are the bakeries that have changed the baking world. These small operations run by people who have no familial baking pedigree but just the passion and bravery to turn a hobby into a career. These are the bakers who have torn down the topless calendars, who challenge previously accepted bad behaviours and practices, who make us rethink and wonder. And the industry follows their trends now, desperate to discover the next sourdough flavour or shape.

The micro-bakery will usually bleed into a market stall as an avenue to sell the bumper load of weekend loaves. The solo baker will prepare the day before, bake in the early hours and then spend the day freezing/boiling to death while trying to explain how each loaf is made to customers. At the end of the day, they will be the first port of call for other traders wishing to swap goods.

The next rung up the ladder is a high street bakery, or some kind of 'bricks-and-mortar' operation. Up to this point, the baking adventure has been an involved hobby. You could stop at any time with very little impact. Once you commit to a building, however, the costs are everywhere. Suddenly your life is spent worrying about the average sale price and number of sales per hour. It seems everyone wants a piece of you. And after all the effort, it's impossible to predict if the customers will buy what you've made. Some days you'll sell out quickly and wish you'd baked more, and people will get mad. On others, you'll end up with lots of waste and then *you* will be mad.

Employees, taxes, sickness, holidays, broken equipment, leaks, and the cost of wheat in China also come into play – and the life of a small bakery owner can spiral out of control pretty quickly. If you are prepared for it, of course, have a plan and about five hundred contingencies, then you'll probably make more of a success out of it than I did. If I had just needed to make great bread to be successful it would have been much easier: it's not the baking that is difficult. It's everything else, so be prepared for that, if you're considering any of the above ventures.

There is another option, if you can't bear all the uncertainty, and that is to open a wholesale bakery, usually found on an industrial estate, a metal shell of a building with open plan concrete floors and doors so big you can drive a lorry in. These are cheaper to set up and run, with lower rent and rates. They have fewer tax implications and more predictable production schedules – really, what's not to love?

Well, you'll get squeezed on margins by all your suppliers for a start. Most of your customers will want delivery at the same exact time, with periodic threats that they will leave if you don't improve some aspect of the service. You also don't get as many of the tasty add-on features with a customer-facing store, like coffee. Many bakeries couldn't survive without coffee.

The bonus of a wholesale bakery is that, every day, you know exactly what to make and you can plan staffing around this. The savings on efficiencies will mostly be eaten up by the discount you feel obliged to give, however, and yet there isn't the wastage to deal with when there's a rainy day and no one wants any bread.

A way to provide a full price loaf to a customer without the upfront costs of an actual bakers' shop is to utilise the power of the internet. Online bakeries can remain fairly small but reach a national customer base. Usually, bakeries will do two or three deliveries a week and release stock at a certain time to be gobbled up by a baying mob of customers.

You'll have to invest a lot in social media and that isn't easy. On-call at all times, replying to customers queries and various banal requests. If you blow-up and become uber-popular then customers will get frustrated at missing out on bread and you may need to employ someone to look after the social media accounts.

Most often bakeries will hedge their bets and mix the shop, wholesale and online aspects into their business. This is a pretty neat way of doing it if the balance can be struck. Wholesale to pay the bills every month, the shop gives access to value added services and the online is an extra sweetener so you can save for the tax bill at the end of the year.

Sourdough bakeries will commit themselves to using only strains of yeast held in a sourdough culture. These bakeries make long-fermented breads and will normally refrigerate the dough overnight to create a flavour and texture that is impossible to replicate using faster methods. Sourdough is a process, not a product or style of bread. It is a way of leavening that develops flavour and changes the chemistry of the loaf. The problem for a baker is that it takes more time, and costs more to produce. This is why a sourdough loaf will be more expensive – gram for gram – than a yeasted loaf. The term 'sourdough' relates to an absence of commercial yeast but there is no current protection for the term, so consumers have to be savvy to spot imitators. Ask questions, request ingredient information and if they try to give you the 'it's a secret recipe' line, you can be pretty sure there's something in it they need to hide. There are no secrets to good sourdough, it just requires practice, sacrifice and a lot of hard work. It doesn't matter how old your starter is either, a culture that's a month old and kept with care and precision will outperform a 5,000-year-old starter found in the tomb of a pharaoh's favourite baker, every time. It's just not as Instagrammable.

Yeasted bakeries will use a fresh cake of commercial yeast to leaven their bread. Sourdough processes can take anywhere from

34 | BREAKING BREAD

twelve to seventy-two hours, but with commercial yeast you can get bread from raw ingredients to finished loaf in as little as one or two hours. Some bakeries use commercial yeast judiciously and stretch the fermentation to get the advantages of a reduced process and longer fermentation. Many bakeries use both sourdough and yeasted processes with skill and care. If a bakery makes sourdough, they will understand fermentation and will most likely be using commercial yeast in a considerate way.

While many bakery terms are not protected, 'organic' is. If a bakery wants to have an organic product, they will have to go through an accreditation process proving that their bread can't be cross contaminated with other non-organic ingredients. These flours have lower yields and therefore the price of the raw material is more expensive which is why organic breads command a higher price tag than non-organic bread made from wheat grown in a conventional system.

A 'scratch' bakery is one that makes its breads using separate ingredients as opposed to one that uses bread mixes, usually containing a host of additives. Every bakery should be a scratch bakery but, in reality, there are many that are not.

Small bakeries can use a method for making bread called 'ADD', or Activated Dough Development, which mimics the large industrial bakeries. It's a way of making bread with low grade flour very quickly. I know some bakeries that use this method and the dough moves so fast they don't even need a prover. If a bakery can give the appearance of a scratch bakery but use this method, they can make a lot of money because they can hit a price point that the customer feels is good value for what is a handmade loaf without any of the associated costs.

Supermarkets and larger stores may have in-store bakeries that provide freshly baked bread. Unfortunately, while they may bake it fresh, in many cases it comes part-baked and frozen from a distribution centre. The advantages to the store are huge because the customer believes they are getting the real deal, all those smells piped into the shopping area and the sight of seemingly fresh bread. In reality, the bread is an additive-packed junk-food.

With any of the above bakery options, if the bread is sold unwrapped by the company that made it, ingredient information is not required – in the UK, at least. That is another advantage for the in-store bakery as most customers will assume such bread is made fresh from raw ingredients. An assumption that carries a lot of revenue.

Then there are factory bakeries that employ industrial systems such as the Chorleywood method in the UK, which I talk about later, to make millions of loaves rather than hundreds or thousands. These 'plant' bakeries will usually replace bakers with machines to scale, shape and even pack the bread they make. Every second on the line will be precious due to the huge costs involved. As such, engineers will be on site to monitor, maintain and fix the bread making mechanical beast.

The most traditional bakery is a woodfired one, but these are now fairly rare. Using the energy of a wood fire to heat the oven, it is then swept out and every last joule of bread-baking heat is used on a selection of products. It requires a true master to make bread in this way and if I ever get the chance to buy a loaf of woodfired bread I take it, paying whatever I'm asked.

Just as there are many kinds of bakeries, there are many kinds of bakers. People join the profession for all kinds of reasons and different kinds of bakeries will tend to attract different baker

36 | BREAKING BREAD

personalities. I've been lucky to work with a mix, from highly engaged people with precision perfect skills to slovenly grotesque characters who are the baking equivalent to Shakespeare's Falstaff.

I'll start with the kind of baker that I am, a family or generational one. I've been learning how bakeries work since I could toddle through one, stealing gingerbread men and wondering where the chocolate buttons were kept. The long, antisocial hours and lack of breaks have been normalised by my parents. You'll rarely get a complaint out of bakers like me. We usually have a very personal, emotional connection to baking and that passion is at best inspiring, at worst intolerable.

Old school bakers tend to be people who have decided they want to be bakers. They normally will have some qualifications and will stick pretty close to the style of baking they learnt when they first started. These bakers will rarely embrace new ideas or change and are best suited to a formulaic environment. In my experience these are also the bakers with the most 'sayings'.

The antithesis of the old school baker is the hipster baker. Usually found working in an urban environment, if they weren't baking, they'd probably be up all night anyway with other pastimes. Often stereotyped as plaid-shirted and left-wing leaning – and beardy in a groomed way – these bakers are more likely to care where their flour is grown and take more of an interest in the craft. They will see baking as a sort of living pottery, enjoy experimentation and a diversity of tasks. Their journey into baking is usually through a combination of having no job, needing money and knowing someone who works in a bakery already.

There are mercenaries in any trade, and baking is no different. These people don't care how the bread is made as long as they get paid on time. They will talk about what hard work it is and often are the first to slack off when the management is out of the room. And don't be surprised if you see them selling waste bread at a market on their day off, side hustlers extraordinaires. More often than not, they couldn't tell you anything about the technical aspects of baking; they are just hands-for-hire and they are firmly entrenched in the job market as good bakers are hard to find. They will often slink from job to job, answering the call of whoever pays the most.

The last category are TV or social media bakers, such as Brad Leone or Claire Saffitz. This type of baker is fairly new to the game but has a lot of influence when it comes to bakery trends. They tend to use the finest ingredients and some of them produce wonderful breads. They come under fire from the jobbing bakers, some of whom think their lack of actual bakery experience and surplus of good looks and sleep makes them somehow inferior. And yet, arguably, their endeavours create money, jobs and opportunities in our industry. I take my hats off to these baking nymphs. I've made a few videos and it's not easy. And while I may never get to taste the bread they make, it inspires me to make my own versions, and isn't that the point?

I wanted to get a window into the world of baking for the screen. So, I reached out to one of the most successful bakers in this field, Edd Kimber, baker and food writer and the first winner of *The Great British Bake Off*.

Since its first screening, *GBBO* has become a global sensation, delivering a national and international audience with a vision of Britain everyone is extremely happy to accept. Namely, a bunch of pleasant, smiley, slightly odd people who like to drink tea and

38 | BREAKING BREAD

eat biscuits in green and pleasant lands. I, certainly, identify with the tea and biscuits bit.

Edd Kimber, the show's first winner, in 2010, and I meet up. I'm keen for his thoughts on the show and baking. I ask him my break the ice question, something I think is important. What comes to mind when he thinks about bread? Edd replies, 'When I hear "bread" I think of a stereotype of a loaf. Very white, very soft, smells of nothing,' adding, 'I don't even think we went to a bakery for bread.'

This bland depiction is at odds with the baker Edd has become. As 'The Boy Who Bakes', he creates wonderful bread, and his recipes strike the optimum balance between achievability and desirability. Edd muses on this contradiction. 'Your whole life is set up by those scenes and memories you get as a kid, and it's really hard to break out of those. Sometimes your tastes change but you still have a nostalgic craving for something like that.' This brings back a memory I have of begging for mum for 'sheep bread', as we called it due to its soft woolly crumb. Occasionally, she would give in and buy some for us. We had access to all the bread we wanted made by Dad, yet still felt the allure of that fluffy wrapped bread our friends ate.

It's funny I say Dad – he was the professional baker – yet for so many of us, our baking or cooking memories are connected to the women in our households growing up. This strong connection between domestic baking and women is deep rooted. So often I have spoken to people in baking class scenarios where they tell me how they used to bake with their mother or grandmother, but rarely a male member of the household. One of my earliest memories is licking the spoon of something my mother or nanna had made. The act of baking has traditionally been heavily gendered in our society, especially in the domestic sphere and Edd experienced this attitude firsthand after he won *The Great British Bake Off*. He tells me, 'People wrote articles about how unusual it was for a man to win a baking competition,' an idea that feels like it would be more at home in the 1950s, but isn't.

My own experience of home baking as I've said was with my mum or nanna or sisters. The exception seems to be bread, and despite Mum being a brilliant cook it's the only home bake that my dad will still insist on performing. Edd has similar feelings coming from his own teaching experiences with home bakers. 'The amount of men that would tell me "I only bake bread", as if there was an unspoken rule that bread was manly and if you baked cakes or something else, it was very feminine.'

My experience of the family bakery wasn't any different. This was an environment dominated by men and this seemed to be predicated on two things: first, that it was nightwork and second, that it involved carrying heavy things. I remember the outcry when the flour sacks were reduced from twenty-five kilos to sixteen kilos, which was seen by my father and the other bakers as a blatant attempt to get more women into baking. An idea they clearly didn't support. The air there was heavy with toxic masculinity.

My parents had four girls before me and none of them was allowed to work in the bakery, despite them all being extremely talented. They had to work in the shop which was 'all female'. They were allowed to work in the bakery when they were older, but the male bakers never accepted the idea and it was only tolerated because they made sweet things, not the bread itself.

The night work was seen as a more resilient barrier to female entry to the workplace than the weight of the flour, the male

40 | BREAKING BREAD

bakers feeling that women should 'stay at home with the kids'. Yet, if I were going to assess the bakers I've worked with over the years and choose my best team, I'd pick mostly women. The laziest, most unreliable, poorly skilled bakers have often been men, in my experience, and perhaps a feeling of entitlement is a leading cause in these examples. Edd had a similar experience of working in a Michelin-starred restaurant that had only one female member in the kitchen team, and she was often given the 'afternoon tea' section. Surprise, surprise.

'The homophobic and sexist jokes made me reconsider a career as a pastry chef. Food production seems to have been enshrined in toxic environments,' he adds.

Perhaps, when I think about it, the desire to industrialise the baking environment was, in part, a quest to make the process more masculine. To exclude women from masculine spaces. Noisy, difficult spaces full of monstrous men discussing sports and their sexual conquests. Places using chemicals, additives, potions and powders to improve sloppy attempts at breadmaking. The bakers in my family bakery would rate each other based on speed rather than quality.

When I was around twelve-years old, I was criticised for my piping skills on that basis, despite already being better than most of the adult bakers with decades of experience. *Very neat, looks like a machine did it, David, but you're too slow, we've got homes to go to,'* I can remember one of them commenting, my dad following behind with, '*Get good, then get fast.'* I think I was the only one who listened to him.

I've never had any formal training myself and have definitely suffered Imposter Syndrome on many occasions, especially as my place in the bakery was telegraphed as nepotism rather than meritocracy. I was interested to hear what, if any, challenges Edd had encountered, as an amateur baker, with receiving respect from the industry, even after proving himself on national television.

'For a while I felt like I wasn't allowed to call myself a baker,' he responds and I wonder if this influenced the title Edd uses, 'The Boy Who Bakes'.

'Paul A. Young, the chocolatier, was one of the only chefs who took me seriously, never patronised me,' he continues. 'I asked whether I should go to school to get a qualification because lots of people had a preconceived opinion of me and it was hard to get a foot in the door. He said, "No, don't do it. It's a complete waste of money. You'll find somewhere that rates your inquisitiveness, your willingness to learn and your love of what you're doing." Sometimes when people go to school it makes them rigid. They assume that they know everything, and they aren't willing to learn new ways.'

This has been something I've come to learn, especially within the food industry, that passion and attitude are more important than any qualification. As the late, great American chef Anthony Bourdain says in his book, *Kitchen Confidential*, '*Skills can be taught. Character you either have or you don't have.*'

Bake-off has had a huge impact on getting people of all descriptions and ages into the kitchen to make bread, particularly through Paul Hollywood's influence. He, like me, comes from a baking family. The bread made on the show is very limited however, due to the constraints placed on it by the filming schedule. Edd recalls: 'When we were doing bread week, multiple people asked to make sourdough, asking if they could bring their starter in, but they said, "No. It won't fit in the time we have to film the show." They've never done anything without commercial yeast.'

We have all witnessed the contestants attempting challenges that can't be completed to any great level in the time they have been allotted, and so the show's desire to justify the format gives a simplified impression of not just breadmaking, but other baking too. My good friend Chris 'Chops' Taylor, who worked behind the scenes on BBC's *Masterchef* for a decade, sums it up for me. 'The problem is that people think these shows are about cooking or baking. They aren't. It's all about entertainment. Producers are aware they are cramming too much in for the time because it creates drama. We all want to see people running out of time, making mistakes.'

Is that an indictment on human nature? That we want the drama of people failing or succeeding, not just getting on with it. These shows have certainly hooked me in and I know the reality of it, the graft it takes to make a decent loaf of bread, not least a magnificent one. I can't count all those times I've exclaimed at the television, begging the contestants to change tack, to ignore Paul Hollywood's advice or just start again. Edd explains how this can contribute to viewers being misled. The *GBBO* has 'given people a false education because things get said on the show that aren't true, because of editing or because a contestant believes something to be true, says it and the voice over backs it up'. So where does that leave us? How can we possibly have a real idea of what a good loaf should be? And how does social media play into this?

While television shows like *GBBO* have been hugely influential, social media platforms such as Instagram or TikTok have done far more to shape our collective baking consciousness. Reaching a global audience of billions, these platforms deliver ecstatic visual bombs and have had a huge impact on the way we digest and absorb content. Edd comments on the advantages of these platforms: 'The positives are that you can connect with people all over the world. It's inspired me to make things I'd never have heard of before.' And that's good, isn't it?

We have instant access to all this diverse information in a way our ancestors never would have. Historically this kind of information would have to travel with people at the pace they could be transported, in recipe books or via excursions away from home. Now that information can reach thousands, millions even, within seconds.

'The negatives can be when I post something, and I get a barrage of comments saying I've done it wrong because it contradicts what they've read or seen on the TV or whatever,' Edd says ruefully. 'It can remove context and detail. It can lessen people's attention spans. It's all about instant gratification.' And that's true. In my experience, there will always be someone ready to let you know when you've challenged their baking beliefs or done something 'wrong'.

An example that Edd gives is making sure the salt and yeast don't touch in the mixing bowl, something that Paul Hollywood and others repeat as a 'golden rule'. And yet, it's a fallacy. Edd has done experiments with leaving salt and yeast in contact for various periods of time and shown the results in his Substack newsletter. He found that even when he added five times the amount of salt it didn't kill the yeast. This is especially true when using dry yeast because often the little granules are coated to preserve them. When I worked at Lily Vanilli, a much-loved bakery, in east London, we had a motto, 'If it works, it works', as a defence against all these baking myths, whether that be the idea that salt kills yeast, not stirring caramel or that the protein percentage on a flour sack tells you how much gluten is present.

I was told the latter for a long time, and it is true. To a point. If comparing two flours milled in the same way, you will be able to see which has the higher gluten-forming proteins, but if you have two bags with identical protein numbers and one is roller-milled and the other stoneground then the roller-milled one will have more gluten forming proteins. Roller-milled flour was invented in the nineteenth century largely to create finer flour for pastries by crushing the grains between two steel cylinders, sifting to remove the wheatgerm and outer bran – which increases its longevity – and then regrinding, resulting in the white flour most of us have used in our lifetime. Stoneground flour, even if sieved, will include protein from the wheatgerm, which is 25 per cent protein. None of that protein is gluten forming so it dilutes the strength of the flour. Everyone loves a tip, trick or soundbite but we should always be wary of them and discover the truth for ourselves.

Social media really came into its own during the Covid pandemic Lockdowns and Edd saw a huge increase in public interest for breadmaking videos, especially with sourdough content. He also saw a shift in the way users interacted with his posts. They were less judgy, responding to more detailed explanations and instructions. People had time to burn and responded to more delayed gratification, to quality over speed or ease.

'I filmed a big "how to" on sourdough,' he explains, 'going through the process of initiating a starter. Every day, I would spend hours responding to questions and queries on it. People started engaging in a way I hadn't seen before. It felt like a once-in-a-lifetime moment.'

In a world that was being forcibly disconnected, social media offered a way for people to connect, and it seemed that one of the most popular items they chose through which to do so was sourdough. Slow fermented bread, taking days to make and years to master, sourdough suddenly hit the mainstream, and those with the knowledge to help do so were actively sought out. I remember getting messages from people I hadn't seen in years, asking me about particular aspects of the process, requesting some starter and asking me to diagnose failed bakes.

All this connectivity is a gift, spreading information far and wide, allowing people who would never previously have had a way of sharing their knowledge to pass on valuable information. When this information becomes super-focused in the form of trends, it can have the opposite effect though. Edd is keenly aware of this, 'When trends become international rather than local we see a flattening of culture. With Basque cheesecake, for example, or laminated pastries. The whole giant croissant thing just drives me crazy.' I, too, feel frustrated watching bakers striving for a viral sensation, especially when it is just for show. It's hard enough baking a perfect, regular-sized croissant and most of the giant ones I've seen have claggy crumbs and over-baked exteriors.

When certain topics start trending there is always a merry gang of people waiting to capitalise on the clicks, the bandwagon piles up with bakers sharing similar pictures of breads, inspiring other bakers to make the same breads. This creates a bready hall of mirrors that becomes hyper-focused on 'the perfect ear', the best lamination or the cringeworthy 'crumb shot' – a loaf being cut down the middle to reveal the honeycomb texture within. I've fallen into all the traps, and it felt good at the time and yet now looking back, I wonder if my time would have been better spent doing something else, revealing something my dad passed onto me, for example. Where is the baking in all this? The creating?

46 | BREAKING BREAD

One of the big divides in bread identity recently is between sourdough and yeasted bread. Another misconception is that all bread before the introduction of commercial, industrial yeast in the 1920s was sourdough. Even in ancient times, bakers would use brewer's yeast to leaven their bread. *Saccharomyces cerevisiae* is the specific strain that is used by brewers and bakers alike. It is a punchy little so-and-so, delivering a virile population of yeast that can help dough rise in a timely fashion.

As a baker however, it is not beneficial to have the dough ready too soon. The batch must be hand scaled and shaped, eventually baked in batches, and a too rapidly moving dough causes all sorts of issues. As a result, it's used in a measured way, often being made into a 'sponge' or preferment and allowed to ferment over a number of hours at a consistent, considered pace. With the advent of various baking technologies during the nineteenth century, yeast began to develop, with dried yeast becoming available in the 1820s. Cakes of yeast were then invented, such as you'll find in most bakeries today.

The issue isn't really the type of yeast though, but the amount used. If a long fermentation schedule is adhered to then the variety of yeast cells shouldn't be a bone of contention. Often however, I've witnessed the smugness of a baker who wouldn't touch commercial yeast with a bargepole. They are often the same ones that care too much about the age of their starter and how big the holes in their bread are.

I make sourdough panettone for Pump Street Bakery, often considered 'the Everest of baking'. The starter, or *Lievito Madre*, must be gently managed with precision and lots of attention, the balance of yeasts and lactic acid bacteria versus acetic acid a tightrope that has seen many bakers tear their hair out. My own baldness probably owes something to the task of maintaining a well-balanced starter. After days of preparation, even when it all goes well and you're faced with an aromatic sweet-crusted balloon of bread, I do wonder if it's worth it.

But does the world really need more complicated bread? Or do we just need better, more simple, tasty and nutritious bread? The skills of a sourdough baker should be appreciated, there's no argument there, but equally the skills of a baker who can use commercial yeast with a delicate hand to yield a loaf that is healthy and accessible to large parts of society should be the Holy Grail of baking. Surely?

Even the Real Bread Campaign, launched in 2008 by Andrew Whitley, of *Bread Matters* fame, and the food and farming charity Sustain, tries hard to soften the divide between yeasty bakers and sourdough ones, stating that 'real bread' can be made with yeast. Driving a wedge between these two disciplines isn't helpful in my opinion and does more to isolate 'good bread' as a preserve of the elite. I have a wonderful recipe for ciabatta that uses a sourdough preferment and a yeasty one. I know many bakers who use both as tools to create delicious breads in a timeframe that allows them to charge a little less. Is that wrong?

My default perception of bread is that it is a distinctly European food. I know how ridiculous that is, to think that a food developed in Africa from a grass cultivated in what is today Iraq should be somehow European. Bread is a global food and once you start looking, the variety is huge. I can't go through all the world's various specialities, but a particular area of interest for me is the bread of Southeast Asia.

48 | BREAKING BREAD

I contacted Christopher Tan, author of *The Way of Kueh*, *Nerd Baker* and many books on Singaporean cuisine, to find out more about how bread is viewed and digested outside of my own Western bubble. I asked him what bread means to him. Although he has lived in the UK for eleven years, he told me bread has no particular structure for him, adding, 'Through my work I am familiar with so much of the extended worldwide family of breads, the word carries almost no Platonic freight in itself,' meaning through his vast experience of so many kinds of bread he is unable to settle on a simple visual definition of the word. He appears to have escaped the Proustian attachment to childhood bread, that luxurious memory of hot buttered toast.

It is too easy for me to think of bread as a colonial hitchhiker, when bread cultures were strongly associated with almost every corner of the globe well before British or European conquest. Christopher, too, tells me that he is surprised at the lack of knowledge shown by 'certain TV baking show judges' when it comes to the bread heritage of Southeast Asia.

I view with interest the British attempts to make *Shokupan*, which is a Japanese white milk bread. Even the idea of a 'Japanese Milk Bread' is a Western construct to add spice to what was essentially a staple European product when it was first introduced. Writer and baker Dan Lepard tells me that '*Shokupan* means "white bread", it doesn't mean anything more than that and it doesn't pertain to a recipe. [The bread] doesn't necessarily, or even often, contain milk, cream or butter. If you go to Japan and ask for Hokkaido Milk Bread, no one knows what you're talking about, because it's not a thing. It's only a thing in New York, Los Angeles, London, Paris and so on.' In Japan it is often sold, defined by its Englishness, a wartime import, during the First World War when

Britain and Japan were allies. Or so the story goes. In Japan, many people dispute its Western influence, some claiming it first appeared in Yokohama in the 1890s.

I ask Christopher about different baking traditions in Southeast Asia and he sends me a video of a bakery in Malaysia, Kim Hock in Ayer Tawar. It's a family-owned business, spanning three generations, and using the wood from local rubber plantations to fire the ovens and stoves. It reminds me of my own family's bakery, not in any physical sense, but in the attitude – the wishes and anxieties are familiar. It was the British who taught the family to bake the anglicised bread when the owner's father was working as a cook. The bread they make is chosen to fit their schedule of four bakes that the residual heat of the oven supplies: first rolls, then loaves. The baking times extend as the oven cools, defining what their products will be.

Christopher tells me about Harbin in China, on the Russian border, where they make beer and bread in the Russian style and I think about how the consumption of bread colours my perception of a place. This bakery is like a portal between cultures. I think of Russia as more European than China even though they both occupy much of Asia. Yet China is the biggest grower of wheat in the world, followed by India and then Russia, the latter of which has 75 per cent of its land in Asia.

In many Asian countries there are examples of fermented grain products, like the south Indian dosa for example, made from rice and urad dahl. In the Americas they have corn tortillas made with nixtamalized masa – a process native to Mexico whereby an alkali solution is added to dried corn kernels to make them more tasty and malleable – and I wonder about these flatbreads in relation to Mazoh or pizza. Almost every settled place has some processed grain culture. When I was young, I thought my family's bread was so boring, but when I think of all the various kinds of bread in the world, made to innumerable family recipes, spoken in whispers from one generation to another, I'm amazed by it all. I feel lucky to be part of that bank of recipes connecting so many people to each other and the land. I feel guilty for ever asking my mum for 'sheep bread'.

The Philippines has a wide range of breads, from *bonete*, *kababayan*, *Pan de Regla* and *putok* to *pan de sal*. While these breads have roots in a colonial past, they are distinctly Filipino. The way that bread, once accepted by a nation, will weave itself into the food culture is part of its success story. Similarly, hybrid bread products like *ampan* in Japan, which uses a rice sourdough starter and red bean paste in a similar way to a moon cake but with a wheat-based dough, show how breads can adapt and integrate into even the strongest cultural identities.

Many national cultures are shared throughout the world, in the first instance, through the selling and sharing of food. It is a way of connecting. When diplomats come together, so often it is at a dinner table. Breaking bread is a powerful act – which is why the phrase has come to be part of our everyday language – perhaps wheat's success owes something to that. You can't share rice in the same way, or millet and even corn tortillas are usually individual morsels, yet pizza and injera, for example, are all about sharing, and used as a serving utensil as well as a bread to soak up different dishes. While teff, the flour used for it it, is gluten free, it is often the very gluten that holds breads together that can be used to bring communities together. Equally it can provide a prize to be fought over. Good bread is worth fighting for and when bread is the reward we are often quick to absolve the sins of the ones who procure it.

*

Bread is a shapeshifter, the chameleon of the culinary world. It can be breakfast, lunch or dinner. Savoury or sweet, basic or celebratory, common or elitist. It is a reflection of the people, processes and cultures in which it is made. For all these reasons I find it fascinating.

My story is bound up in bread. Without it I would be a very different person. As a baker, it defines me both professionally and personally. I am a third-generation baker, so it also defines my family. It was bread that lured my grandfather away from market gardening and the coal pits of Northumberland. Bread brought Granddad and Grandma Mim to Suffolk with my dad, aged just six months old.

Bread helped the business survive over seven decades and it was bread that captured my interest in running the family business. In recent years, I have defined myself by the failure of our bread and business but am hopeful that won't last. Every baker is as good as their last loaf and so I continue to bake.

Every night I will try for the perfect bake, for every last thing to be absolutely optimal. While I've been close a few times, it has never happened, I've never completed it, never mastered it. With breadmaking I have found that it isn't the bread itself that holds the joy, it's the process and the process can always improve. The environment too can always be improved in some way, and this never-ending opportunity for progression – summed up by the Japanese notion of *Kaizen*, meaning that change is good and continuous – is what will keep me baking for as long as I live. Whether that be as a home baker, teaching or running a commercial bakery.

It can be a hard, punishing job to do. The sleep deprivation on its own can lead to a quasi-madness, coupled with the physical strain and temptation to eat sugary foods all the time. So, it can feel like the first circle of hell. When it is good though, when the doughs behave themselves and the bread comes out of the oven looking incredible – on those days, well, I wouldn't swap being a baker for anything in the world. Bread is in my blood.

2

The Wheel of Life
A loaf's cycle

I realised it was time to stop looking outward, thinking about who was going to do something about this. It was time for me to take some social responsibility.

George Lamb, broadcaster and co-founder of
Wildfarmed, October 2021

It's not easy being a baker. I'll be honest, but somehow the attraction, the love, has always outweighed any distaste I may have felt – enough to reel me in and make it my life's work. Bread is a parcel of contradictions. Crunchy yet soft. Simple yet complex. Nourishing yet deficient. Honest yet nefarious. My relationship with bread is complicated, but, I love it deeply. I love making it, baking it and teaching people how to bake their own version at home. I speak its language, have learned not just to hear it, but to listen to it, its foibles, its wants, needs.

For me, the beauty of bread lies in its completeness. Recognising the connection between the natural world, the farmer, the miller, the baker and bread itself. How realising that all the energy we take from a bite of succulent toast was once bound up in the sun changes things. Seeing how that energy has been transmuted through many living organisms to end up fuelling humankind.

This journey is not a straight line, but a circle. Botanist Sir Albert Howard, one of the great elders of organic farming, refers to this as 'an ever-recurring cycle, a cycle which, repeating itself silently and ceaselessly, ensures the continuation of living matter'. He goes onto say that this cycle is one of 'birth, growth, maturity, death, and decay'. This 'Wheel of Life' is also, I believe, the *weal* of life, its source of happiness. And mine. The cycle starts with the soil and ends with bread.

In the following section, I want to show you the who of it all – the people who are making bread more beautiful and the processes they use. Farmers, millers and bakers who want to be part of a sustainable system of creating, making and baking. And perhaps, if you put your ear to the ground and listen, you may hear a rumbling, the stirrings of a revolution.

First meet Wildfarmed. They are taking on the farming system in the UK. Who are they? Well, they are a headstrong group of farmers, millers, chefs and bakers who are using and applying their combined, extensive knowledge of agriculture to make the best possible flour. Formed in 2018 by musician Andy Cato, corporate financier Edd Lees and broadcaster George Lamb, Wildfarmed's mission is to grow wheat 'the right way' and make 'regenerative flour and bread that tastes better, is better for you and for the planet'. Andy told me that he was most influenced by father of sustainable farming Sir Albert Howard who promoted the refined soil management skills he learnt in India, in the early twentieth century, when he was supposed to be teaching local farmers about Western industrial farming methods.

I was invited to Wildfarmed's place in Oxfordshire in June 2023, a day dedicated to showing fellow bakers exactly what they are trying to achieve and how they are going about it. It looked like all the farms I had played on as a child, with barns full of knick-knacks and dusty, broken-down tractors. The yard was a collection of concrete slabs, each one at a different level. There the similarities between past and present ended, however.

We were herded into groups and sent off into the fields with our guide, the man behind it all, Andy Cato. Probably better known to many people as one of the iconic 1990s electronic music group Groove Armada, Andy is a 6 ft 8, scarecrow-esque man, with a straw hat that he used to point at hedgerows and field margins, grazing cattle and medieval ridge and furrow formations. It had rained heavily just hours before, but now the sun was out, the humidity on a par with what I experienced the first time I stepped off a plane in Vietnam.

Walking through wheat fields, blooming with flowers and various companion crops, I was greeted by crowds of insects. The fields of my childhood were inert, lifeless places, populated only by burgeoning heads of dwarfish wheat. These were the opposite and I wondered if we had been led into the fields to distract the flying creatures from the crops.

'The landscapes that grow our food should be full of life, from birds, bugs and bees to hedgerows, flowers and trees but right now the industrial agricultural system is killing us and our planet,' co-owner George Lamb explains when I ask about their aims. They hope to change this through regenerative agriculture. I asked George to explain what this means.

56 | BREAKING BREAD

'The Wildfarmed regenerative standards combine five principles; no 'cides on the growing crop, companion crops, nutrition based on need, cover crops at all times and integrating livestock.' The ''cides' George is referring to are insecticides, herbicides and fungicides, the main agents of control in the conventional agricultural system. 'Right now, there's no official certification,' he adds, 'so we have to hold ourselves to the highest standard.'

Companion cropping is nothing new, and one of the best examples comes from Mesoamerica (Central America), with the three sisters' system of planting maize, beans and pumpkins together. These three crops provide the soil's nutrition and feedback different elements which benefit each other so the soil maintains its balance without becoming depleted.

In the Wildfarmed system, legumes such as beans are interspersed with the wheat crop to perform the same function, and as these kinds of plants are nitrogen 'fixers', there is a reduced dependency on fossil-fuel derived nitrogen. Nutrition based on need allows for some nitrogen use but only what is necessary to kickstart natural systems. It involves a fraction of the amount used by conventional farming.

Cover crops aid the sequestration of greenhouse gases that would otherwise leach into the atmosphere if the soil was left uncovered. The mix of clovers and other leguminous plants help refuel the soil while it rests.

Integrating livestock helps with fertilising the soil naturally and controlling the vegetation in fallow areas while offering a revenue stream for resting arable land. Wildfarmed don't rely on adding huge amounts of ammonia-based fertiliser to boost yields, so takes full advantage of fixing nitrogen and recycling it through animals.

THE WHEEL OF LIFE | 57

They don't have a commitment to any particular varieties of wheat or the way that the wheat is milled. Wildfarmed talk openly about getting their flour into industrial baking systems and have recently begun to roller-mill their flour to offer the consistency that plant bakeries require for their products. The rationale is that the more flour is being used, the more land is being managed in line with their systems, and the bigger the benefit to the natural world.

As you might expect, this strategy has left them exposed to criticism from both sides with hardline organic, stoneground flour proponents suggesting they aren't doing enough and the more commercial enterprises picking up on their lack of certification. Part of the problem with farming is that the certification is either misleading or not fit for purpose, and Wildfarmed prefers to resist reducing farming to a set of rules, adopting a more holistic approach that considers all the contributing systems rather than just the physical product.

Andy Cato, who started the Wildfarmed project, sold his music publishing rights to begin his farming journey. A move akin to the lad who sold his family's prize cow for some magic beans, he has spent the best part of two decades waiting to climb the beanstalk to agricultural supremacy.

He was prompted to start on his farming journey in Gascony, France, where he lived with his family, after reading an article while returning from a gig on a train, in 2007, that changed the course of his life. It ended with the line *'If you don't like the system, don't depend on it'*. For someone who started his music career playing trombone in a small northern colliery band and who has since headlined in front of hundreds of thousands at festivals and stadiums globally, what to many might seem a daunting journey forward, to Andy seemed possible.

To better understand what Wildfarmed seek to achieve I went to meet one of the people who helped shape their goals, Tim Williams, one of the original thirteen farmers that adopted their system in 2021. I visited Tim's farm, Crocadon, in Cornwall, which has, according to its website, '*a collaborative approach to food and farming, working together to explore and celebrate a brighter vision for food and agriculture*'. Crocadon is a fine example of agritourism, boasting a restaurant that won a green Michelin star in 2023, under the stewardship of Dan Cox, and a fine bakery and a café, where I sat waiting for him to arrive.

The businesses were closed, and I passed the time by trying to throw pebbles into a courtyard drain. It was a mild Monday in October and apart from the clinks of stone on metal, the only sounds were of birdsong from the many species that call this land home. The rumble of a diesel engine broke the almost magical spell, and there was Tim coming down the hill in his tractor.

Tim has over two decades of farming experience in both his native New Zealand and in the UK. Regarded as a grazing expert, he advises, mentors and experiments in regenerative agriculture, seeking to restore the health and vitality of the soil. Doing no harm isn't enough, farmers such as Tim argue; it's their mission to repair the damage done by previous generations.

We go into the café through a small kitchen with a box of soil-covered vegetables on the central prep table. Tim says he'd offer me a coffee, but he can't work the machine, but luckily I can after working some coffee jobs to get me through university, and we sit down at a pine farmhouse table with cups fired from local clay. Tim is slight, with sun-tempered skin and enough furrows on his brow to believe him when he says that farming is a hard profession. His voice is quiet and understated but he speaks with passion about agriculture, and when he hits a seam of conversation that is important to him, the authority of his words is palpable.

'I've come late to the party,' he comments. 'I'm livestock turned arable. Basically, because it's more fun riding tractors around all day – killing animals isn't so much fun.' He opens up about the human side of agriculture, believing a lot of the issues arise from an emotionally repressed root. 'There's a lot of frustration in farming, and a lot of intergenerational trauma. There's people who are farming who aren't natural farmers; they're just doing it because they are expected to, dealing with the bad relationships they had with their fathers. Playing it all out in the fields.'

As a third-generation baker myself, I am all too familiar with this. The competition that can play out between father and son when they share a profession is not usually healthy. My father wanted to join the army as a PT instructor but couldn't sign the forms himself as he was too young. My grandfather flatly refused: 'You're a baker' he said. And that was that. I'd always wanted to be a theatre director and after a promising start in the industry ended up letting go of the dream, trying instead to patch up a family business that had suffered from years of poor management in the absence of my ageing parents, as they struggled with their own physical and mental health challenges, my mother attempting suicide at one point. There was a surplus of negativity from my parents to me, and in the face of such emotion, that doesn't provide a solid foundation for progression.

'With each generation it gets magnified', Tim goes on, explaining that the cocktail of the trauma that comes from the stresses and daily grind of farming, capitalism and the narrow scope of academia when it comes to teaching young farmers, all of which have led us to a bottleneck.

60 | BREAKING BREAD

I'm surprised to discover that Tim is incredibly sympathetic to the high-input farming he opposes, believing solutions to come through compromise. 'To elicit change on any scale you have to be obliging to the conventional system. That's the only way farmers are going to change.' he explains. 'Let's say you can reduce nitrogen and other chemicals by 50 per cent, environmentally, on a global scale, that's huge.'

The nitrogen he's talking about is synthesised using fossil fuels, and a lot of fuel is needed to break the triple-bonded nitrogen in the air to create a soluble ammonia-based fertiliser that can be spread onto fields. Back in New Zealand, Tim's family stopped farming in the 1990s, and since that time, just in that country alone, nitrogen use has increased an incredible 600 per cent. It's no wonder that global farming is responsible for 20–30 per cent of all carbon emissions. One per cent of all the fossil-fuel energy on Earth goes into this process, first developed by Fritz Haber and Carl Bosch early in the twentieth century. It feels a no-brainer that we should be moving to a more sustainable model, away from oil-derived inputs and back to a more harmonious system. But it needs support to make that happen, a lot of support.

Tim explains that 'with conventional wheat, if you throw everything at it, you'll be pushing nearly 10 tonnes to the hectare, if you get it right. So, at £100 per tonne who cares? . . . You're getting paid.'

The grains grown by Tim include a heritage variety named 'Red Lammas'. It costs £850 per tonne and although it commands a high price to specialist food producers, the yields are a quarter of those enjoyed by conventional farmers. The difference between them is the cost to the soil. High yields with so-called 'Borlaug' – common wheat varieties, which rely on lots of chemical inputs, either through fertilisers or pesticides, have produced a bubble in the farming world. The wheat variety takes its name from influential American agronomist and Nobel Prize winner Norman Borlaug, instrumental in the Green Revolution. He said: 'The Green Revolution has won a temporary success in man's war against hunger and deprivation; it has given man breathing space.' Borlaug saw his achievement as a way to buy time to transition to a more sustainable kind of agriculture, not a solution to the problem.

Wildfarmed are hoping that they can offer the long-term solution, providing systems successful both naturally and commercially. At the time of writing, they have loaves of bread in the UK supermarkets Waitrose and M&S. The M&S loaves are made at The Village Bakery bread plant using 10 to 16 per cent regenerative flour in each loaf. The other 84 to 90 per cent of the flour comes from Marriage's Millers. Their 'Life-Changing Sliced White' is made using their own flour completely, with the addition of extra vital wheat gluten which comes from conventionally farmed wheat. The idea of taking regenerative wheat, roller-milling it, adding in extra gluten and flour enhancers to make a white sliced loaf for a supermarket shelf is a bold move. Many artisan bakers who signed up to the Wildfarmed movement found this hard to swallow, that they could supply a premium product on one hand and use it to make a version of what many see as the anti-Christ, on the other. Just as Tim Williams suggests we must be obliging to the industrial farming system, we may have to be just as obliging to the industrial baking system.

Bread begins with flour and water so, of course, I have to visit a mill to see for myself how the flower of the field is converted into the flour in the sack.

62 | BREAKING BREAD

Marriage's Flour was used by my family bakery for more than fifty years. Most of my relatives have, at one time or another, scooped powdered wheat from a Marriage's Flour sack and turned it into bread, so there's a personal connection to the place I am going to visit.

Their own story is some two hundred years old. Milling in Essex since 1824, the company is now run by a father–daughter combo that represents the fifth and sixth generations of the family. Under George and Hannah Marriage, it produces around one per cent of all UK flour and while, undoubtedly, it's an industrial scale operation, it's by no means one of the biggest.

I squeeze my ageing Volvo between the Victorian brick buildings; on one side a complex of apartments has taken over a former ball bearing factory in the town of Chelmsford. On the other is the 'new' mill that was built by the Marriages in 1899, at the time in the middle of a field, far outside the city. The bricks give the tall factory the look of a restoration project, with lovely pale lintels and more modern temporary additions that have corrugated roofs and look awkward cuddled-up to their better-looking siblings.

Marriage's mill is ideally placed to take advantage of East Anglia's bounty of wheat, and testament to this is the number of other large mills still operating in the area. The Romans brought their wheat to the UK and set up their first town and capital in nearby Colchester, or Camulodunum, as they called it. The colonising Romans viewed the eastern counties with covetous eyes, salivating at what they could see as the grain-growing potential from the quality of the earth. Flat and fertile, with links to the continent, the land was ideal for grain production that could help feed the Empire.

A majority of the wheat milled by Marriage's is grown within a thirty-five mile radius. They have relationships with over four hundred UK farmers, while also importing wheat from Canada, Romania, Sweden and Lithuania. Historically, they have also imported grain from Kazakhstan, but those Black Sea supplies have become difficult since the war between Russia and Ukraine escalated in 2022.

Marriage's is a 'gristing' mill that mixes grains from different fields before milling, as opposed to the bigger 'blending' mills that grind the grain in separate batches and mix it afterwards. As I followed the process from delivery of grain to finished flour, I was amazed by the volume.

As a planet, we eat an astonishing amount of bread, around one hundred million tonnes a year by some estimates. Some 99.8 per cent of UK households buy bread compared to 90 per cent in Australia and 97 per cent in the United States. How wondrous were those humans who first looked at wheat grass seed and thought *'let's crush this into a dust, mix it with water and bake it'*. I can imagine other members of their group telling them to stop playing with their food. There must be something inside us that wants to atomise and then reconstruct everything.

One of the most influential changes to the breadmaking process took place in nineteenth-century Europe with the advent of a new kind of milling. Since the first millers had crushed grain by hand using quern stones in the Fertile Crescent,* or even before then, the First Nations Peoples, as Bruce Pascoe suggests in his 2014 book, *Dark Emu: Aboriginal Australia and the Birth of Agriculture*. Milling had not changed all that much. The efficiency had improved without doubt as the Greeks developed the

---

* The Fertile Crescent, an area encompassing modern-day Iraq, Syria, Lebanon, Palestine, Israel, Jordan and northern Egypt, where the first settled agricultural communities arose *c.* early ninth millennium BCE.

BREAKING BREAD

hour-glass mills powered by animals, then the Romans harnessed the power of the waterways to keep the millstones turning around the clock or sundial. Essentially, though, the end result was similar.

With the urban relocation of rural people that came as part of the Industrial Revolution in eighteenth–nineteenth century Europe, mills had to be moved into the cities, away from waterways and sheltered from the wind that could power the mills famous across the flatlands of Holland. Steam-powered mills, fired with coal, provided the energy but still were used to drive millstones. Even in thousands of years of development, this was still seen as the best way to turn wheat into flour.

In Switzerland, Austria and Hungary, around 1820, milling wheat using a series of rollers was trialled and for the first time the endosperm could be released from the germ and bran. These are the three parts of the wheat kernel. This is the baking equivalent to splitting the atom, the result a change in process used to this day. The first set of rollers cracked the kernel so that the endosperm could be singled out for separate milling. Rich in starch and gluten-forming proteins, this makes the white flour found on most supermarket shelves all over the world. The fractured wheat can be milled in isolation and then reconstituted (or not), depending on the requirements of the baker (or factory).

Without this advance, you'd probably never have eaten a croissant, or any other viennoiserie for that matter. Vienna was where this highly technical flour was first showcased. The process generated a lot of heat which was an issue at first, until it was eradicated by passing chilled water through the cores of the rollers. It also generated a different kind of heat with traditional millers who lost their monopoly on the flour business.

While the efficiencies of roller-milling make the flour cheaper to buy, and the resulting bread is softer and whiter, our bodies are getting short changed. Those early adopters who gorged on white refined flour, made from the endosperm, were at risk from deficiency diseases like pellagra, which is fatal if untreated. It is characterised by such symptoms as diarrhoea, dermatitis and mental disturbance – all as a result of a lack of niacin. The parts of the grain that spoiled more rapidly were also the ones that contained the most nutritional diversity.

So North American and British millers were forced to add some of the nutrients extracted back in. Instead of being scandalised, marketeers pounced on the opportunity to take advantage of fortification by raising prices. Capitalism at its best – solving a problem created by the same industry that caused it, and getting the consumer to pick up the tab.

The white flour I have in my cupboard is fortified with niacin, calcium carbonate (chalk), iron and thiamin. The stoneground wholemeal flour that sits alongside it has none of those additives, because – you've guessed it – it already contains them. The gluten content can also be carefully managed in roller milled white flour and if a particular harvest has lower than required levels for processing, extra gluten is added. When not properly fermented, our guts are forced to work overtime, sometimes resulting in health-related issues.

Vital Wheat Gluten, or gluten as it's more commonly known, is expensive however, so the mills that do most of this balancing will use the cheapest grain they can get their hands on. As they are required to fortify it anyway, they don't need to worry about its original nutritional value. Marriage's has added gluten to some of its products but they are typically ones required by the plant bakeries that make the soft wrapped bread for supermarkets.

Mills that supply plant bakeries require equipment to generate exact results for the performance of a particular flour using a mixer that can measure gluten development to a precise degree. Marriage's technical manager Simon Fortis showed me theirs, which can mix a dough that weighs around one hundred and fifty grams, or just over five ounces in old money. It produces an exact assessment of the flour's properties that can be used to calibrate the bread plant machinery and maintain consistency, efficiency and production flow.

The technology of the mill is an interesting mix of ages. Grain is sorted through a bank of cameras that reject any kernels that are too dark in colour, suggesting ergot, a fungal disease that can cause sickness, hallucinations and even death at high enough concentrations. In the Middle Ages, it was called 'St Anthony's Fire' as the people consumed by it felt as if they were burning to death.

The mill is controlled by a computerised system, and I'm allowed to step inside the nerve centre of the operation, which reminds me of Homer Simpson's workstation. A semi-circle of screens, with various graphics that wouldn't look out of place in an arcade, indicate silo levels and encoded information to allow the miller to keep track of everything that is going on.

We walk down the original wooden staircase to a modern on-site laboratory that tests for gluten content, purity, protein levels, nitrogen markers and enzymatic activity. It's the same space that houses the £42,000 bread-lab that can only make a quarter of a loaf of bread. There's a stack of printed A4 sheets next to it giving the precise technical analysis that is required by big robot staffed bakeries.

The main Büler roller-mill is omnipresent, whirring and sending vibrations through my entire body. In another space, I see five Victorian French burrstone mills slowly grinding away, each one sitting on a wooden stage strengthened by steel that was machined in Suffolk sometime in the nineteenth century. Simon explains that the stones can never be replaced. 'Hitler flooded the only quarry in France where you can get the stone.'

The whole mill perfectly represents the modern baking environment, as we sit today with all the spoils of modern technology and yet still hang on to the last frayed ties to the past. The Marriage family saw the wave coming in the late 1800s, so they abandoned their water mills and their windmills dotted around the Chelmsford area and invested in the future. A state-of-the-art roller-mill, powered by steam, turning black coal into white flour, their goods sent back to London on the same trains that dropped off the fuel.

Simon lets me feel some of the flour that is still warm from the mill. The first is at a semolina stage, like fine sand, not yet ready for the paper flour sack. It goes through more reducing rollers, into gigantic sieves that look like gyrating sheds. What comes out is finished white flour that I spread across my palm with my thumb like soft butter over warm toast. In a side room, the master miller, who has been with the company for some thirty-eight years, is fixing broken sieving frames with his apprentice who is almost the same age. Different grades of net are stretched across frames and glued in place with little brushes imprisoned to keep the powder moving through the process.

The humming mill looks like an imagined contraption. A piece of set from the 1971 film *Charlie and the Chocolate Factory*. This is not for show however, the company that made Marriage's latest

68 | BREAKING BREAD

roller-mill, Büler, has 65 per cent of all the wheat on earth going through one of its machines. Pressured air pumps grades of flour through shoots, an Archimedes' screw mixes in fortification powders and when Simon opens the inspection hatches to let me see the shiny spinning cylinders, I have to use all my self-restraint not to reach out and touch them.

But it's those heavyset burrstone creatures that really set my mind into action. One of the stones is being 'dressed', a process of chipping away at the surface of the stone to create a pattern that will radiate the grain from the centre to the open edge. The tool used is a wonderfully ancient-looking thing, all wood except for some high-grade steel that forms a double-headed chisel. Called a 'mill bill', it pecks away at the stone to give the kind of precision we can't yet match with modern tooling. The stone itself is made up of pieces, fused together with Plaster of Paris and contained by a metal hoop. I wonder if France's access to premier milling stones has anything to do with their national bread mania?

When the masonry is complete, the stone is polished with a sacrificial piece of burr, and as I hold it in my hands, I'm lit up by the resemblance to bread itself. It has a honeycomb crumb, irregular and a creamy colour that varies by area. The crust is thin and smooth, and the piece weighs less than I had braced myself for. Simon explains that this piece has been exposed to the elements at one time or another and is now useless as a mill stone. 'Once the rain gets to a millstone if you try to use it, it will shatter. That's why when these stones go, we can't replace them.' Three have already been replaced by composite stone mills made from a blend of quartz and cement. When there is an issue with one, the whole unit has to be replaced.

THE WHEEL OF LIFE | 69

It is possible to make wholemeal flour using a roller-mill. It just involves putting all the pieces of the grain back together once taken apart. It's a bit like the difference between an omelette made with a real egg and one made using liquid egg, or even worse, powdered egg. They may be technically the same product but spiritually, they're very different.

Simon looks at the bran from both roller-milled flour and stoneground flour under a microscope, and finds a difference. The stoneground bran has softer edges, less likely to disturb gluten development unlike the 'tiny razorblade-like' pieces that are produced when the wheat is ripped apart in the rollers.

The last thing I'm shown is a bag attached to one of the shoots of the Büler mill; it contains what looks like golden confetti. I'm not sure what I'm seeing initially, then it hits me: it's the germ. The fatty nutritious part of the wheat that is milled into the flour during stone grinding but is taken out by the more modern mill. When the germ is included in the flour, the shelf-life is reduced by around three months because of all the fatty acids it contains, but it's also the part of the wheat seed that has life in it and that life is valuable to us. Its value is certainly recognised by the millers.

'What happens to the bag when it's full?' I ask Simon.

'One of the Marriages will take it home,' he replies. They scatter their porridge with the super-nutritious golden germ, a perk that keeps them in good health.

As I collect my belongings from the Marriage's boardroom, watched over by paintings and photographs of all the previous directors, I ask whether they have any plans to mill regenerative wheat. 'We have a meeting booked in with Wildfarmed,' I'm told by their flour sales manager.

It is mills like these that recognise the value of old methods but also have the capacity to mill large quantities of flour that can make a positive difference to our bread – and to our personal wellbeing, it seems, if we have access to those loaves.

And so, to my next visit, to my friend, Oliver Hornsey-Pennell, head baker at Hylsten Bakery in Devon.

'Hylsten' is old English for 'stone baked' and all the bread at the bakery is made with domestically grown wheat, with a majority coming from the South West Grain Network, a group of farmers, millers and bakers taking active steps towards an alternative, more sustainable grain economy.

I drive the three hundred and sixteen miles to see what kind of bread can be made with traditionally milled local flour. For this opportunity, I've agreed to help Ollie bake all the bread, using stoneground flour, for the following day. I arrive in time for dinner and we sit together with some of his friends, discussing the bakery and listening to a 1970s' recording of old locomotive engines. It's the kind of hedonistic extravaganza that bakers are famous for. We're in bed by 10 p.m. A baker's day starts early.

Of course, I am already awake when Oliver knocks on my door at 3 a.m.

'Do you *need* anything to eat?' he asks politely. I say no, although I could eat something. Coffee is far more important. 'Good. We don't have time anyway.'

We drive down the dark, deserted lanes from his house to the bakery. As we approach the town of Buckfastleigh, I start seeing the word as 'Breakfastleigh' but soon put that out of my head. If I want some toast, I am going to have to bake the bread first.

We wind our way over the hill to where the bakery sits, helter-skeltering through streets until we turn into the half-Victorian, half-new build business estate where Hylsten is based. There are various enterprises there, including coffee roasters, tent makers and the Fresh Flour Company run by Andrew Gilhespy. I trip over a pallet of his flour as I enter Hylsten.

When I ask Ollie what he imagines when he thinks of bread, he says a classic country loaf with a dark bubbly, caramelised crust dashed with a tiny bit of flour, a long loaf with a single ear. Inside it has a creamy, porridgy crumb, not too open but with a good amount of wholemeal. It's the bread he makes along with Kate Marton who now runs the bakery operation after spending time at artisan bakeries such as E5 Bakehouse in London.

At just twenty-five, Ollie's young to be in the position of head baker – a hundred years ago he'd still be an apprentice – but within his field, he's extremely skilled and experienced, having been exposed to the cosmopolitan melee of sourdough bread with stints at Dusty Knuckle, in London, and Ten Belles, in Paris. Every bakery is different, and every artisan bakery is custom-fitted to its bakers, so I must learn how he does things. My own experience means I know the right questions to ask as we fire up the ovens and check the dough.

'Hmm,' Ollie grumbles, head in fridge, 'the dough is a little over.'

The dough has fermented more than he would like. He predicts the bread won't have the maximum volume it could as a result. The acidity will be higher and the crumb will have a sharper, zingier flavour but the same acids that bring the flavour will have also denatured the gluten a little more than is ideal and the balance will be out by an amount only Ollie will notice.

He makes a flurry of micro adjustments in his head for the next day's dough. 'We shaped them too slowly. I knew it. How do you make people faster?' It's a rhetorical question. This kind of constant analysis is the cheaper, human version of the dough lab that sits in every industrial mill across the world.

While the ovens are heating up, Ollie performs all sorts of tasks to prepare for the next day. Checking orders, printing delivery notes, wiping off the numbers on the whiteboard. I don't interfere too much and snoop around the long, narrow bakery space that smells grassy and sweet.

Ollie is going through his process like a sprinter before a race, visualising his day, focusing on what he needs to achieve and unfortunately for me he forgets about that coffee. The office area is on a mezzanine at one end. The only other place I've seen that layout is E5 Bakehouse, where Kate had worked. The whiteboard has notes of all the adjustments made to account for temperature, hydration and fermentation times. A daily organoleptic calibration, using all the analytical potential of the human senses, chasing the golden loaf at the end of the rainbow. The coffee has to wait, the ovens are hot.

We wheel out the steel racks, full of inverted dough slumbering in bannetons, the baskets that the dough proves in. Wobbling like well-made panna cottas. Now, I can see what Ollie meant when he said the dough was 'over', and know instinctively we will have to take extra care in turning them out. Ollie has already found the best layout to get the ideal bake while using every inch of oven space. I commit the patterns to memory, so I don't have to ask him later.

The dough eases from the banneton to the peel, the wooden board used to load and unload the oven. Ollie makes the first cuts, showing me exactly what he wants. Not just the number of cuts but the depth, length, angle and positioning. I do a couple and he corrects me until he's happy. Lifting the boards to the top deck, we slide them in and pull them out, leaving the bread in the oven. It's a bit like that tablecloth trick, you know the one.

The oven door is closed and steam injected into the chamber. It hisses and whistles as some leaks from around the door seals. In the first twenty minutes, the dough will expand, springing from the hearth. Heat energy flows directly from the stone into the bread. The crust is kept supple by the humid environment and the dough expands. Maillard reactions, the ones associated with the deliciousness of browned foods, take place that give the crust its distinctive flavour and appearance. It is the conclusion to a flurry of small chemical reactions that occur on the surface of the dough as it bakes, the reason the crust and the crumb don't just have a different texture, but a completely different flavour too.

The dough ruptures along the cuts we have made and when we inspect the oven again, it has jumped considerably. After twenty minutes, Ollie pulls the dampers out which opens flaps at the back of the oven, releasing the trapped steam and allowing the bread to finish baking in a dry heat. It is in these conditions that the reduced sugars from the Maillard reaction can caramelise giving the bread a sweet, crisp crust.

Finally, the bread is unloaded and placed onto racks to cool. The smell is incredible, a wash of warm honey, toasted nuts and deep almost meaty notes. As the crust contracts, it cracks, with thousands of tiny pops. Ollie smiles. This is the joy of being a baker, the little wins that can't be replicated or shared.

Once Ollie is happy leaving me working the oven alone, I finally get my coffee, and the anticipation makes it all the more

74 | BREAKING BREAD

delicious. Yet the excitement of working in a new space and successfully baking with Ollie has already given me a high. He starts mixing dough for the day shift and packs rye sourdough into brown bags, labelling each one by hand.

I stack the bannetons upside down on top of the oven so they can dry before being filled again. A pyramid of brushed-out wood pulp. As the bread bakes, and dawn approaches, Ollie makes me a breakfast of warm bread, butter and jam.

The bread is a delight, a creamy bran-scattered crumb that resists my bite but isn't chewy in the least. A paper thin, deep flavoured crust balances the sponginess, and the acidity comes in at the end to wash the palate clean. Worth every one of the three hundred and sixteen miles it took to get here and all made with flour milled by stone, naturally fermented, raised by hand. Ollie's hard work the day before in mixing and shaping the loaves, the tinkering of water and silent beady-eyed officiating of the fermentation, the cold, blind prove that misbehaved ever-so slightly, the care in scoring the dough and watchfulness as the bake progressed are all in that mouthful. The story of hard graft, expertise and sheer will, written in a language that only the tongue can understand. Bread, making more life, with its release of energy in the eater.

Once we finish our shift and the daytime team takes over, we swing by a farm shop that Hylsten supplies. The bread we baked has already been delivered and is being snapped up while we're waiting for our sausage rolls to warm through. It's priced at more than double that of the most expensive supermarket loaf, but isn't in the same spectrum.

It is a difficult fact for bakers to realise that their produce will always be compared to the SKUs (stock keeping units) on supermarket shelves. We don't make these comparisons with other products like cars or televisions, where we accept some brands are more focused on quality than others, and therefore more expensive. With bread, we want it all – to be the best quality possible at the lowest price.

Kate Marton has a wonderful graphic on the Hylsten website that shows exactly where all the money goes when you buy a loaf of Hylsten bread. Forty-eight per cent of it is spent on wages, otherwise known as 'people'. Skilled people who can handle the complexities and inconsistencies of nutritious flour, who live in communities and have families and pay taxes that support domestic initiatives.

The way Hylsten makes bread isn't the way most is made. Our food systems lack diversity, and when any large systems become homogeneous, the danger of disease and decay is ever present. There is always the question of how we should eat and the expectation is that there's one answer, but this mindset is the problem, we got into the pickle we are in by reducing the collective diet. We need to eat in different ways at different times, we need small, medium and large producers to work in concert, not competition.

If the system that produces our bread is to be cyclical, then it must be a series of cycles. Not a single circle, but a Spirographic web of nuanced systems. Each one, tailor made for the place it feeds. The beauty of bread is its adaptability. Six thousand years and counting, it has adjusted to environmental and anthropological system changes. It is never one thing, and as we move into a new age of food production, brought about by necessity, I'm excited to see the creative ways in which our daily loaf will keep us fed.

3

Frankenloaf

Science and the perfect bread

Hateful day when I received life! Accursed creator!
Why did you form a monster so hideous that even you
turned from me in disgust?

– Mary Shelley, *Frankenstein* (1818)

Frankenstein: Or The Modern Prometheus is a warning of the unbridled potential of science when coupled with the ego. A desire for notoriety which spread through the scientific world like wildfire, leading to bigger and bigger challenges being taken on by its creators. Mary Shelley's character Frankenstein, the scientist and not the monster as most people mistakenly believe, performs a shamanistic necromancy by raising a lifeless corpse to life. In doing so Victor Frankenstein believes he is creating a human, but his fault lies in leaving humanity itself out of the recipe. Ashamed of his actions, he denies the 'wretch' a companion – indeed any element of happiness, which in the end turns his pleading creation into a destructive force. How does that translate to bread, you may ask? Well, we have created a 'Frankenloaf' to supersede our original breads, arguably devoid of its heart, soul and essence required to make it special. Science explains that it has all the properties of bread, shouting about the added extras, the 'benefits', but it only adds up to a fraction of the handmade loaf, in my opinion.

The story of Frankenstein's creation, like the story of modern industrialised bread, has become skewed over time. We have grown to fear the monster when perhaps we should be more concerned with the fault in the maker. The enemy is seen by many as the cheap, sliced white loaf that we find lining supermarket shelves and stomachs all over the world. Perhaps the only fault with the soulless bread is that it is too keen to serve us, its master. Science is brilliant, don't get me wrong but the truth is that this super bread is a step backwards, unpicking the sutures of modern medicine. If it wasn't so wonderfully profitable it would have been discarded well before it hit the supermarket shelves. Money beats quality and health.

The most logical (and easiest) way of cooking grain is to make a porridge: simply add water to the grain and heat until soft and thick. The resulting meal works so well that it survives to the present day in several forms globally – oat porridge, pottage, rice pudding, risotto, paella, grits, polenta and pearl barley, among others. Far from simple carb capsules, these grains have a complex mix of fats, amino acids, nutrients, protein, sugars and, of course, carbohydrates.

The next evolutionary stage involves mechanically crushing the seeds before cooking to release more of their natural potential. When water is added to ground wheat flour, two proteins, glutenin and gliadin, come together to produce a gluten network that encapsulates moisture and turns porridge into parchment. The dough that forms can be stretched to make thin unleavened breads such as wheat tortillas, piadina, paratha and chapati.

When the dough is left to ferment, the gluten, enrobing the moisture pockets, begins to inflate with the carbon dioxide released by the metabolising yeasts. The tiny balloons make a dense loaf softer and easier to chew, and the yeast has friends working alongside it to lessen the burden on our digestive system.

Ever eager to please, a scientist will seek to solve any problem for us, even when the solution may end up being a bigger problem than the original. Unpack that if you will. Bread is a perfect example of this. A foodstuff that's survived adaptation to a great extent, for thousands of years, before we looked at our old pal and thought, *you deserve a makeover*. Once we'd made all our 'improvements', the finished article was worlds apart from the original. More concerned with how to get the dough through all the machinery without it causing damage, we ignored the fact that the damage might come later – to our own internal machinery.

I'll revisit this idea, but a loaf of bread is a whole thing. It's a complete meal that can keep us alive for a whole day. We can eat some bread and turn that energy into all the joys, sorrows, mistakes and achievements that life has to offer.

The kernel of the wheat plant is a marvellous thing and bound up within it is a complex recipe for life. Everything from the outer bran to the nutritious endosperm and germ combine to produce a whole meal. It can be helpful to think of the seed as an egg, with the bran representing the shell, the endosperm played by the white albumen and lastly the germ mirroring the yolk. The bran is made up of around 42 per cent dietary fibre (mostly insoluble), 15 per cent protein, with the rest made up of fat, B vitamins and mineral content. The fibre is essential for keeping the colony of colonic microbes in your gut happy and healthy; it wicks moisture to your digestive tract and keeps your bowel movements regular. While it doesn't pack the nutritional bomb of the other two components, it is sorely missed when sieved out of wheat flour, as we shall see.

The germ is the seed within a seed, loaded with an alchemist's shopping list of proteins, fat, B vitamins and minerals. This embryo initiates the transformation from dormant capsule to a living plant. While only making up around 2.5 per cent of the kernel, it is indispensable – or at least should be. It has life and this is a problem for an industrial process: it spoils, the fats turning rancid, reducing the best before date of stoneground flour by three months.

The final part is the endosperm, a starch-rich cluster of energy that is bound up with two very technical proteins. The siblings of the endosperm have a good dose of protein themselves – in the germ it's 25 per cent (about the same as a steak) but the ones that are present in the Big Brother form the membrane that is essential for breadmaking as we know it. This is what gives our bread volume and the strong, rubbery consistency required for shaping by hand, or machine. This last element is 75 per cent starch and interspersed with glutenin and gliadin, the two gluten-forming proteins. I like to think of these two proteins as a two-part glue, entirely inert when in the packet but when combined with water becoming strong, fixing the structure of our dough. In too high a concentration, however, the adhesive can damage our gut lining, causing cracks that let undigested elements into the bloodstream.

There are other catalytic ingredients such as the enzymes amylase and lipase which play pivotal roles in the process. The takeaway here is that wheat has three principal components that work in harmony together and only when this balance is maintained do they provide their full nutritional promise. Phytase is a particularly essential enzyme present in many plants and in wheat it neutralises the phytic acid during fermentation. The latter acts like a wall that restricts our body's access to all the nutritional content. Short-fermented bread may contain the same nutritional elements as long-fermented bread, but they are not as accessible.

Bruce German, a food scientist at the University of California, reminds us: '*If [he] gave you a bag of flour and water you could live on it for a while but eventually you would die but if you take that same bag of flour and water and bake it into bread you could live indefinitely.*' So, although the potential is all there in the flour, we have to unlock that through the process of breadmaking and if we take shortcuts the resulting bread will not release its goodness into our bodies.

Let's make some naturally leavened bread together, a wholewheat (or wholemeal) sourdough loaf that will be risen using a starter dough and nothing else. Some of this may sound overly complicated and as dense as a pumpernickel, but at its root, breadmaking is a simple art. There are two goals we aim for on our journey, one is to create a structural network of gluten to hold carbon dioxide, and the other is to facilitate the conditions for the creation of carbon dioxide through fermentation. Put simply:

Make gas. Catch gas. Bake dough. Eat bread.

The true benefits of bread eating are byproducts of those human aims. We see a dough rising and are content and yet if it's rising as the result of obscene quantities of yeast rather than the interplay between microbes and cereal elements, we have a problem. Much in the same way as artificial nitrogen breaks the relationship between soil and plant in the farmer's field, when accelerated leavening is used, it can break the relationship between the seed and bread. What we end up with appears to be bread, but a much poorer version.

Developing our sourdough starter takes time. By taking a small amount of wheat flour (or any cereal flour really) and mixing with an equal measure of water, the flywheel begins to turn. An active starter is a soup of bacteria and yeasts that lives in a home furnished by the combined gloop. While there are more than 1,500 named varieties of yeast, the ones most common to sourdough all have incredibly complicated names that neither you nor I could probably pronounce. On a basic level, we are dealing with a combination of more than one yeast.

These yeasts can be derived from a number of sources – from the environment of the bakery or home to the baker's hands, but most commonly from the bran of the cereal grain. The skin of organic fruit is another fantastic source of natural yeasts as winemakers and brewers know. The reasons most instructions for making sourdough starters from scratch call for 'stoneground', 'organic', 'wholewheat' flours are that the bran is the most densely populated source of natural yeasts. If organic, they won't have been killed by pesticides or other chemicals and stone grinding flour is done at a lower temperature to other milling methods so maintains more of the yeasts.

In the mills there is a zero tolerance for pests in the delivered grain. Conventionally farmed grains can be gassed with phosphine or another fumigant. Organic wheat can be treated with carbon dioxide at the very most. This is one of the reasons that organic grain offers more diverse yeast strains. The sourdough process is a story, from soil to sandwich and each chapter can be told in full.

Chris Young, co-ordinator of the Real Bread Campaign, sums it up when he tells me: 'sourdough bread is not a look, it's not a style, it's not a shape, it's not a fashion – it's a process. We are surrounded, in us, on us, all around us, by microorganisms, yeasts, bacteria and fungi. There are certain groups of these yeasts and lactic acid bacteria that are actually really good for bread making. Conveniently, they tend to hang out on the surface of grains.'

The Real Bread Campaign aims to find and share ways to make better bread for people, communities and the planet. And when Chris answers my question, what he thinks of bread, he imagines a cornucopia of loaves, all sorts and shapes of sourdough and yeasted breads, made using traditional methods, by hand and far from the factory floor.

So, on Day One we add our organic wholewheat stoneground flour to some spring water – this is because tap water contains traces of chemicals with the job of killing the type of cells we wish to propagate. Once the starter is active, tap water is not an issue but in these embryonic stages we want to give our sourdough baby the best start in life. For the record I have used tap water to initiate a starter and it does work just fine but let's be fussy – because we can.

When you first add the flour and water together nothing much will happen, or at least not to the naked eye, but on a microscopic level the yeast spores are awoken from their slumber by the hydrating effect of the water. Once so, the prospect of lunch is their first priority. They like sugars, just as we do, and you

84 | BREAKING BREAD

will have noticed there is an absence of sugars in my detailing of the contents of our wheat kernel.

Enter amylase, triumphantly. This enzyme is part of the seed package and has a special talent that is essential to the whole act of making bread in general. For anyone who can't remember their school science lessons, an enzyme very simply turns one thing into another thing. Amylase's party trick is to turn starches into sugars. With the addition of water to the mix this all happens concurrently. The amylase lays the table with sugars and the yeasts feast. The result of this meal is that the single cell yeasts gain the energy to metabolise, in simple terms they divide and multiply, doubling with each generation. A byproduct of all this splitting is that they release carbon dioxide, the same gas that puts a tingle in your soda. It is also the gas that gives us wonderfully light, leavened dough.

As our yeast population grows, we need to refresh the dining table for them to continue their exponential expansion. If left unfurnished the cells would exhaust the supplies of sugar and turn to cannibalism, which as you'd expect is not ideal. By adding some more flour and water the cycle starts again and the activity builds, by Day Four or Five you'll see bubbles appear, and after a week or two, the primordial broth will double in volume after two to three hours sitting in a relatively warm place. Once this occurs your starter is 'ripe' and ready to use.

While the yeasts are getting active, there's a subplot developing alongside the main action. A very special bacteria has hitched a ride. *Lactobacillus acidophilus*, an acid-loving bacteria, has been busy helping the fermentation and keeping the gassy slop food safe. This lactic acid bacteria enjoys anaerobic (without oxygen) conditions which the carbon dioxide from the yeasts provide.

FRANKENLOAF | 85

This is 'good' bacteria which will complement your existence rather than the 'bad' bacteria which seeks to end it.

As the bacteria itself multiplies, feeding on the same sugars, it produces lactic acids which give sourdough its sour flavour and provide an environment that pathogenic (food poisoning) bacteria find intolerable. The party-pooping, panty-pooping bacteria don't compete well; they are socially anxious, so by creating an environment populous with friendly ones we keep ourselves safe. Often only a small amount of pathogenic bacteria can cause serious sickness, and when we create sterile environments that seek to eliminate all bacteria whether good or bad, we actually increase the risk of getting ill. I know this because I had to have the highest level of food safety for manufacturing environments qualification and the course leader, a lovely lady called Jean, confessed to eating natural yoghurt way past its best before date for this very reason.

Many are fascinated by how much water they can get into the dough but true breadmaking experts are more concerned with starter health. A well-kept sourdough starter will yield beautiful bread. It begins with adding a little water and flour together, an act that can easily be performed by a toddler, and a simple process that will keep you intrigued, beguiled and mystified for the rest of your life.

When it comes to making the dough, the first stage is to mix more flour and water together and then leave the resulting mass to perform '*autolysis*', from the Greek meaning 'self-digestion'. As we now know, the amylase is kicked into action by the addition of water and a sugary banquet is then prepared for the yeasts and bacteria ahead of their arrival. Much like a slick catering outfit preparing tables with cut sandwiches, coffee and individually wrapped biscuits for a business conference lunch.

86 | BREAKING BREAD

The water in the dough brings together the glutenin and gliadin proteins to form gluten strands. At first these pieces are small and disconnected but over time will link to form ever longer chains, transforming a shaggy clump into a homogenous silken dough. This pre-soaking of the flour gives a boost to the fermentation and reduces the mixing time. After thirty minutes, or as much as six hours, the ripe sourdough starter is added to the dough and mixed in. The gluten strands bond together and these long protein components make the dough tight as they demonstrate their elastic properties to the baker.

Lastly, salt is added to provide taste and texture. At low concentrations, salt will cure protein, in our bread it toughens the gluten strands. It is added at the end to allow the glutenin and gliadin to come together first, before strengthening them when in combination. You can just add the salt in at the start, true, but this is the optimum way of extracting the best performance from the flour. The sourdough starter having inoculated the dough begins to tuck in to the spread of converted starch and once again uses this energy to divide, multiply and repeat. All the time, cells are burping out carbon dioxide and the developing gluten network catches this gas – *et voilà*, we have lift-off.

The dough then ferments at a rate dependent on the temperature of the environment and the dough itself, ideally between 25 and 28 degrees Centigrade for around three hours. The dough must also be kept in humid conditions to prevent a skin forming on its surface and restricting the growth. Every so often the dough is folded in on itself to regulate its temperature and further elongate the gluten strands. When the dough rests, the elasticity decreases, and the extensibility of the gluten comes into its own.

Gluten is brilliant for making bread because of these two properties, being both springy and stretchy.

The *Lactobacillus acidophilus* bacteria continue to multiply and the resulting acids soften the gluten, essentially pre-digesting it so our own gut doesn't have to work so hard. If we overload our intestines with unfermented gluten, it gets clogged up, downs tools and we feel the effects. This could lead to anything from a sore tummy to dry skin or headaches.

At the end of this 'bulk fermentation', the dough can be shaped and left to rise a final time before baking. If left too long the dough can become overly acidic and the gluten structure will degrade. Many a novice (and professional) sourdough baker will attest to this, as they turn out their dough for baking only to watch it deflate before their eyes. Managing the acidity of the dough is one of the great skills of the artisan baker and this mastery is valuable. Just ask anyone who has been brave enough (or foolish enough) to attempt the Everest of baking – sourdough panettone. I should have included a trigger warning for those bakers still recovering from the trauma of an acidified first dough.

Baking is the real showstopping transformation, the initial bake stage is hot, sweaty and energetic. The outer skin of the dough is slashed and kept moist so that, with the addition of extreme heat, the dough 'springs' and grows considerably in size. The crumb sets and sugars continue to develop at an ever-increasing rate both inside and on the outer crust where simpler sugars caramelise – thus browning.

What takes place is a Maillard reaction, named after the Frenchman Louis-Camille Maillard, who first got to grips with it. It happens to lots of food, not just bread, and requires humidity, proteins and extreme heat. A steak searing over fire, french fries, coffee and more examples all get their complex flavours from this chemical wonder. Sometimes I will raise a freshly baked sourdough to my nose, inhale deeply, close my eyes and marvel at how it smells like a banquet of foods.

Once baked, the resulting bread has an acidic complex flavour with a dark sweet crust, its chewy crumb will stay supple for days and the natural pH levels prevent moulds from moving in as they do with other foods. After becoming stale, it can be used to thicken soups and stews and can become an ingredient in many other dishes. Nothing needs to be wasted, and with all the effort you don't want to.

The truly magical element of this is that most of the effort is made by the bread itself; we humans are required to process the grain and mix the ingredients, but the intricate complexities are performed independently. That's sourdough bread, the bread on which empires were built and which, for thousands of years, was the companion to all of humanity's great endeavours. So, the question is if it wasn't broken, why did we try to fix it?

The answer that springs to mind is that it's punishingly hard work. While the ingredient list totals just three for the bread explained above, getting to grips with the process can take a lifetime. Most artisan bakers I know still get stumped on a regular basis by their bread, and just when you think you've got it sussed something will jump up and present a problem you have to solve. Real bread, and by that I mean bread that doesn't rely on the catalogue of additives to nullify all of bread's wonderful complexity, is the child that never flies the nest. It will keep you up at night (or more accurately during the day, when us bakers are supposed to sleep), and I'm speaking from experience, questioning the balance of acids and yeasts, feeding schedules and even the specific pH of each stage.

Customers demand fresh bread in the morning, so bakers must work at night to accommodate this desire – in my case from the age of thirteen. Even the schedule is a sort of imprisonment, and every bakery I know battles to keep hold of good bakers by trying out all sorts of shift patterns. The bottom line is that this kind of bread is the Boss, and humans must adjust to its schedule. Offering a baker the chance to improve on this is the Holy Grail and it's really no surprise that when the representatives from large companies come knocking (just when the baker is most weary-eyed), the promise of fast bread becomes supremely tempting. Or is it? I called one of my baking heroes, Dan Lepard, to find out why the world needs science to improve on nature.

Dan is a well-known baker and his books have sat in my various kitchens over the years, and now look very well-worn and used, with their sun-bleached spines and flecks of various doughs and batters encrusted throughout. He writes and teaches all over the world, having worked in some exceptional bakeries and kitchens, so if anyone would have a comment, it would be him.

When I ask Dan what he thinks of when he imagines bread, his answer is a simple flatbread, made from a dough of flour, water and salt. *'I probably think of unleavened bread as essential bread. There's something really basic about it that I love.'* I guess it makes sense. This kind of bread is the alma mater of baking, would surely have been the first born breads. Cracker style or soft blankets of pitta, depending on the heat treatment used, they have served humanity well as a rich source of sustenance.

Dan has made a lot of bread, most of it wonderful and most of it leavened. His books have provided expert advice to thousands of home bakers who wish to make their own loaves. Dan has also advised professionals, and been brought in as a poster boy of the

90 | BREAKING BREAD

baking scene in the UK. His advice hasn't always been welcome though. As my dad would often say, 'You can lead a horse to water, but you can't make it drink.'

Dan recalls working with The National Association of Master Bakers (now the Craft Bakers Association) in the UK, as a rising star of the baking world, and speaking with old-school bakers in the late 1990s. 'The bakers told me, "We don't want to do all the processes, we don't want to do it the old way. What we want is more money, less hours, to get in and get out." I think that was driven by very human reasons . . . [being] a modern artisan baker, it sucks up all your life. I think of it as akin to being a performer in a West End or Broadway show that's at the top of its game. Everything is so physical. Everything is a performance.'

Dan asked me why I became a baker myself after seeing two generations before me struggle with the job. I didn't have a good answer for him. The more I thought about it, the more it seemed to have parallels with Prometheus's punishment of having his liver pecked out on a daily basis, chained to a rock. The bakers who worked for my father had the same attitude as Dan's discussion group – which was arguably what led to the end the bakery, but I'll talk about that later – and that's no surprise when you've experienced firsthand how hard traditional processes can be, both physically and mentally. But what can be done? Are our choices really that we make good time-consuming bread or make money? Is it really that basic? Yet how realistic are our expectations? Tell me, who has ever made a loaf of bread at home that looks like an emoji or a store bought one? Sliced, with a bleached complexion and consistent in every way. Technology and science have allowed us to dream away the parts of bread we are dissatisfied with – mostly relating to all the time and effort spent – and unfortunately most of the elements that are left on the cutting room floor are the ones keeping us in good health.

Science first helped us solve the economic problems with bread, the processes, the look and feel. Yet as science has continued its deep dive into the crusty companion, new lessons are being learnt about the effects on our health and though the robot bread produced might seem to have a small down payment, it's definitely a case of buy now, pay later.

In 1859, Scottish chemist John Dauglish sought to solve the principle drain on profitability in breadmaking, the time it requires for dough to rise. He laid out a corpse of dense dough and pumped it full of gas. He was unimpressed with the bread he had experienced in his homeland which was too dense, too hard and too, well, nutritious. Curious of mind, he set about understanding the process, dissecting it, improving it. All the manual handling required in a bakery made him queasy as did the soup of bacteria and yeasts he saw as unhealthy and dirty. (How my tutor, Jean, would disagree.)

In the industrial world, with all its innovations and new techniques, he thought there must be a better way of doing things, a cleaner, more sanitary way. Dauglish bypassed the elements that led to the release of carbon dioxide and found a way of adding it to the dough during the mixing stage. Clever man that he was, success was inevitable. He founded The Aerated Bread Company, which went on to patent an almost completely automated system that saved on materials, time and labour. It was reported that two sacks of flour could be converted into four hundred two-pound loaves in forty minutes, and the dough was untouched by hand. In comparison, the ordinary bakers' process required about ten hours.[*]

---

[*] *Bread: A Slice of History.* p.80

92 | BREAKING BREAD

The predigestion of fermentation was marketed as stealing away calories from the consumer and with all the gluten intact rather than softened by the acidic conditions of traditional methods, the bread produced was seen as far superior to anything existing. It wasn't. It was a recipe for sickness and stomach cramps.

His bread was cheaper though, driving other bakers to slash prices and scramble for efficiencies just to stay afloat. For nearly a hundred years, the company produced bread without fermentation, well known for its 'A.B.C' tea shops across the UK and Australia. While the running costs were mouthwatering, the capital costs were eye-watering. Only a handful of bakeries were set up and they never gained a stranglehold on the market, and yet it stands as an important moment in bread processing history, one that paved the way for the future of mass-produced loaves.

Artisan bread is not exclusively sourdough bread and for a long time baking and brewing have shared a strain of yeast called *Saccharomyces cerevisiae*. It is the same strain that is referred to as 'commercial yeast', whether fresh in claylike blocks or dried, in the sachets often found at the back of our cupboards. Despite certain corners of the baking community suggesting it is a bad actor in the piece, bread can be made in a sympathetic way with this yeast.

Long-fermentation, sometimes overnight, will develop characteristic flavours and acids that will soften the structure of the flour. In the traditional 'sponge and dough' method a portion of the dough is made the day before and left to ferment before being added to the final mix and processed after further fermentation. It's a method I've seen countless times and requires time and space to make the dough in advance. The chemical reactions take place naturally as with the sourdough method and condition the dough, giving a soft bread with a certain amount of bite.

Commercial yeast does have to be used sparingly to achieve this result and the problems come when the potency of this leavening agent is used to speed up the inflation of the dough at the expense of the natural fermentation process. American basketball coach John Wooden said: 'A true test of a man's character is what he does when no one is watching.' Well, bakers work when everyone else is sleeping, and I can tell you from experience that there are some terrible characters out there. Those with the attitude: 'More yeast. Less time. Get in. Get out. Get paid.'

Electrical engineer Charles F. Wallace and chemist Martin F. Tiernan met in 1909 and shared an apartment in New York, where they found initial success by using chlorine to purify water in response to the epidemics of waterborne diseases at the time. From water their gaze shifted to wheat, using chlorine again in the form of Agene to bleach and artificially age flour. Dan Lepard educated me on the advantages of bleached flour, when we spoke. Aside from its whiteness, it gives bread a finer, softer texture. The way the flour behaves changes after treatment and while all bleaching has been outlawed in the UK since 1998, it is still permitted in the US, Brazil, Japan, among other countries. The specific practice of using Agene was banned in 1949 after dogs fed on the stuff started having running fits. After feeding my kids certain ultra-processed foods, I witness these same behaviours and am pretty sure we haven't solved the problem yet. It was through this chemical dive into grain that the two bleach enthusiasts, Wallace and Tiernan, became associated with John C. Baker, a cereal chemist

94 | BREAKING BREAD

and inventor.

Together they sought to reduce the time it took to make bread and stitch together the various processes of a batch approach into a continuous flow. They met their goals, reducing the time it took to process the dough from many hours to around twenty minutes, the system was capable of producing a 'no-time' dough that could yield six thousand loaves an hour. To give some context, a really good baker can make three hundred loaves in an eight-hour day. It was successful in the States and a plant was set up in the UK which was operating commercially in 1959. The British palate wasn't suited to the cake-like texture though. The idea of piggybacking on this project to create a loaf that was suited to a European style of bread was an open goal however, and the scientists based at Chorleywood, just north of London, were only too pleased to capitalise.

Wallace and Tiernan allowed one of the scientists working on the Chorleywood process to use their mixer as a comparison to other options. That led to the 'Tweedy' mixer being used, which was capable of the extremely high-speed dough development required. Additives, such as the oxidising agent ascorbic acid (vitamin C), hydrogenated (trans) fat and enzymatic agents suspended in soya flour, were included in the early tests. The breakthrough was the conversion on the mixer to provide a partial vacuum, which generated the close crumb structure that was desired.

Britain now had a process that could be used to bake fluffy white bread, using domestic wheat. Imports from the US, Canada and Australia could be scaled back, which increased domestic food security. This process was so successful, it is still used by the UK's biggest bakery brand, Warburtons, which use it to bake over two million loaves a day. Yet, the Faustian pact required – selling the soul of the bread, the flavour and nutritional elements, in order to use lower quality ingredients and create a cheap mass-produced loaf – has proved too good to be true for customers.

Dan Lepard has explained the impact that the Chorleywood process has had on the smaller UK bakeries, and how it has contributed to Britain being characterised as having terrible bread, a label that has been hard to shift but which Dan, like others, strives to do.

'It devastated many of the small, hands-on bakeries, and they didn't have a way of producing very white, very soft, fluffy bread. So, the National Association of Master Bakers went to their chemists and asked if there was a chemical way of producing softer white bread that would compete with the Chorleywood process. They came up with a combination of basic improvers and chemicals that could be put into bread so that the high-street baker could produce a loaf that rivalled the Chorleywood process bread without the huge capital investment.'

This all rings true from my own family's history. When my grandparents set up a bakery in 1946, they were one of seven bakeries in the town. By the time I was working there as a teenager, there were just two left. Cheap, sliced white bread made with all the efficiencies of a mass-production unit was very difficult for the small high-street baker to compete with. At the end of the Second World War, Britain had around 35,000 such small bakers; by the Millennium, the number was down to 1,500. France had a similar number in the 1940s and their number increased over the same 50-year period. One of those countries is renowned for world-beating bread and the other is Britain.

Activated Dough Development, or ADD, was also developed at Chorleywood, in 1966, by using the work of the Foremost

96 | BREAKING BREAD

Technical Centre in Dublin, California. Their 'instant dough development' used a heady mix of additives that performed all the tasks previously allocated to time. Gluten was developed, dough oxidised and, to make up for the lack of natural softening, extra water was added which increased the yield. And, more importantly, the profitability.

The most curious ingredient, though, was the amino acid L-cysteine for which the industrial source is hog hair and poultry feathers. It's also found in human hair, nails and skin. This first incarnation was banned in 1998 due to the inclusion of potassium bromate (yummy). In the UK, with the wholesale deregulation of enzymes in 1996, it was possible to make the dough do everything that was required. As an added bonus, when any of these enzymes was deemed to be a 'processing aid', rather than an additive, the manufacturer wasn't required to list it on the ingredients label – still the case now.

ADD was taken up with enthusiasm by small family bakeries and in-store bakeries. No sooner was the dough mixed, it was scaled off and plopped in tins, given a short proof and baked off. Colloquially referred to as 'make and take', the process has been derided by artisan bakers who view their counterparts as chasing a quick buck at the expense of the reputation of small bakers everywhere. When I returned to the family bakery after working in London at some of the country's best sourdough outfits, I was shocked to see the bakers using this 'gunpowder' as they called it. Growing up I was told by my father how important integrity and honesty was, and now, even we were making bullshit bread just to keep the doors open. Every step I tried to take back to long fermented, additive free, bread was boobytrapped and sabotaged as the bakers kept returning to these shortcuts. It was a sickness from which the business never fully recovered.

The influence of science and technology on the bakery industry has been all-consuming, yet the act of making bread hadn't changed all that much for thousands of years. A baker in 1850 could feasibly step into a job in 1950, but since then everything has changed beyond imagining. The industrial bread now is not bread in the same way that a glass of orange squash may not be orange juice.

In the 1970s, acclaimed food writer Elizabeth David asked the question at the heart of this in her book *English Bread and Yeast Cookery*. While the loaves that would dominate 80 per cent of the UK market might be a technological triumph, there was no taste, so, '*Should it be called bread?*' A question that I think needs answering.

When bread transitioned from produce to a product, a chasm opened up that still exists today, producing industrial bread so far removed from the traditional breads our species has grown up on that perhaps it's no wonder our bodies now reject it. We may have been foolish enough to let it share the name of our founding meal, but our bodies know the difference.

It isn't just the big factories either but the smaller high-street and instore bakeries that play out the pantomime of a bread production fuelled by additives that require no explanation as long as the bread remains unpackaged. Once wrapped, labels including all the ingredients, except so-called processing aids, must be displayed in the UK at least. These bakeries compare themselves to truly artisan outfits which spend good money on high-quality ingredients and skilled labour. With no protection,

98 | BREAKING BREAD

the customer is fooled into thinking this bread is something it's not. Unable to make an honest choice, we have been misled by science. We may have cheap bread, but at what cost?

I like to compare the industrial progress within breadmaking to that of Frankenstein. Our own 'Frankenloaf' has followed a similar trajectory to the 'monster'. As he became a destructive force within the story, so too has modern bread begun to cause problems within society. Gluten has become one of the villains of the piece, with countless sources advising against consuming it at all. But isn't that assuming all gluten is the same? Is the gluten in 'no-time' bread the same as gluten in a long-fermented counterpart? The science suggests not. The natural processes that occur through fermentation soften it and they predigest it, to a certain extent. This allows us the opportunity to benefit from its nutritional bounty.

Science, I would argue, has made a monster of bread. That very word 'monster' meaning to 'show' as in demonstrate, it shows us what we have become – a people that values appearance over character, price over value and volume over substance. In Mary Shelley's story, the monster kills its maker so perhaps we should take heed before it's too late and take better care of our food system before it does the same to us.

Andrew Whitley, co-founder of the Real Bread Campaign, paints a gloomy picture when he states in his book, *Bread Matters*:

> *Bread is a nutritional, culinary, social and environmental mess – made from aggressively hybridised wheat that is grown in soils of diminishing natural fertility, sprayed with toxins to counter pests and diseases, milled in a way that robs it of the best parts of its nutrients, fortified with*

just two minerals and two vitamins in an attempt to make good the damage, and made into bread using a cocktail of functional additives and a super-fast fermentation (based on greatly increased amounts of yeast), which inhibits assimilation of some of the remaining nutrients while causing digestive discomfort to many customers.

Unfortunately, the picture isn't much rosier eighteen years after these words were originally written. There are more artisan bakeries opening, true, but the volume is a drop in the ocean compared to factory made bread. Most of the artisan spots rely on selling coffee and pastries with bread as a requirement for making their own sandwiches. The truth is that, as well as the nutritional value, all the perceived value of good bread has been stripped away. It is inconceivable for many to spend upwards of four or five pounds on a loaf of bread, when we can pick up a sliced white one for a fraction of that cost. And, of course, with the money that we've saved, we can buy all the vitamin supplements we now need, as a result. Plonk, plonk, fizz.

4

Sicker by the Slice

A marriage not made in heaven

Even the bread, which is the simplest form into which human ingenuity tortures the flour of wheat, is, by other causes besides the concentration I have named, too frequently rendered the instrument of disease and death, rather than the means of life and health, to those that eat it.

– Syvester Graham, *A Treatise on Bread* (1837)

There are so many kinds of bread, so many ways of making it, that to suggest bread as a whole can be either healthy or unhealthy is dangerous. It's not that simple. As I've already stated, when bread is good it can be very good, but when it's bad, it can be very bad indeed. Not just in taste, but for us humans, the impact can be physical, mental and environmental. In this chapter, I want to look at how bread can affect health, which aspects are associated with different outcomes and how individuals have shaped the discourse on bread and health. Aside from the ailments and metabolic boons linked to eating it in its myriad forms, I want to dig into the issues that can arise from making bread. At what point does the staff of life become a rod for our backs?

102 | BREAKING BREAD

In most cultures, bread is the foodstuff on which people rely. Whether in Ethiopia, where sharing bread can be a utensil as well as a vital foodstuff, or in a Michelin-starred restaurant in London, you can be assured that this simple carb is part of the meal. And yet, throughout history, the amount of bread we have eaten has often equated to status. During the Industrial Revolution in Britain, for example, there was a clear link between how much money you had and how much bread you ate. The poorer the household, the more bread was consumed as a percentage of total food. Around the middle of the nineteenth century, the diet of the working class was founded on bread, potatoes, dripping and extremely weak tea. They also had the worst health outcomes. But are the two linked? Does this show that a diet founded on bread is inherently bad for us? Or was the health of the poor being propped up by the bread, a noble pillar of nutrition fighting against all the other negative factors – such as poor housing, working conditions, nutrient deficiency and lousy sanitation? I would argue that the relationship between commodity bread and the poor has had a lasting impact on health, especially as eating habits are passed down through generations. The idea, too, that simply supplying enough energy constitutes a fulfilling diet has led to the confusing situation we find ourselves in now, where somebody can be simultaneously overweight and undernourished. Food by numbers doesn't work.

A simple bread made with stoneground wholemeal flour, water, salt and sourdough starter is often considered the healthiest of breads. If you add some potato to the mix for a vitamin C boost you could live on it for quite a while. Served with some fat, like butter, beef dripping or olive oil, and we are approaching the kind of energy-dense food that can keep the human machine functioning all day long, as history has shown us.

Maestro Charlie Chaplin recalls, in his 1964 autobiography, that he lived on little more than white bread and beef dripping while growing up in Lambeth, south London, at the turn of the century. It was all his family could afford at times and yet this diet doesn't appear to have held back the creative genius of one of the most influential minds in entertainment. I'm not suggesting this as some kind of creative diet fad, but Chaplin is proof that perhaps people can thrive on a bread-rich diet. Yet, the sad truth is if Chaplin were a young boy today, he'd be more likely to be eating an ultra-processed diet that would give him more chance of adolescent type two diabetes than a profession as a movie star.

Most bread today isn't 100 per cent wholemeal. The extraction rate of flour is a key indication of how healthy the resulting bread will be. White flour tends to be around 70 per cent extraction, which means that it uses 70 per cent of the whole wheat seed. The 30 percent that is left behind accounts for some pretty significant losses, however. Essential B vitamins such as thiamine (77 per cent loss), riboflavin (80 per cent loss) and pyridoxine (72 per cent loss) are all depleted in roller-milled flour. There's 76 per cent less iron, 60 per cent less calcium and 86 per cent less vitamin E. The list is long, and reads like the side of a multivitamin packet. Quite challenging figures, if we think about it. With quite significant results.

The biggest loss is all the dietary fibre contained within the bran layer itself, the fibre that keeps microbes in the gut fed and contributes to better overall health. The bran surrounds the super calorific and nutritious elements of the wheat seed, protecting it from pests and disease. When consumed, bran benefits our digestive system by attracting moisture, making more of the nutritional elements available and keeping the trains running on time, so to speak.

104 | BREAKING BREAD

Small amounts of artificially manufactured versions of the really essential vitamins and minerals are added back into the flour. This 'fortification' stops you getting deficiency diseases from eating all white flour that can be found in over half of the products at the supermarket. By law in the UK, white flour must contain added niacin, thiamine, iron and calcium, but a further fifteen vitamins and minerals, such as zinc and magnesium, are present in whole grain flour in significantly increased quantities.

There are elements within wheat flour that keep us healthy, and by choosing to remove them through roller-milling and sifting, we have created a problem that still needs to be artificially fixed to this day. Deficiency diseases are those of nutritional absence. Most grains when processed in the proper way have the ability to sustain us and when supplemented with a variety of other foraged, farmed and reared food can allow people to thrive.

When flour is sifted to exclude the wheatgerm and bran what is left is dangerously low in iron, niacin, thiamine and calcium. The resulting deficiency diseases include pellagra, anaemia and beriberi. Pellagra, which I've mentioned before, is the result of niacin deficiency and is more commonly an issue with diets high in un-nixtamalized maize. Symptoms can include delusions, confusion, skin conditions and diarrhoea. When Europeans discovered the Mesoamerican bounty of maize in the sixteenth century, they gorged on it, but without the careful, essential processing known as nixtamalization, it made them sick. This process involves boiling the grain in water containing wood ash, otherwise known as lye water.

Anaemia is a condition that results in a deficiency of iron and is manifested in low energy levels, headaches and poor concentration among other symptoms. In 2021, 1.92 billion people had anaemia globally, with the main cause being iron deficiency in their diet. The nutrients in food are only of any use if they are accessible to the body. The way we process our food is important as it impacts on its nutritional content.

Beriberi is a deficiency of thiamin, or vitamin B1. It can result in inflammation of the nerves and heart failure. It can have a significant impact on the brain, and you may have noticed that each of these major deficiencies has a symptom related to mental health. The gut and the brain have a strong connection, and it's a relationship that will reveal just how important our diet is to every aspect of our health. Bread is not just an important source of these vitamins and nutrients, of course, but when made properly can, arguably, be a preventative medicine.

It was the US that first fortified their flour against these diseases during the Second World War after they discovered that certain diseases were preventable in their men, and in the UK it is mandatory to add these micronutrients to any flour that isn't 100 per cent wholemeal. That's why when we look at the ingredients list for a true wholemeal flour it will simply read 'wheat flour'. Unless we buy flour from a small mill with a low output that makes them exempt, it's the only unadulterated flour on the UK market. Any country importing white flour into the UK must also make these additions since Brexit.

My mum used to cook a lot from *The Cranks Recipe Book* for us when we children and would use wholemeal flour wherever possible. I can remember the crumbly shortcrust pastry she would make and how nutty and aromatic the flavour of the flour was. My dad, too, knew the benefits and would seek out small mills to supply freshly ground flour. When he tried to start selling organic sourdough in the 1980s, he was a bit ahead of his time.

106 | BREAKING BREAD

Millers are due to be required to add in another juicy ingredient – folic acid when legislation changes. Folic acid helps in utero babies develop healthy brains and spinal cords, and the hope is that by adding folic acid into a product that features in around 60 per cent of all food products, incidences of the condition of spina bifida will be significantly reduced. Spina bifida is caused by the under development of a baby's spine and symptoms include issues with movement, and the bowel and bladder.

Again, this won't need to be added into wholemeal flour and there is a small-scale milling exemption for all fortification so that anyone milling less than five hundred tonnes a year won't be required to make these additions. That's a sizable amount of flour considering a large-scale artisan bakery like Dusty Knuckle in east London gets through between 260 and 300 tonnes a year. I guess it allows for bakeries or farms that want to mill their own wheat without the hassle of calculating quantities of micronutrients.

Enough wheat is grown on Earth to feed eleven billion people every year, and the total global population sits at just over eight billion as I write this. We put all the extra grain to use in animal feed, cosmetics and a host of non-food related uses. If we all ate 100 per cent extracted flour in our bread we would be healthier, better nourished and could farm it using much less land. That doesn't happen though, bakers are reluctant to give up on the lower extraction flour because it performs better when we consider attributes like texture, appearance and volume. Who wants to give up their croissant?

The wholemeal flour also sells, from a financial standpoint, making more wholemeal bread would be wonderful for a baker's bottom line. Wholemeal flour is cheaper per kilo and really good wholemeal loaves are hard to find, so it should be the aim of any baker worth their salt to master the art of making it. All those super open crumb loaves on Instagram are the result of engineered roller-milled flour, the airy focaccia drowning in olive oil struggle to achieve the same gaseous expanse with whole grain flour. Some bakers have taken up the challenge however, and I was keen to speak to one of them about the joys and challenges of using wholemeal flour.

Wing Mon Cheung has worked for some of the finest bakeries in Europe, including Ten Belles in Paris, Brickhouse Bakery in London and Landrace Bakery in Bath. She set up Cereal Bakery in the southwest of the England. When she thinks about bread, the first thought that comes to mind is the bread emoji, a homogenous slice of white bread that exists only on screens. This is an interesting juxtaposition for someone who is baking some of the most flavourful and nutritionally valuable bread on the planet. Wing Mon spent most of her early career making the kind of hearth-baked sourdough we can see on any popular social media feed. A blend of roller-milled, high-performance, low-extraction wheat flour that is dressed up with a little stoneground grain for the hashtags. When she set up her own place with her partner, Niall, they made the decision to use 100 per cent whole grain flour for all the baking.

Wing Mon confesses that she initially spent a month making loaves that were 50 per cent wholemeal and 50 per cent sifted heritage flour but after some deep questioning decided to go cold turkey. Sifted stoneground flour is very different from the white roller-milled flour that goes into a sliced and wrapped product. It maintains lots of the nutritional elements of the whole grain with the germ being crushed into it.

108 | BREAKING BREAD

Wing Mon explains: 'There was some piece of me that thought I had to use at least some sifted flour', but she found the 100 per cent loaves were super moist and stayed fresh much longer than the cavernous, crumbed sours that light up our Insta stories.

'Social media is amazing,' Wing Mon continues, 'but it ends up with us making quite a homogenous product.' The loaf at Cereal is baked in a tin, which can confuse some customers who wonder where the sourdough is. 'I [have] had to explain that sourdough is a process, not a shape or style,' she says, echoing Chris Young of the Real Bread Campaign's words.

By baking wholemeal sourdough in a tin, more moisture is maintained within the loaf and you can get more loaves per bake and the slices make more egalitarian sandwiches. 'If you try to make five sandwiches from a one-cut batard sourdough loaf then a couple of people will get tiny ones and the one cut from the middle will be massive,' she explains. This also solves the problem that most hearth-baked sourdough slices don't fit in the toaster. The requisite pampering to turn the slice halfway through and risk burning it is avoided. So, Wing Mon has taken a piece of industrial baking equipment and used it to make her bread more accessible; it also delivers a softer crust and her older customers definitely appreciated it. The one-cut batard is a leaf-shaped loaf that is sliced lengthways, and the baker hopes that its crust will resemble a breaking wave. It's less practical – more enticing.

One of Wing Mon's challenges is getting enough flour. Only through close relationships with Somerset-based Fred Price of Gothelney Farm and Rosy Benson (another E5 Bakehouse alumnus), who bakes and mills at Field Bakery, was she able to get the quantities required. 'We have to show farmers there is a demand for this flour. Cann Mills did a project with farmers growing heritage grain and they sold out really quickly.' Proving there's obviously a need for it.

The process takes time and millers, bakers and customers will need the patience to see it through. The bread that comes out of this flour is wonderfully tasty and beneficial to all sorts of human systems aside from the obvious local economic ones. Wing Mon selects her grain based on personal relationships rather than technical qualities. It's more important that the people growing the food share the same beliefs and hold themselves to the same standards.

The grain is more expensive and the bread commands a high-ticket price but it keeps for much longer than other more open sourdoughs. 'Customers used to tell us how the bread would stay fresh for so long, which is probably to our detriment as people didn't need to come back every day.' Cereal Bakery is relocating to Tongue, on Scotland's north coast and Wing Mon and Niall will struggle to find the flour they require so are looking at the option of installing a mill and getting grain shipped in.

The bakery definitely has a more prosperous customer base, demographically speaking, with lots of customers following Tim Spector (see page 118) and doing the Zoe app thing, they are, as Wing Mon comments 'BBC Radio 4 listeners for sure'. The dilemma of creating healthy bread that is accessible to all weighs heavily on her, and it's hard to communicate the benefits of the bread to those who aren't in a specific glutinous bubble.

Either people need to make their own bread using high-grade flour or the government needs to step in. If a sugar tax can be organised, then why not a white bread tax, I wonder? Setting a limit for whole grain inclusion would surely see the biggest shift in bread for decades. The money harvested from refined white

110 | BREAKING BREAD

products could go to offset the 100 per cent whole grain ones, support smaller supply chains and boost the income of farmers who want to diversify away from commodity grain. If more of us ate increased quantities of carefully grown whole grain products, especially those that have been properly fermented, we would see reduced incidences of diabetes, reduced rates of some cancers and better overall health.

This is spelled out in T. Colin Campbell's book *The China Study*, which claims to be 'the most comprehensive study of nutrition ever conducted'. The book also spells out why the message isn't getting through, with almost every major nutritional study being funded either directly or by less transparent means, by the industrial food system. Dr Chris Van Tulleken's *Ultra-Processed People*, similarly, shows the extent to which processed foods are not only devoid of positive nutritional elements but are actually demonstrably harmful to health. So, the game is rigged. Even the politicians are powerless to a concerning extent. As Jean-Claude Junker said of European economic reforms, '*We all know what to do, we just don't know how to get reelected after we've done it*'. Van Tulleken digs into the massive influence of pension providers who are seen by some as the puppet masters of our modern nutritional crisis. With investments in ultra-processed food manufacturers and simultaneously holding stakes in the big pharma businesses it is a win-win.

Former UK Prime Minister Boris Johnson declared, in 2024, that ultra-processed foods should carry 'tobacco-style warnings'. A strong statement and one I agree with, but if he feels that strongly about it, why didn't he do anything when he was in power? Are our leaders unwilling to put their money where their mouths are? To make simple changes that would fix many social, economic, health and environmental issues?

One of the principal issues that modern developed nations face isn't deficiency of any kind, it's quite the opposite. An excess of refined carbohydrates is clogging up more than just intestines. Our health services are overwhelmed with patients that have preventable diseases associated with highly processed foods.

Food writer Michael Pollan in his book *The Omnivore's Dilemma* lays out the problem of the 'fixed stomach' in which food companies must find ways of getting more food into our stomachs than can possibly fit. The answer is to refine. If we can only eat a kilo of wheat, then by refining it to 700g there is room for another 300g. In the same way that I stamp down the cardboard in my recycling bin after Christmas, every financial year big business must make a little more room to facilitate next year's bonuses.

The added advantage of taking out the bits that are essential is that they create new opportunities to sell you solutions for the problems the industry has caused. Food companies need to demonstrate growth to their shareholders, and this is one of the ways they have been able to do it. Pollan gives various examples of products derived from maize, such as high fructose corn syrup all the way to corn starch and biofuels. We can buy, right now, a kilo of pure gluten. That gluten typically represents 70 per cent of the protein present in the wheat flour, totalling around 8 per cent of the already refined flour. So we need over twelve kilos of flour to get that kilo of vital wheat gluten. The cost of all this super refined grain? Our bodies.

The irony is that it's more risky to make bread without fermentation. When dough is made in a factory environment with flour that has been balanced with extra Vital Wheat Gluten the proteins remain pretty much intact. It was this property that was heralded as a triumph in the early days of industrial bread production, with no loss of nutritional value it was thought.

It's precisely this predigestion that unlocks the nutritional potential of flour however, and it has been seen that fermented foods deliver a bigger percentage of a food's potential and require less energy to do it. Unfermented gluten can cause more of an issue in the gut as it damages the lining of the intestines leading to a 'leaky gut'. This allows undigested elements into the bloodstream and can trigger seemingly unrelated reactions such as headaches and skin conditions. The change from long fermented, whole grain bread to ultra-processed white bread with added gluten has caused a great deal of unnecessary pain and suffering.

I went to see a doctor who works as a GP in London to find out if there really is a problem with the bread most of us are eating. When Dr Seb Ambrozie thinks about bread, he imagines a white farmhouse loaf but this homely vision is then hijacked by the advert for Mighty White from his childhood. I, too, remember the adverts that purported to give children superhuman strength by adding a speckle of rye and adding a little fibre back into a soft industrially made white loaf. Dr Ambrozie works at the First4Health Group in the east London borough of Newham, and he has around ten thousand consultations a year. He also likes to make sourdough for his family at the weekend and I've tried his bread and it's delicious. A tangy white boule made using a no knead method over a couple of days.

I wanted to know if he thought there was a link between the increased consumption of refined white flour products and gluten intolerance. Dr Ambrozie thinks that to a certain extent people were more likely to accept minor symptoms of IBS (Irritable Bowel Syndrome) caused by gluten sensitivity in the past. 'Younger adults now are not prepared to accept feeling even slightly unwell. The media, information and misinformation surrounding food have contributed to an increase in patients self-diagnosing with coeliacs disease.' This affects around 0.5–1 per cent of any given population and is a condition affected by specific conditions. It is an autoimmune condition where the body attacks healthy tissue in defence against a perceived infection caused by gluten. It can be debilitating and even a very small amount of gluten can trigger a reaction.

Dr Ambrozie makes around one or two positive diagnoses of coeliacs disease a year, but often none at all. This is the result of over more than 100 screening blood tests a year, 60 per cent of which are at the patients request. Of the negative ones, many do report feeling better after cutting gluten products such as bread from their diets but Dr Ambrozie says that usually people make a number of changes at the same time so it's hard to definitively say that gluten is the issue.

The much bigger issue is type two diabetes and this is very specifically linked to sugar and refined carbohydrates. 'I don't think many doctors differentiate between types of bread when they give advice,' Dr Ambrozie says. 'I have an interest in bread and am only recently becoming more aware of the effect of ultra-processed foods on diet related health.' There is no distinction therefore between a loaf of sourdough rye bread and the Mighty White that popped into the doctor's head at the beginning of our conversation.

Doctors in the UK at the time of writing only have a short amount of time with patients during GP consultations, ten minutes in total, so it's unsurprising there isn't time to dig into the fine details of diet and specific choices within groups of food. Many people are also from economic groups that don't have the option to buy artisan bread – for them it's a choice between own-brand supermarket bread or no bread. In that situation, a blanket rejection of bread makes perfect sense.

The acceleration of type two diabetes is an avoidable situation, the doctor believes. 'Bread has been around for thousands of years, but it's only in the last thirty to forty years that type two diabetes has blown up. It can't just be related to bread and carbs. There are many other factors around the way we live and the way we manufacture our food that have tipped the scales.' In east London, where he's situated, the most commonly consumed bread products are chapatis, an Indian unfermented flatbread typically made with white flour and fried in oil or ghee. Without the flour going through the fermentation process where starches are broken down, the body recognises breads like these as complex sugars.

Dr Ambrozie comments: 'It's hard to advise people to stay away from foods that make up such a large part of their communal diet. It isn't realistic to tell people to eat more expensive foods, because for many that isn't a possibility.'

Many people are also victims of their location, with a lack of access to the variety and lower prices attainable at larger superstores or in other towns due to their travel constraints. Smaller retailers offer fewer options and usually at a higher price which compounds the issues around diet and health, these places will tend to stock longer life bread products as a defence against wastage, but they are more often the highly processed, super-refined products that exacerbate the problems of intolerance, sensitivity and blood sugar levels.

The concern around refined wheat flour is not new. Sylvester Graham published *A Treatise on Bread* in 1837, less than twenty years after the invention of roller-milling and fourteen years before it was demonstrated at The Great Exhibition of 1851.

John Harvey Kellogg also published a number of articles and books from the late 1890s through the 1920s. These two had a big impact on the way the public viewed health and wholemeal – ironically the former is associated with the biscuits that sandwich malted marshmallow and chocolate in a 's'more' and the latter has his name emblazoned on some of the unhealthiest items you will find in any supermarket. Graham was particularly concerned with adulteration, the addition of potentially harmful ingredients that improved the flour's performance or visual appearance. Graham cites '*alum, sulphate of zinc, sub-carbonate of magnesia, sub-carbonate of ammonia, sulphate of copper, and several other substances,*' as well as chalk, Plaster of Paris and many more.

The chalk that was derided is now mandatory, given that it helps boost the calcium content of refined white flour. The Plaster of Paris would have been easily explained by the miller as it is the material used for filling the joints between the sections of millstone and minor repairs in the surface. The traditional method for setting this bonding agent was urea and this was provided by the miller who would keep a small pot of urine for such a task. Ah! The good old days. Alum would assist the baker by extending the time they had to shape the mass of dough into individual loaves. With no quick fermentation options, usually there would only be time to make a single batch of dough and if the dough fermented too quickly then the bread would be ready all at once and if the oven was already full then the baker would quickly be out of pocket. The restrictions that came from the Assize of Bread (see pages 165–66) placed pressure on the bakers and with only a small profit margin of 13 per cent allowed for, the bulking agents, it could be argued, are the result of over-zealous policy rather than the greed of the bakers.

116 | BREAKING BREAD

There's an organic farm about half an hour from my home in Suffolk, Maple Farm in the village of Kelsale. It is run by William Kendall who has run some pretty big food businesses including Green & Blacks chocolate and the Covent Garden Soup Company. With those both sold he now concentrates on his organic farm, producing cereal grains, eggs and vegetables and mills flour on site. He has also branched out into Kombucha and has a new farm shop after seeing the success of other agritourism sites in the UK and America. I met him at his home, where I was accosted by his two extremely affectionate Labradors. William made some tea while I handed out some tummy rubs – to the dogs, of course. Later, we sat down in a quiet part of the house bathed in autumnal light from the large sash window. The table between us was stacked with books that were in the process of being sorted, covering the kind of topics you'd expect from a farmer – dogs, birds and food.

When I ask William what he thinks about when I say 'bread', he considers the origins of bread in northern Africa before being drawn to his childhood, visiting his granny's house and queuing up outside the baker's shop for freshly baked rolls. The sheer pleasure of buying a dozen warm rolls and having them with jam in the kitchen. It's exactly the answer you might expect from someone who straddles the worlds of big business and small-scale producers.

William grows a number of heritage varieties of wheat, including April Bearded, Orange Devon Blue, YQ, Miller's Choice, Red Lammas and Maris Widgeon. The names themselves are delicious enough. William recalls getting his mill from Austria after deciding he'd had enough of selling his organic grain through conventional channels. When he enquired about buying a mill from the company in East Tyrol, they divulged that they'd only sold one of their mills to a UK buyer. While their other international sales were healthy, at the time the UK market wasn't interested in freshly milled stoneground flour.

'I was one of the first to buy a mill like this and use it to mill my own wheat. They were selling one a week to America, dozens to Italy and supposedly every Austrian and German hospital had one to grind fresh flour to feed the patients,' he comments.

The idea of a British hospital milling fresh flour or even baking fresh bread is almost beyond imagination. When my children were born, I took bread into the hospital so that their first milk wasn't fuelled by the low-grade industrial bread they serve. I'm not bread shaming the NHS, which is incredible and, incidentally, my wife's employer, but the bread is some of the worst I've ever seen.

William tells me that in Austria they have this 'weird belief' that if people are in hospital, you feed them good food to help them get better. 'Whereas in British hospitals they think if you feed people things that are alien to the common diet, it'll be a shock to them and they won't get better.' When an increasing amount of British patients' poor diets are contributing to their poor health this is quite hard to digest. When William told this story to BBC journalist and presenter of the Radio 4 show The Food Programme, Sheila Dillon, she found it to be largely true when she produced an episode on the subject.

Perhaps if there was a big movement to consume healthier bread among the populace they would require better bread in public institutions, using their own logic. My little county of Suffolk has a deep connection to organic farming and one of the most influential individuals in the movement was Lady Eve Balfour who William cites as a hero. She stated: 'If a nation's health depends on the way its food is grown, then agriculture must be looked upon as one of the health services.'

118 | BREAKING BREAD

The COVID-19 pandemic saw a huge number of people take up baking and especially sourdough. For many people it was the forgotten skill that lockdown afforded them the time to learn. Maple Farm was inundated with requests for flour. 'We had queues of people here, some driving from London for our little mill. We would have stopped milling if it hadn't been for Covid,' William says.

My own experience resonated with William's: instinctively consumers were keen to bake their own bread and use the best flour they could get their hands on. I was bagging up hundreds of flour orders a night during the pandemic, partly because the country seemed to have run out of small flour bags and partly because the supply of factory-made bread had diminished.

I was making loaves to plug gaps in local supermarkets which couldn't get their orders fulfilled from the giants of the industry. A single factory may have had the equipment to make two million loaves a day but during the pandemic, production was scaled back to allow for safety measures and the smaller bakeries across the country picked up the slack.

It was during Covid that I started watching the *Bon Appetit* YouTube channel as an escape from the mayhem around me. The New York-based magazine has a test kitchen housed on the thirty-fifth floor of One Trade Centre in Manhattan and I watched pretty much every video they put out. I wasn't alone: they reached unmatched viewing figures during the first wave of the pandemic. I was working seven days a week and a particular favourite was Brad Leone's spot 'It's Alive', a show concentrating on fermented foods.

I spoke to Brad over Zoom to get his perspective on bread. He has since left *Bon Appetit* and has his own YouTube channel that allows him to spend more time outside of the city in rural

Connecticut. I couldn't get enough of watching him making sourdough doughnuts with fellow food writer and baker Claire Saffitz or noodling for catfish with chef Matty Matheson, better known for his work on the hit TV series *The Bear*.

When Brad thinks about bread, he imagines the twenty-inch long pullman tinned loaf he makes for his family, pretty simple but adorned with a shoyu glaze and bejewelled with poppy seeds and sesame seeds. Brad made a video showing how he makes this loaf on his channel, Makin' It. He points out that one of the attractions of bread is that anyone can make it. 'Well, anyone can make bad bread. It takes a lot of effort to master it.' He says that growing up, he didn't have the same access to great tasting fresh bread as he does now, but his mother can't really eat it. 'I think she's full-on coeliac, but she still eats my bread and she says it definitely doesn't cause the same reaction as store bought bread.' This kind of anecdotal evidence reminds me of Andrew Whitley's book, *Bread Matters*, in which he recalls the same thing, specifically that when those with gluten sensitivity consume long-fermented wholewheat bread their symptoms reduce to a tolerable level or cease completely.

Brad's own experience of Covid was similar to a lot of home bakers. 'It was a little annoying,' he says, 'shopping itself was intense. Everyone and their mothers were buying all the flour like the world was ending, so they could make bread.' The market became swamped with people wanting to bake their own, to wrest some control back from a world that was unravelling.

In his distinctive New Jersey accent, Brad adds, 'Lots of people got on the sourdough kick which is absolutely incredible. I want everyone to make bread and enjoy the long, never-ending, road of breadmaking. But I don't miss the food shortages and the flour aisle being barren.'

120 | BREAKING BREAD

I ask Brad why he thinks that sourdough struck such a chord during the lockdowns and he says, 'Folks got into sourdough because it's part of their DNA. They lost touch with it during normal crazy life, plus it's all about the steps and fun. It's like having a little friend that you learn from and play with. Plus, you get rewarded with fresh baked healthy bread.'

While communities were being kept apart, the lure of creating new ones bound up in mixtures of flour and water made people feel better. Many sourdough owners give their starters names (my son named our home one 'Flash') and I think this personification is fairly common. It leads us to care more about this living sludge, which will in turn care for our health.

Brad is famous for his lacto-fermentation food experiments, and will often get concerned individuals in the comments worried about botulism which is an incredibly dangerous yet thankfully rare condition occurring from toxins produced by *Clostridium botulinum*. It's definitely worth understanding if you want to preserve vegetables but, luckily, it's not a concern when it comes to breadmaking. Brad does link the concern over fermented foods with a tolerance of industrial systems, and it's something I have personal experience of too.

Our family bakery began supplying a number of local supermarkets and was required to undergo an advanced food safety audit. During the process the general suggestions were for us to adopt processes in line with larger plant bakeries, I was able to come up with novel ways of getting around this to maintain our standards but as a supplier increases their reach the pressure grows to adopt industrial methodology in the name of food safety. What this means in the bakery environment is more machines and fewer people.

Aaron Bobrow-Strain's book, *White Bread*, delves deeper into the concerns over contaminated bread and the safety that white sliced bread represents. His work shines a light on the bread industry specifically in relation to the xenophobia and racist attitudes towards mixed-race labour producing bread for the masses. By using food safety as a smoke screen, the way we produce food has been altered in unfathomable ways and it's no coincidence, in my opinion, that industrial bread, industrial farming and tight food safety controls all began to exert their influence at the same time. It was the perfect cocktail to feed on the Cold War mentality of the later twentieth century.

The principal risk associated with bread production now, aside from any physical contamination, is probably *Bacillus cereus*, known more widely for the effects it can have when rice is cooked and then not stored properly. If storage conditions of flour or grain are too moist then this spore-forming bacteria can multiply and result in sickness. While it would require a baker to completely ignore the fact their flour's wet and clumpy, it's important as the spores are not killed during the baking process and hibernate until favourable conditions return, when they again multiply. Good stock rotation and keeping flour sacks off the floor are usually enough to mitigate against this.

In earlier times, ergot was a fairly significant problem as it can affect any cereal grain. In this fungal condition, the grain has the tell-tale sign of being black and if bread is made with it and consumed then symptoms can range from sickness to hallucinations and even death by 'St Anthony's Fire', where the victim feels like their flesh is burning. Other bacterial infections of the grain may turn the crumb to slurry and all this unexplained microbiological activity was usually (and erroneously) attributed

122 | BREAKING BREAD

to figures such as 'the corn hag' who could turn children, corn and bread black. Witch trials were commonly associated with some sort of perceived curse resulting in an agricultural blight. When a whole town or village relied on the same grain to survive the winter it was no wonder inhabitants went mad with hunger.

As I wanted to get a clearer understanding of how bread was received by the digestive system and how different styles of bread could be converted into energy, I decided to speak with Dr Vanessa Kimbell to get an insight into her work on bread and the microbiome. She has seen results that show bread can have a positive and negative effect on mental health depending on the kind of loaf one consumes.

She's been a big influence on Dr Tim Spector who runs the Zoe programme that has revolutionised the way that we can analyse the impact the food we eat has on our internal systems. When I ask what image she sees when I say the word 'bread', Dr Kimbell is transported back to childhood, in a sensory rush that resembles the gastronomic reveries that Remy, the rat in the animated movie *Ratatouille*, experiences. A busy French restaurant, voices, smells, the basket of bread, reminiscent of slices of walnut wood with the bark attached. Ripped by hand, its got a sticky, creamy crumb that elicits a sexuality in the food that doesn't exist in the square, insipid slices of gut-clotting bread back in England at the time.

It's safe to say the doctor is a bread person. A third-generation baker, like myself, with Italian heritage and a British upbringing, she runs The Sourdough School in rural Northamptonshire. Dr Kimbell's route to academia began not with the cerebral but the tangible: a love of making bread and instinctively understanding the processes at work had a bigger story to tell. By transitioning into the academic world, she has been able to expose huge areas of nutrition, specifically associated with bread that demand to be explored further. A self-styled disrupter, Dr Kimbell hopes her work will have a legacy beyond her own research and sees those she trains at her school as agents of change, springing forth to spread the new gospel.

The main focus of her work is the effect that bread has on the gut and thence how gut health impacts our overall health. In a statement that reminds me of Tim Williams' assertion that there has been a break between the soil and the plant in agriculture, she tells me how 'the relationship between our bodies and the microbial world has been broken'. The fracturing of wheat and refinement of the flour leaves the gut nutritionally deficient and we are collectively learning the results of this. The countless tiny microbes that break down and unpack our food, making essential vitamins and minerals available to us can't function without the fibre we are removing from our bread. These microscopic, friendly parasites, keep our digestive systems operating efficiently and beneficially. Many, including writers such as Dr Guilia Enders, have highlighted the gut's power on health and disease. When this system is running well, the benefits are significant, the gut being branded as a 'second brain' to help regulate overall health. When the system breaks down, it can have negative outcomes in a wide variety of areas, including mental health.

One of the questions that I keep coming back to is this: why has wheat been so successful despite requiring such focused attention in the growing and processing into a foodstuff such as bread? Rice can be eaten as a grain; pulses and other legumes can likewise be simply cooked and hold a nutritional bounty within

124 | BREAKING BREAD

their fibrous husks. Perhaps the answer has something to do with the fact that eating gluten makes us feel good. Artificially good.

Wrapped up in the seed that feeds so many humans is a drug, named either gluteomorphin or gliadorphin, a sedative-type opioid. Wheat gluten is formed of two proteins, glutenin and gliadin, and the active agent is found in the gliadin protein. Rye flour by contrast has a similar two protein glutenous structure of glutenin and glutelin which accounts for both its density and low consumption rates. It doesn't get high and doesn't get us high. These food-delivered opioid peptides are found in other foods such as dairy products (caseomorphins), with 75 per cent of the standard American diet being formed of foods containing wheat and milk-based products.

Both gliadin and casein have been found to damage the lower intestinal lining and cause malabsorption of essential micronutrients. These so-called 'comfort foods' make us feel good in the short term while causing longer term damage. When you take into account all the other drug addled foods we consume, such as sugar, tea, coffee, alcohol, chocolate, and so on, it really is no wonder they call it junk food. Dr Van Tulleken found many ultra-processed foods pass every stage of the addictive substance test, with refined white wheat flour present in around 60 per cent of all supermarket products, and this addictive element may explain why other grains have been less coveted.

It doesn't have to be this way. If we ate more of the whole grain and consumed higher levels of the fibre and short-chain fatty acids, which Dr Kimbell calls 'the engine oil' in our guts, we could keep our dopamine receptors tickled while keeping our bodies ticking along nicely. Many people have responded to this in the way that an addict might, by going cold turkey. The response to search for gluten-free alternatives to familiar glutenous foods seems a sensible one at first glance. Another ultra-processed fix for the ultra-processed problem in many cases. This kind of reaction is like those people who think the solution to our own problems on Earth is to build a rocket and live on Mars. There are huge problems with a lot of the bread we eat, but the solution comes from changing the current system rather than abdicating to a gluten-free realm tortured by the same problems in many cases. Guar gum, for instance, is used in many gluten-free products but has documented negative side effects, from bloating and gas to diarrhoea and inflammation. We don't need to turn our backs on wheat. In fact, in order to keep populations functioning, wheat is our best hope, yet the way we manage our food systems in general needs a shake-up.

Dr Kimbell asks me about the relationship between the industrial system and the artisanal one and I comment that I think big industry keeps a small artisanal market active to bring up their own prices. She stops me dead in my tracks, when she responds: 'I've seen how the industrial systems works, David, everyone thinks that they are pulling the strings, that they think this or that. They don't think at all. That's the problem.' I'm arrested by her words, replaying the conversations I've had with various agents of the industrial system and her argument sounds increasingly plausible.

It hits me that there are breaks at every level of the system. From seed to soil, ingredients to food, food to gut, gut to body and even the systems outside the natural world such as consumer to product and products to economy. I have been trying to get to the front of the metaphorical train and have just discovered that no one is behind the controls. All the time I have wondered

126 | BREAKING BREAD

how big companies are able to produce foods that they know are harmful to health, I imagined scheming, conniving Dickensian characters with names like Flackstone and Pricksworth sitting laughing at graphs showing increased NHS spending on diabetes medication. We are in the 'good people doing nothing' territory, a benign evil that once dispelled will reveal food execs from all over the world saying that they have been trying to make the same changes for years.

We need to stop viewing those in charge of these companies as the enemy. They need our help, and this could be a huge opportunity for some seismic change. We are all on the same train after all, and if we can foster a collaborative relationship between small businesses that can test new methodology and offer it to big baking then we may be collectively much better off. Dr Kimbell is one person but if her work is scaled up and made accessible to a wide portion of the public then it could have lasting benefits on all aspects of health.

She has come up with a solution. 'Baking As Lifestyle Medicine' (BALM) uses bread as a holistic antidote by focusing not just on nutrition benefits such as higher bran content but also the mental benefits from bread making, including social interaction and relaxation. These 'pillars' of the BALM protocol have been tested and refined (in a good way) over years at The Sourdough School and are a wonderful way to enrich the home baker's experience and intensify their connection to the food they eat and produce. Critics may argue it requires the kind of time that is only available to some members of society but with avoidable diseases ravaging all parts of society any impact would be positive and as her research grows, I'm sure she will find a way to make her approach universally available.

There are ailments that a baker is susceptible to. Conditions such as 'baker's lung' caused by inhaling small amounts of flour particles over a long period of time can lead to respiratory issues. I have always added water to the mixing bowl before the flour to counteract the powder-puff experienced at the start of the mix and refrain from leaning over the mixer for the first minute or two. Fingers crossed, I haven't had any issues but I still have a few decades before retirement age.

'Baker's Knee' is another common condition, a joint issue like tennis elbow that relates to a repetitive action. When I wash my white trousers, they will usually have one dirty knee, my right, from constantly lowering my body to load and unload the lower decks of the oven or arrange trays, breads and tins on the bottom shelf of a cooling rack. After busy weeks, in hot temperatures, cramp can be a problem if the time can't be found to rehydrate sufficiently. I can remember times when standing in front of the oven for hours, I would constantly be filling my water bottle, drinking up to eight litres in one shift and still cramp up as soon as I sat down back at home. It is a physically demanding profession for sure and when baking in traditional ways, hand moulding bread over decades can lead to arthritis in thumb joints, worn out hips, knees and just about everything else.

One of the worst health impacts of being a baker has got to be night work. BBC Radio Two presenter, O. J. Borg calls them 'dog hours' because any hour worked at night feels like seven daytime hours. His show runs from midnight to 3 a.m., the self-styled messiah of the 'midnight massive', the stable of nocturnal workers that keep the country moving while the majority sleep.

When O. J. thinks of bread, he experiences the constant warm hug that has been ever present in his life. He's reminded of eating

128 | BREAKING BREAD

the warm centre of a loaf from a hole-in-the-wall bakery in Malta and baking his own sourdoughs at home. He'd rather have a warm slice of buttered bread than go out for a three-star dinner. He lets me know via WhatsApp that night work is 'the preserve of cat burglars, bakers and the criminally insane. There are upsides to beavering away when the world sleeps. Yes, you may be depressed and die way younger but at least you didn't have to deal with the rush hour.' According to a 2022 study, between 15 per cent and 20 per cent of workers in industrialised nations work nightshifts, with an average life expectancy that is around fifteen years lower than their diurnal compatriots. I present the following evidence to support that statistic.

Last week I was on nights, starting at 10.30 p.m. and finishing at around 7 a.m. That's nine-and-a-half hours if you're doing the payroll. *Not that bad, stop whinging!*, I hear you cry. I will arrive home at 7.30 a.m., so my wife can leave for work at the local hospital, I then have a coffee and some toast to give me enough energy to get the kids ready for school and walk them to the gates in time for 8.45 a.m. Normally the small one requires carrying for a distance due to a self-diagnosed condition called 'fizzy legs'.

Back home just after nine, I race to bed and try to get to sleep, battling the coffee, daylight, dog and the monologue in my head that is reminding me of all the things I haven't done. I will then wake up after four hours to feed and walk the dog before collecting the children at 3.30 p.m. They then require all manner of *amuse bouche* before being fed and watered. Billie, the love of my life, will arrive home at 5.30 p.m. and after discussing the ins and outs of a day in nuclear medicine, feeding ourselves (and secretly eating biscuits while our children watch cartoons), we combine our powers to get them bathed and in bed for around 7 p.m. I then usually fall asleep after reading *Hooray for Bread* (yes, really) and am woken up an hour-and-a-half later to spend some quality time with Billie before leaving the house at 10 p.m.

At work, I will drink coffee and lots of water and O. J. keeps me awake through the really sticky patch with his radio show. I am allowed breaks but never take them because then I would fall asleep and all the bread would burn. If I get really tired, I take a minute to eat something sweet or perhaps a warm bagel. The schedule is tight and you can't just stop for twenty minutes: it would require learning all the languages the micro-organisms in the bread speak to get them to also stop working. They don't stop so I can't stop, especially when I'm working on my own. Finally, after all the bread is baked, packed and out the door, I leave with a warm loaf under my arm. To do it all again.

Many bakeries try to mix up the nightshifts (or eradicate them completely) to benefit their people and keep their mental health in check. I remember a six-month period during the coronavirus pandemic when I was working seven-day weeks and refrained from counting the hours I was doing because I knew it would send me crazy.

I have, at various stages, required antidepressants and counselling sessions, both of which were in large part the result of my schedule. A toxic environment that is often passed down through the generations in the way that older high-school kids justify bullying the new students, it's a 'if I had to live through it then so should they' attitude. And founded on the idea that fresh bread is required in the morning, with wholesale customers often prescribing delivery times that will mean the baker will not get to read a bedtime story to their kids. I know from speaking to bakers from across the industry that this is not uncommon, an added personal cost to the warm bread you see on the shelf as the shop opens. Makes a £4 loaf seem cheap at twice the price, doesn't it?

All aspects of the breadmaking process can have an impact on health. Whether that is for the benefit or detriment of the eater and maker is a choice. I often wonder if this information were laid out simply for consumers, if the costs were more explicit, how many of us would choose to eat ultra-processed bread over one of Wing Mon's loaves?

5

Big Bread

Industrial vs artisan bakeries

*I do not believe that there is anything inherently
and unavoidably ugly about industrialism.*

George Orwell, *The Road to Wigan Pier* (1937)

David vs Goliath. A story every child is familiar with, the little man triumphing over adversity. An example of how a small, unburdened and skilled boy is able to take down a technologically superior, gigantic warrior. As humans we love an underdog story, whether it's Rocky Balboa, the Karate Kid or my personal favourite, the 1980 US hockey team beating the USSR in the Winter Olympics, in what was called the 'miracle on ice'. We must be wary of seeking out the conflict in these relationships, as too often happens with big bread and little bread in the media.

Pitting artisan and industrial bread against each other may prove a surefire way of getting engagement on some editorial content but it's a cheap shot. Our world needs both the adaptability and creativeness of small food systems and the ability to scale

132 | BREAKING BREAD

them up so that everyone can benefit. I do not believe these aims are mutually exclusive.

I want to try to understand these two camps and see whether they are truly separate, or if they are pieces of the same puzzle. Can a unification of artisan and industry solve our food production problems? Will industry always dominate the artisan? If they fight it out, who will win? Can a few shiny artisan pebbles bring down the polished sword of industry?

In our family bakery, at around five in the morning, after all the mixing had been finished, my father would get himself one of yesterday's sandwiches so that he could take the handful of pills he needed to keep him baking. A pick 'n' mix of joint looseners, pain suppressors and anti-inflammatories tossed back in the fashion that Americans like to eat peanuts by making a fist-shaped cup that was energetically levered into his face, all washed down with a swig of cold tea from a chipped mug.

The old machines got their gears greased once a week, but the old baker needed a more regular service. At the end of the shift, the bakers would all go to the pub, to decompress from the night's labours. I'm sure it wasn't advisable to drink with all the medication but it's not advisable to bake for sixty years either.

Dad's doctor couldn't understand why his body was in such bad shape so eventually agreed to watch him at work. It was like a deleted chapter from H. G. Wells' *The Time Machine* as the Eloi doc observed the Morlock baker in his dark, claustrophobic workplace – dragging mixer bowls full of dough, carrying buckets of water and lifting two or three bags of flour at a time (each bag weighing sixteen kilos). A grotesquely cut figure making beautiful bread for the diurnal townsfolk. He had won a national baking award in the 1980s, Britain's Best Baker, and his prize was to be chained to the oven until his hinges finally seized up for good. Now it was my turn. Oh goody.

All of the unexplained symptoms were answered as the doctor watched on, he was surprised my dad was still functioning at all. The tons of cumulative flour that had compounded joints, millions of repetitions that had left cartilage worn to a whisper. Could any of this be changed to make it less physically strenuous? The question was moot. This was the way my dad had worked for over half a century – what was the point in changing now? The damage had been done. I was another matter.

In 2017, five years after I had returned to the family bakery, I attended the Baking Industry Awards. I was a finalist in the category for 'Best Baker' along with two others. The judges had come to our bakeries and we had demonstrated our skills as best we could, performed all the requisite schmoozing and ventured to London from our respective corners of the country to find out who would win.

Walking into the hotel that was to host this showpiece of the baking industry calendar in my rented tuxedo, I felt out of place. I had moved the bakery into a more spacious building, with better conditions for the baking team and the ability to move the flour on pallet trucks to reduce the strain. The cramped conditions of the Victorian brick building were replaced with a repurposed space on a former American military airbase nearby. The production capacity had increased so that we were getting through two tonnes of flour a week and we had become more focused on distribution. The quality was good enough to see me invited along to the shindig in the capital and while this was an honour, I was looking forward to

134 | BREAKING BREAD

getting out of the black tie and into my whites. The only sensible course of action seemed to tuck into all the free booze and enjoy the show.

Incomprehensibly the theme for the evening was 'The Wild West' and all of the cardboard cutouts were smothered in the names of the biggest corporations that extract their income from the bakery sector. I could tell from looking at the hands of those around me that very few of the attendees were actual bakers, their soft, slight Eloi fingers delicately pinching stems of Champagne flutes filled with a less expensive sparkling wine.

Representatives from national and multinational companies filled the main room where we sat, and Denise van Outen hosted the whole spectacle after busting out a couple of showtunes. The décor was more in line with a special screening of *Back to the Future III*, old hat British pantomime versions of corrals and cowboy memorabilia. Hundreds of people from all the big mills, big bakeries, supermarkets and bakery chains. There were sprinkles of artisan bakers, but this was really an evening to celebrate the might of the industrial sector.

It struck me that nearly every award was sponsored by a giant of the food manufacturing industry and won by a small- or medium-sized business. All of the finalists in my category were small-scale bakers, representing an impossibly tiny crumb of the market share. Yet, where were the bakers from the Chorleywood plant bakeries who make 80 per cent of the nation's bread? Was the industry admitting that its products were inferior? Lacking in skill? I ended up winning the award and swiftly ruined the moment by treading on Denise's foot as I collected the trophy.

So, here I was, that year's 'Best Baker'. Then why did it feel like a Pyrrhic victory? I felt extremely hollow, and like the whole thing was a performance that had been rehearsed by the biggest players in the industry to demonstrate their credibility.

The baking industry is primarily made up of large-scale industrial bakers and supporting industries. A few giant mills supply animal feed, the brewing industry and bakers nationwide and this is replicated in various other nations across the world. Baking factories kick out millions of loaves of bread every day to keep packed lunch boxes filled, toasters stuffed and butter knives busy. Around 20 per cent of the bakery market is reserved for smaller bakers, the kind that appear on television programmes and are usually what we imagine when someone says 'bakery'. Most of those small bakeries are really just satellites of the industrial operations however, selling bread made with mixes from the big mills, additive-packed bread made on a cute scale.

What's left are the artisans, masochistic Spartans who enjoy spending their lives perfecting their craft using high-quality ingredients. They are the ones that pop up on your Instagram feeds, but they can't feed the nation. The systems they rely on are too small, enfeebled by the gargantuan operations that demand low-cost, low-quality commodity wheat to produce artificially acceptable bread at artificially low prices.

The principal difference between the two models is the use of bakers. Industrial bread is made by machines, supervised by technicians. Artisan bread is made by people with the support of machines. An artisanal baker can make around three hundred loaves a day, an industrial bakery with a fully mechanised bread plant can make two million. The goal is to get calories wrapped and on the road

136 | BREAKING BREAD

as cheaply as possible in a format that is acceptable to the end consumer. But this does not equate to good health, just big bucks.

A Warburton's TV advertisement from 2015 exemplifies these aims. It opens with a branded lorry exiting the factory gates as a telephone sounds and a member of the company bursts into Jonathan Warburton's office announcing Sylvester Stallone – yes, that Stallone – is on the line. He takes the call, a movie pitch from the man who played the ultimate working-class contender. The idea borrows heavily from the Rocky franchise, with multiple references to Bolton letting us know in a heavy-handed manner that the sixth biggest brand in the UK hasn't forgotten its roots. And all with an emphasis on '*fresh*' bread. Stallone proposes he plays a driver, delivering bread to thousands of stores every day. We see some fleeting shots of bread being baked, which accounts for less than 5 per cent of the total running time. Then a platoon of drivers run to the delivery trucks, and Stallone seamlessly transitions into a Rambo-esque figure. He jumps from his jammed-in truck stating 'it's time to earn my crust' and proceeds to run over the tops of cars, carrying a crate of bread in his arms, then through town and country until he reaches a local shop where he hands it over to a swooning employee. The proposed title for the movie is *The Deliverers* and as Sly wraps up the pitch he asks 'Johnnie' Warburton for his opinion. '*Tell me the bit about the bread again,*' Warburton replies. The investment in getting someone like Stallone on-board for ads shows how much money is involved in producing bread on this scale.

Warburton's are not alone in this focus on delivery; one of Britain's favourite adverts ever is the 1973 Hovis ad. Here, we see a young boy pushing a bike, post-war, loaded with bread, up a steep cobbled hill. Exerting himself to make sure 'old Ma

Peggerty' gets her bread on time, to the sound of a brass band playing 'New World Symphony' by Dvorak. Directed by none other than Ridley Scott, the voice over is in the kind of lilt that my ears were familiar to growing up as a boy, the men who worked as farm hands and would visit the local pub on a Saturday after helping out with the pheasant shoot. It was filmed on Gold Hill in Shaftesbury, Dorset – less than an hour from the south coast and historically associated with milling wheat flour.

Indeed, the post-war era was a new world and in no more a demonstrable way than in its production of food. The voiceover is from the boy as an older man, dripping in working-class nostalgia. In Britain, the sound of brass bands are heavily associated with industries such as mining, so this is intentional, just as using a Hollywood actor, associated with health and strength, to endorse a product is.

The Hovis ad was so influential that the British Film Institute (BFI) restored it in 2019 as a sample of only twenty-five from its collection of many thousands of adverts. Described as 'heart-warming' and 'iconic', it laid the blueprint that Warburton's and other companies followed, with a focus on working-class, salt of the earth heritage and emphasis on delivery over production.

In 2013, Hovis turned the nostalgia up to eleven with a nationalistic romp through the twentieth century. Our northern lad picks up a loaf from the baker's shop in the early 1900s, running home past posters for the *Titanic*, suffragette demonstrations, First World War soldiers on parade, bombed out terraces, street parties celebrating victory over Nazi Germany with snippets of Churchill, a Spitfire flying by, through the decades to a Union Jack-smothered car full of men celebrating the 1966 Football World Cup win, past a 1980s' stand-off between striking miners

138 | BREAKING BREAD

and riot police, with a final incongruous night time run set against a backdrop of Millennium fireworks, only to return home. It ends with the unchanged strapline: '*As good today as it's always been.*'

While fairly recent technological advances have driven the scale of individual factories, industrial-scale baking is not a new phenomenon. The Ancient Egyptians required two loaves per day for every worker who helped build the pyramids. Given their scale, we can deduce that's a huge requirement of bread. Even undertaken by smaller bakeries, the organisation must surely be classed as industrial. Sitting here, it's just hit me that those incredible feats of architecture, visible from space, were built by people who were fuelled by bread. This isn't to say that the industrial scale of these ancient bakers meant that they weren't also skilled artisans. Yet it begs the question, if the Egyptians had access to the Chorleywood process, might they have built a factory next to every pyramid? The mind boggles.

It was in North Africa that bread baking technology advanced, in a form that is still recognisable today. The tomb-esque ovens of the pharaohs gave rise to loaves worthy of recording on their hieroglyphs. Later, the Greeks would put animals to the task of milling grain, improving efficiency and output as well as freeing humans from the laborious quern stone. The Romans advanced this further by employing water and wind to take the place of bestial power, with each successive empire growing more cereal grains, milling more flour and baking more bread. Populations rose alongside the proving dough, this growth in capita was, at once, a result of the increased production and the driving force for continued output.

The large-scale bakeries of today require huge reserves of skill and hard work to keep them producing such vast quantities of bread. The difference, for me, comes from the intention that the baker has when making it. An industrial baker is focused on output, and all other concerns such as variety, quality and the provenance of raw materials are required to bend to this aim. The peak of the mountain is a number that can be measured in units for an industrial baker. For an artisan, the focus is on quality, sourcing, relationships and emotion. They must hit certain numbers to keep the business operating but they live and die on the quality of the bread, not the number of loaves.

For the artisan, the peak of the mountain is measured by the view. Lots of bakers will juggle these two opposing forces within themselves, and the best artisan bakers will draw on certain skills associated with industrial operations, such as keeping wastage to a minimum, sourcing ingredients at the best possible price and maintaining a clean and safe working environment.

An example of an artisan who has become industrial without losing the core of the business would be that of the American baker Dave Dahl from Portland, Oregon. Chef Brad Leone mentioned this bakery to me when I was suggesting a dearth of good industrial bread in the UK. Dave's Killer Bread is the US's number one organic sliced bread, selling loaves in every state, as well as Canada and Mexico.

Like me, Dahl was born into a baking family, and saw firsthand the level of skill and hard work it takes to run a bakery business. His path was anything but smooth. Dave started a relationship with illegal drugs and crime that would lead to him serving fifteen years in prison. Through his rehabilitation, he learnt the discipline and skills required to take a good local bakery that responded to customer's requests and turn it into a leader in the industry.

Dave's Killer Bread began, like so many bakeries, as a market stall venture. When customers couldn't wait for market day to get their next bread fix, Dave began supplying stores directly. The brand now sits under the Flowers Foods' umbrella, after being bought in 2015 for $275 million, and the bread is made industrially in a factory environment. In many ways, it mimics operations such as Wonder Bread but it is made with organic ingredients, has a focus on customer health and accepts that it will always be more expensive than its competitors. In fact, when Dave was trying to develop a 'diet' bread, instead of compromising on the quality of the product, he simply used a thin cut slicer. That might be a lesson for our time.

The bakery also has an altruistic arm that seeks to give rehabilitated offenders a second chance, and 30 per cent of the employees have been through the prison system. All in all, it doesn't feel like a typical industrial bakery and shows that industrial methods don't all lead to the same end. Critics would point out the high level of sugar in the products, which is no doubt there to keep the bread soft as it travels across state lines. Five grams per slice does seem pretty steep, but it is organic cane sugar rather than high fructose corn syrup and compared to other breads with a similar distribution it is in the nutritionally elite.

In the UK, there are brands on the market that look to provide a similar offering. Jason's Sourdough is a supermarket brand that has one of the smallest ingredients' lists you'll see down the bakery aisle. Their standard white sourdough contains the following: wheat flour (wheat flour, calcium carbonate, iron, niacin, thiamin), water, rye flour, salt, fermented wheat flour. The supplements in the white flour are a legal requirement.

This is a bread that is distributed nationwide through some of the country's biggest retailers. It contains no fats, no sugars and no additive package to boost fermentation or keep quality. It is undoubtedly produced on an industrial scale but has the provenance and process of an artisan product. This is a growing business and obviously a successful one, as shown by the announcement in 2024 that they will be investing in a new eight-million pound state-of-the-art bakery to double their production capacity, after a bumper year which saw growth of 132 per cent.

The eponymous Jason is a fourth-generation baker from Leicestershire, and there seems to be a link between the clean label, store-bought loaves and family businesses that have been squeezed into a small corner of the market, which break out to capitalise on the fertile ground occupied by the bigger bread brands.

Bertinet Bakery follows a similar pattern. Founded by Richard Bertinet, a baker famous in the UK for bringing French flair to the 'dourdough' of the British bread board in the late 1980s, and for his cooking school in Bath, Somerset, the Bertinet Bakery brand was sold in 2018. Although Richard hasn't been involved since 2020, the bread carries the same simple ingredient list and authentic sourdough credentials despite it being manufactured in great numbers and sold in supermarkets and online stores such as Waitrose and Ocado. Dr Vanessa Kimbell, who specialises in the link between bread and gut health, chose Bertinet's seeded sourdough as the best supermarket loaf in a 2024 article for the *Telegraph* newspaper.

I've tried both these breads, and although they feel familiar to me, they both suffer from an inescapable hurdle to mass distributed loaves – they aren't fresh. I know that some industrial bakers get annoyed at claims their bread isn't fresh because they do a wonderful job of getting it out of the factory gates and into big stores in an impossibly short space of time.

The freshness I equate with bakeries is what I grew up with – taking the bread out of the oven, walking ten or so feet and

142 | BREAKING BREAD

putting it on the shelf for customers to buy immediately. I know what it's like to take a baguette from the oven and slice through the sweet porcelain crust to receive a face full of fermented steam. It has ruined me. I've eaten from the tree of fresh bread and I know the difference. If you do, it's almost impossible to settle for anything else.

The process of staling is mainly the crystallisation of starches, like when honey seizes in the jar. With bread, the crumb goes from soft to firm. A kind of necromancy can be performed to bring the bread back to life, toasting a slice will do this for instance or taking a whole unsliced loaf, running it under the kitchen tap and baking it again for ten minutes. Be warned though, much like Cinderella, time is sensitive: you have to get it while it's hot before it turns back into a dry, unappetising loaf.

The artisan loaf is a performance, the customer requiring the same hit of nostalgic charm that Hovis provide in their TV spots. The smell, temperature, sounds and even humidity of a bakery can't be replicated in a sterile store environment. Even the in-store bakeries at the back of supermarkets don't fool many. Chris Young, founding editor of *True Loaf* magazine and co-ordinator of the Real Bread Campaign, calls these 'loaf tanning salons' when they are used in the pantomime performance of re-baking industrial dough products that were originally manufactured elsewhere.

When you walk into a small baker's shop and see firsthand the mixers spinning, the shaping of the dough, fresh loaves peeled from the oven straight onto shelves, you realise all of this is impossible to replicate. There are many places like this, across the UK, and the numbers are growing. And their impact often goes beyond just the provision of fresh bread, made with well-sourced, good ingredients, they reach to the wider community.

BIG BREAD | 143

Let me take you to one I know personally, one I have taught at, the Dusty Knuckle bakery, in east London, to show you what I'm getting at. To get there, we have to take a turn off Kingsland High Street, between a McDonalds and a modern high-rise complex, down Abbot Street. We walk past the back gates of a Sainsbury's supermarket and as the road narrows, we go down a tight slope which opens up into small metropolitan oasis. Now filled with a bakery, a brewery and a BBQ joint, it was, not long ago, a ratty, neglected carpark. Now it's a bustling paradise of snacks and beverages – and it all changed when friends Rebecca Oliver, Daisy Terry and Max Tobias had a dream, and put two shipping containers in that space space to start a bakery.

Those containers are now the classroom where members of the public can learn to make bread the Dusty Knuckle way. Taking very basic ingredients and turning them into the most delicious bread, with very little equipment other than a bowl and a pair of hands. On a Saturday morning, there's a queue that stretches all the way out to the main road. The bakery itself is now in the main building, and as we approach the glass doors, a wave of freshly baked and baking bread hits us.

The multi-storey Victorian brick office space is run by the Bootstrap Charity which supports young people who want to start businesses or social enterprises. Much of the ground floor is now taken up by the Dusty Knuckle bakery and café. Inside it's usually a mosh-pit of customers, scrabbling to get to the counter before all the bread and pastries are gone. Opposite the bakery counter, the small energetic kitchen makes beautiful food to complement the bread, most famously in the form of a rolling menu of focaccia sandwiches. Bakers with dusty blue aprons drop off crusts for serving with homemade soups.

144 | BREAKING BREAD

At the back, sacks of flour are lifted high onto the bakers' shoulders, then poured into the gaping mouths of mixers and guards pulled down before the giant metal hooks start combining the flour and water. Puffs of cereal dust escape as the process starts. Simultaneously we see tubs filled with dough, stacked to the sky, wheeled, one-by-one. The stretchy contents are folded by hand and a metal table is filled with hundreds of dough balls that are shaped and placed in bannetons that will go onto racks and be rolled into huge walk-in fridges.

An oven timer pierces the chorus of the bakers' chatter and as the metal door of the deck oven swings open, there's a burst of steam before hundreds of freshly baked loaves are unloaded. Bleary-eyed bakers move through the space with timeless grace. It's a routine they know so well, having played all the parts before, so no words are necessary: the symbiotic relationship between the bread and the bakers is really something to wonder at.

The bakery is popular and the bakers apologise regularly for selling out of their stock so early, but they couldn't work any harder, faster or more efficiently. I'm certain that one of the reasons for their success is that they lay it all out on a platter, allowing customers to see everything, to share everything, all that joy that comes from how the bread is created, by real people, shaped by flour-dusted hands. It shows bread is the food of love, created with love. This epitomises the best of artisanal production for me.

The bakery makes thousands of products a day, everything from pastries and cakes to breads – but that's not all they do. They feed the community in so many ways. Like the American Dave's Killer Bread, Becca, Daisy and Max offer second chances to vulnerable young people, many with little or no education or with criminal records, people who face barriers getting into the workplace. The mentality of an artisan bakery is that you are only ever as good as your last loaf and that keeps you focused on the present and future. For those with difficult pasts, it provides mental training to look forward by creating something that others can enjoy. It gives people purpose. Dusty Knuckle's record for getting young Londoners back on track is astounding. In their 2024 impact report, they cited having 180 young people in their programmes and of those that stayed for the full duration, 90 per cent went into full time work or further training. One of the alumni said: '*I always knew I could do good, I just needed someone to give me a chance.*' This resonates with me. My family's bakery supported local groups and activities in our community, especially those relating to youth, in sports, the arts and through work experience provision.

There are also parts of the business that depend on the industrial. They use a mixture of stoneground flour and roller-milled flour in their breads for instance. They analyse their production flow and use various machines to assist the operation of the bakery. While mechanically assisted, it is also people-centred, and it's the family environment that is the real engine room behind the bakery's success. They don't just supply the queues of customers that hand over their hard-earned cash for bread and pastries; there's a long list of wholesale accounts that receive freshly baked bread at dawn. Lots of bread.

I covered a bake shift at Christmas a few years back for Daisy Terry, the force of nature behind the bakery arm of the Dusty Knuckle. It was the Christmas party and they wanted to make sure all their team could make it, so I took a busman's holiday and baked the bread for them on my own, with drunken text support from Daisy whenever I needed it. Daisy and I are old

146 | BREAKING BREAD

pals, since working together at Lily Vanilli and, as anyone in hospitality will know, when you find good people who have your back, it's always reciprocated. So, when she asked if I'd provide cover, of course I said yes straight away, even though it involved a two hour-drive each way.

Looking at the Dusty Knuckle's packing slips I could see more than seventy sites, among them some of the capital's most prestigious restaurants, delis, cafés and stores. The wholesale side of things has been capped off for about five years so they can balance the business with their own two outlets, mobile milk float (they don't sell milk from it) and the youth programme.

It was a gruelling shift. Despite freezing temperatures outside, I was overheating as I ran between fridges and ovens, loading, unloading and stacking bread. Standards were high and it was essential I maintained the level their customers expected which isn't easy in an unfamiliar space and I can't overstate how difficult it is to maintain the level of production in a bakery like Dusty Knuckle without slipping up on quality and consistency. It takes artistry, skill and dedication. A few minutes can carbonise a previously perfect batch so cups of tea are most often enjoyed cold by a baker.

I did my best for Daisy, determined not to let her down. Still, I was admonished by the packer in the morning for not baking the loaves in the usual order and putting things in inconvenient places. Otherwise though, I escaped with my reputation intact. I drove straight home to Suffolk afterwards, and it gave me time to think about the business and the decisions they'd made. Very often a successful bakery will be faced with having either to concentrate on their own shops and open more of them or chase more wholesale accounts and move to a bigger production unit. We can see this illustrated by the two DKBs – the Dusty Knuckle bakery and its American counterpart, Dave's Killer Bread.

Dave's Killer Bread went down the volume route, seeking to reach a point where the low margins per loaf were offset by sheer volume of sales. Dusty Knuckle decided to maintain a balance, concentrating on added value items such as food and classes. Both maintained their core beliefs; both had to make compromises along the way; both are successes. Arguably, each example maintains a healthy relationship between the industrial and artisan. It's sometimes easy to think of these terms in their extreme sense, polarised like two entrenched enemies with a vast no-man's land between them. The future of bread will depend greatly on managing the opposing forces to provide future humans with bread that nourishes bodies, communities and that can be delivered daily in the volumes required by our burgeoning populations.

In order to meet this need, we have to consider the ways that bakeries will have to format our bread. If we want universally good bread, will we have to sacrifice some of the aesthetics of an artisan baker's loaf? Important issues that need to be discussed.

The way that we bake has changed. The Industrial Revolution and the introduction of new technologies and economies of scale, allowing businesses to produce larger quantities of product for less money, of course, has fed into that. There is a piece of technology that has been instrumental in the making of the modern industrial loaf and, perhaps surprisingly, you'll find it in both artisan and plant bakery kitchens. You probably have one, or more, in

148 | BREAKING BREAD

your cupboard at home, especially if you watch the GBBO or *Masterchef*. What is it, you may ask? Well, it's the humble bread tin. A rectangular, pullman-style tin.

Today's bread is mostly angular due to the shape of the tin, but the ancient, more traditional method was to bake a 'round' of dough in the oven, and depending on the quality of the flour (and the baker), the breads would range from pancake flat to full and fluffy. And if you look at old prints and photos, rarely do we see depictions of bread that are anything but round. Every nation has a variation of a round – the Moroccan Khobz, Arab Khubz, English Cobs, all signify a circular shape of bread. When I was a boy, in the family bakery we would make Cob loaves which were simple rounds (Cob is Old English for 'head'), and when we made rolls, the dough would be divided by hand into large rounds to be processed. 'How many heads did we get?' the bakers would ask. Today, however, most bread isn't made like this: around 70 per cent of the bread eaten in the UK is tinned loaf bread. Why the change?

It's especially perplexing when we consider that when baking bread in a tin, the margin for error, across the board, increases. The quality of flour, mixing, shaping, proving and baking can all fluctuate to a certain degree and the result will be consistent. I can tell for instance which loaves I have shaped when making free-form bread compared to my fellow bakers, but with tinned bread it's harder to discern who has shaped which loaf, and there is less opportunity for the skill of the baker to be made manifest.

Tinned bread allows loaves to be baked closer together as there is no danger of the dough fusing together in the oven, although care must be taken to allow some air to pass between the tins to allow an even bake. To help this, metal 'straps' were added to bread tins that set a number of tins in a frame for consistent baking as well as faster loading and unloading. A sandwich loaf, or 'pullman' is baked with a lid on top to give an entirely straight-edged bread that is ideal for slicing and dominates the market. Bread baked in a tin also has a thinner, softer crust so it won't dry out like a traditional boule.

While bread tins are relatively inexpensive, the most expensive piece of bakery equipment is the oven, and a good oven will deliver even heat, a sealed chamber and ideally have steam injection – like the deck oven I used at the Dusty Knuckle. If you are baking in tins, though, the oven can be of a lower quality as the tin itself will self-steam the bread as it bakes and the cost of baking tins compared to the cost of a good industrial oven is minor.

At the end of the twentieth century, the artisan movement seemed to kick into gear just at the stage when the industrial sector had a stranglehold on the market. Pale, sliced, square loaves made with low grade flour, trans fats and a long list of additives, which most of the industrial-scale tinned bread, arguably, seemed to be, was increasingly challenged by customers and the new bakers coming into the field. The most influential baker in this movement for me was Chad Robertson from Tartine bakery in San Francisco. His influential 2010 book, *Tartine Bread*, seemed to break every sacred rule of bread production – and my generation of bakers lapped it up.

Here was a baker who embraced life, who said you can do what you love and still have a life. Instead of baking bread for the early morning customer, Chad's bread came out at 5 p.m., in time for dinner. Chad moulded his schedule around his passion for surfing and dismissed the notion that the baker must be a nocturnal beast, operating on a different timeframe to most

150 | BREAKING BREAD

people, including family. And his bread didn't suffer. It had an open crumb, facilitated by the large quantities of water he used in the dough. Of course, that made it hard to shape and it would clog up a factory bread line in minutes. And he challenged perceptions of what many people thought of as bread. Chad's crust was dark, burnished and blistered. Many thought he was burning his bread, so used were they to the insipid ghostly crusts of mass-produced loaves.

He took his inspiration from a late-nineteenth century painting, Emile Friant's *The Boatmen of the Meurthe,* so divorced had the concept of flavoursome bread come from modern civilisation.

Chad's love of water, both recreationally and in his dough, spilled out from every page of his book. When I first read it, I was inspired. Here was a baker who seemed so joyful, so different from the morose and negative individuals I had grown-up with in my parents' bakery. He was happy. The bakers of my childhood were forever complaining, groaning and moaning their way through each shift. Talking about how little sleep they'd had and itemising every bodily defect and fault with a forensic attention to detail. When that's what you experience, that's how you think things should be and while I'd questioned certain behaviours, methods, even, it hadn't really sunk in that being a baker and being happy weren't separate goals. From that moment, I began to see bread and being a baker in a new light.

Just shortly after Chad's book was published, I was given a copy of it. At the time, I was working a three-month placement at E5 Bakehouse in Hackney. This bakery has been instrumental in creating a new kind of baker in the UK, a curious kind, on a journey of discovery. Many of their alumni have gone on to open and work in other brilliant bakeries, such as Lizzie Parle, Eyal

Schwartz and Kate Merton. I decided I wanted to talk to founder Ben MacKinnon to learn more. Fortunately for me, Ben lives on a farm in Suffolk just down the road from the family bakery. He's a Suffolk boy and returned to the fertile plains of eastern England to grow organic produce for his bakery operations and run baking retreats.

Ben is a warm and gentle person. He is also as sharp as a tack and his views on food are always enlightening. When I ask Ben my usual question, what he thinks of bread, he imagines a boule – a traditional French bread, resembling a flattened 'ball', its literal English translation. It has simple slashes and a fine dusting of flour and is baked dark, revealing a brown, creamy crumb that's quite tight. He confesses that while contemplating what bread is, he had flashes of supermarket-wrapped and sliced bread. The very (and ever-present) antithesis of his own bread production.

Ben originally started E5 Bakehouse from his home in east London, mixing loaves by hand and baking them in a wood-fired oven. This is the same way that Chad started his operation on the West Coast of America. Mixing by hand is hard work so the added water helps to alleviate some of the toil required. Ben would deliver his freshly baked bread to neighbours in the surrounding streets, a small beginning that sparked a fervour of demand for the kind of bread that people weren't familiar with, that had skipped a generation (or two) with the rise of branded, mass-produced, low-cost bread.

Eventually Ben opened up a shop, in a railway arch next to London Fields, on Mentmore Terrace where you can still find the bakery today. This is the archetypal artisan operation. Ben grows grain on his farm in Suffolk, supplemented by various suppliers of small batch, heritage wheats from across the country. They

152 | BREAKING BREAD

have a mill in the bakery itself that grinds fresh flour to use in the bread, alongside carefully selected flour from suppliers such as Hertfordshire-based Gilchesters Organics.

The sourdough process follows, and the dough is carefully tracked through its long fermentation before being scaled, shaped and chilled in preparation for baking. In 2011, when I was making bread there, all the mixing was done in bowls. No big mixers. All the recipes were scaled up in those units. *'How many bowls of Hackney Wild?'* was the call. This was all new to me. I was used to mechanical mixers, dealing in sacks of flour. And does it make a difference to the quality of the bread? I would argue, yes. This level of detail matters. It enhances the connection between the bakery and the customer.

Ben confesses that no one at the bakery, in the early days, had any commercial experience; they were winging it, developing the process as they went along. Like Chad Robertson, in the States, Ben had an idea of the bread he wanted to make, but the pathway didn't exist. Yet, it was a well-trodden path, historically speaking, albeit one that had become buried, seventy years of industrially processed bread making it redundant. I knew the path existed because my family had been stubbornly walking it all that time. Under an avalanche of fluffy factory bread, Grandad Jonty and my dad, Peter, had refused to use the new bypass. And just when my parents' health was failing and their bakers had abandoned the old ways, a new wave of artisan bakers like Ben appeared to take on the mission to keep real bread alive.

At E5, in Hackney, sustainability has always been at the heart of the bakery, with a keen eye on the impact the business has on the environment. It's what led Ben to purchase a mill so he could buy grain directly from small farmers who had no way of getting the flour to market through the handful of big millers that dominate. Much in the same way that specialty coffee is directly traded from farmer to end user, it appears wheat is following the same model.

'The flour feels like it's got more life in it,' Ben explains as we talk about the joys and challenges of baking with freshly milled flour and his impact on the stable of British artisan bakeries. He is proud of the legacy provided by former E5 people going on to open successful bakeries. Yet there have been issues, including one former employee reportedly photographing recipes from E5, before setting up his own operation on the south coast.

'The secret isn't in the recipes,' Ben's adds. 'You have to actually make the bread, day in day out for years to even begin to understand it. Knowing how to fix it when it deviates, dealing with oven breakdowns, changes in seasons. It takes at least five years.' While it may take five years to begin to understand the craft, I know that the lessons never cease. My dad would often remind me that he was still learning fifty or sixty years into his career and in order to enjoy the job, it's important to love this aspect of it, the constant development, the never-ending change. That bread is slightly different each day and has a slightly different message for the baker who is humble enough to listen out for it.

This typifies the challenges of artisan production. In an industrial environment, everything is contained, controlled and consistent. In an artisan bakery everything is moving, variables are ever shifting, a room full of spinning plates that must be carefully considered afresh each day. Every batch is different; every day teaches a new lesson. It's life, ever-changing, reshaping, adapting. That's the beauty of it.

E5 has diversified to include a bakery school, coffee roasting, the mill, a café and hosting special dinners. Hackney, in spite of

154 | BREAKING BREAD

gentrification, is ethnically and culturally diverse, with new communities arriving and the bakery's outreach operations reflect that. They run a programme to train refugees, Just Bread, in combination with The Refugee Council, and E5's commitment to nourish the community with more than just bread is reflected in other artisan like-minded operations, not just across the country but across the world.

They have certainly developed a great deal in the last fifteen years and if the swarm of eager customers outside the shop doors indicates anything, it's set to continue. Customers want this. I remind Ben of the time that Chad came to E5 while I was working there and how it created a similar buzz among the bakers. It was on one of my day's off and the feeling of regret was huge. I had to listen to the other bakers tell their stories about him, how nice he was, how they'd shaken his hand. I've still never met him. One day.

Ben nods, then adds, 'He was at the bakery, again, a few weeks ago for a coffee. Everyone was just as excited. I don't think his influence has waned.' He admits that the kind of bread he, Chad and bakers like them make, doesn't appeal to everyone, those American football shaped loaves with burnished crusts and tangy crumbs. It may serve environmental food systems but the high price involved – often necessary, sometimes inflated, depending on area wealth – and the unfamiliarity of the product for some local markets make it exclusive to certain tastes or diets. Artisan bakeries provide a real-world example that high-quality bread can be too expensive for most people, too crusty, too chewy and unsliced. Ben reveals that sometimes when they've donated bread to homeless charities, it goes uneaten. 'For some, the bread isn't recognisable.'

This bread has been on such a journey to survive and after all the sacrifice it has taken from bakers like my own parents and grandparents, the thought that it isn't even seen as bread is hard to stomach. At the same time, it reminds me of why it is important to keep these traditions alive. And yet, they are still endangered, still on the fringes – put simply, there's more work to do.

Back in 2011, while at E5, I baked with a young guy who had a taste for 1990s hip-hop and flamboyant caps, another Ben as chance would have it. Ben Glazer now runs Coombeshead Bakery in Cornwall, which specialises in making organic sourdough goods made from locally sourced heritage flours of wheat, spelt and rye. I caught up with him, keen to get his views on the artisan bread movement.

When I ask Ben what kind of bread he imagines, he says it's the light wholemeal loaf from his childhood: a thin crust yielding to reveal a custardy, porridgy crumb. It's the bread that has inspired his own signature loaf. Like the other Ben – and me – he is also haunted by a white sliced bread emoji, the convenience store bread that keeps inconveniently popping into his head. The bread that drives us all to do what we do.

Ben describes himself as a 'bread geek loner' who has ended up on a Cornish farm in the middle of nowhere, baking just one kind of bread and trying to perfect the process. He really does make just one product which he primarily sells locally and in the West Country and to fancy London restaurants. There's very little industrial about his approach. He works closely with local farmers to source the best grain and tweaks his bread recipe daily to get the best out of it. Ben is happy to share it – because it changes so often even he doesn't know what it'll be tomorrow!

156 | BREAKING BREAD

Looking at the way he works and his commitment to creating bread, I would say central to his success is the way he has built relationships with the humans that support and complement his business. An example of this is Ben's tight bond with Fred Price at Gothelney Farm in Somerset which follows a regenerative model, using few artificial chemicals, enriching the soil and producing some beautiful grain. Ben tells me that the variety of wheat is less important than the person who grows it, in the same way that a sourdough made by an industrial baker will never be as good as one made by an artisan. People are the stitches that hold the world together; as soon as we take them out of the process, everything falls apart. Our collective aim needs to be to celebrate and reward these people, not replace them with machines or AI. I don't want a robot to make my sandwich. I want Ben Glazer to make it.

Fred sees the change on his own farm – their recent shift from tradition to more regenerative techniques – as a positive move from imposing conventional systems onto nature, fighting against it really, to now working alongside nature, in harmony with its systems. And this fits in with Ben's approach to breadmaking at Coombeshead, more about watching and listening to the process than dictating it. The level of attention that this requires accounts for Ben's adherence to a one loaf menu: that one loaf gets all his love and devotion. Ben mills fresh grain which he blends with other stoneground flour that has been diligently sourced, and while the ground grain is lively and can be challenging to deal with, that's the joy. It ferments quickly and in different ways depending on the harvest, the temperature and humidity. It's the black run of baking.

When I ask why he would willingly take on such a laborious process, requiring such dedication and effort he answers simply,

'Because it's more fun' and it's obvious he means it. When Ben sends the van off to deliver his day's bake, he knows that he couldn't have done anything more to produce the best bread he's capable of.

It's not a loaf that can be scaled to feed the nation however and Ben struggles even at current levels of production to get enough grain to feed the bakery. The demand on this kind of regeneratively farmed flour is accelerating but it takes time for farms to transition away from conventional systems of agriculture. The price, too, is a barrier and Ben feels the disconnect between baking in a relatively deprived region of the UK, only to send his daily bake off to a clutch of Michelin-starred restaurants in London.

'I've come to terms with it,' Ben comments. 'I remember an article in *Vice Magazine* about Chad Robertson, where he was defending his choice to mechanise his process. A lot of bakers in the community I'm a part of reacted badly to it, but how else can you reduce costs?' When I look up the article from 2015, I can see why some romantics of the small food movement might find it hard to digest. In it, the man who, for many, represents everything pure and honest about artisan production announces his intentions to go global and the changes necessary to do so.

'The farm-to-table movement is like a one per cent movement,' Robertson says. 'I'm looking at getting better food to different parts of the country, trying to mainstream something that has historically been for the wealthy alone. The most exciting thing I can do now is scale [. . .] We're trying to scale something super artisanal, but take full advantage of all the technology that's applicable.'

So, how can this be? Chad Robertson, the man who launched a thousand micro-bakeries, who influenced the way I think about bread, an advocate for an industrial system? I need to get my head around that idea. How can I marry that with what I do? But the kind of bread, I know I and the people who I've encountered in this book want to make, is expensive. There's no way around that. So, perhaps Chad has a point. Is the use of technology itself a barrier to carefully considered artisanal production? If change is required and if the industrial stranglehold on the market is to be loosened, then it may need a mechanical hand to do the job. It's something worth thinking about.

Yet, the idea that industrial and artisanal models are defined by the equipment used is missing the point, I believe. The spirit of artisan production comes from creating relationships with suppliers who are themselves invested in more sustainable methods, at a scale that supports them, something that people like Ben Glazer and Fred Price are doing. The ingredients, the process and the goals can all be assisted by advanced technology without becoming consumed by the corporate food industry.

Baking is hard. That's important to stress given the halcyon images we see on our screens through shows like *Bake Off*. It is not a job for the faint-hearted and it's one that takes its toll, mentally and physically. My dad needed two hip surgeries before the age of sixty, which is no age now, his hands crippled by arthritis and so acclimatised to opioids that he had to use alcohol to numb the pain. I, personally, had to go to hospital after severe panic attacks and take antidepressants to keep clocking in everyday and the loss of the bakery has, as I've said, caused fissures in the family and impacted on me mentally. Baking can be fun, as Ben Glazer says, but it is also punishing. The idea of machines taking some of the strain is something I can get on board with – as long as they have a person alongside them.

Chad has been at the forefront of the craft movement for the last fifteen years and his 'Manufactory', in the US, is thriving. As he says, 'You can source your grain from a regional economy, you can fresh mill it, and you can bake 20,000 loaves using robots.' If that's true, then there might be a future for good bread that everyone can access.

Big bread is weak bread though, in many ways. The investment requires a mindset that seeks to protect the factory as a whole over the integrity of the final products. If a small bakery closes, the others in the area will take up the slack. When a single super-bakery goes down, the nation starves. Or does it? An example of this can be seen as recently as 2022. In the Russian–Ukraine conflict, many big bakeries were targeted to disrupt national food supplies. Road and rail links were damaged beyond repair and the result was that the small artisans stepped up, local bakeries keeping going, baking through the darkness, feeding the population. With the international and domestic tinderbox that I find myself in as I write this, perhaps we'd be wise to support the opening of smaller bakeries, ones that invest in local systems, ones that can keep people fed when the global systems fail.

6

The Breadline

The economics of a crust

It does not cost much. It is pleasant: one of those almost hypnotic businesses, like a dance from some ancient ceremony. It leaves you filled with peace, and the house filled with one of the world's sweetest smells. But it takes a lot of time. If you can find that, the rest is easy. And if you cannot rightly find it, make it, for probably there is no chiropractic treatment, no Yoga exercise, no hour of meditation in a music-throbbing chapel, that will leave you emptier of bad thoughts than this homely ceremony of making bread.

– M. F. K. Fisher, *How to Cook a Wolf* (1942)

The economic world is built on tangible footings, commodities that are the foundation to all else. When a basic product, a staple food, such as wheat, maize or rice shifts in price then everything adjusts to the new benchmark. As with the princess and the pea, even the smallest irregularity is keenly felt and a few dollars here and there can cause panic in the global markets. This relationship, especially that between bread and money, goes back to the very start of trade and commerce.

Because bread is such an ancient commodity, every civilisation and nation having it in some form, it is a great historical tool,

162 | BREAKING BREAD

allowing us to compare different eras and how they relate to us today, to draw crucial information about standards of living, poverty, food trends. But how can we do this, if the bread of antiquity becomes so divorced from our contemporary factory-made bread as to make those comparisons meaningless?

'Bread' or 'dough' are often-used slang for money. The 'bread-line' is a shifting indicator of financial self-sufficiency, 'breadwinner' used to denote the person financially supporting a family. Where did this relationship between bread-associated words and money begin? When did the bean counters become loaf counters? And why is there such a disparity between breads' value and price? I'm especially interested to find out how much an artisan loaf costs to make and why well-made bread is so much more expensive than the sliced and tagged rectangles that furnish store shelves. We've already touched on this subject but let's look at it more closely.

Before bread can be traded, it must be made, and to make it one must have access to the means of production. Nearly every stage involves negotiation, whether it's about access to grain, flour, ovens or the end market to sell it on. Take the oven though, something we in the Western world, take for granted. As our access to ovens has increased, it seems strange that the tradition of making bread at home has declined, but is that to do with our busy working lives and the fact we have easy access to cheap, industrial made loaves? As we saw during the pandemic, when the world stopped, an oven can turn a home baker into a priest or magician, capable of transforming a living mass into an essential fixed meal. If there's ready, affordable access to the ingredients and equipment, of course.

I was born into baking, as you know, my family entrenched in that world, and my access to ovens, and ovens of an extremely high standard, was complete even before I could support the weight of

THE BREADLINE | 163

my own head. I can remember the big gas 'steam tube' oven we had in our bakery. A Werner Pfleiderer. Five decks of patinated steel, each one capable of holding approximately fifty loaves of bread. It was installed before I was born, in 1980, by an engineer named Helmut who travelled from Germany specifically to do so (where else?) and, after two weeks, it was ready to fire up and give up bread.

Lighting it was like starting a spaceship: bakelite switches flicked on in sequence, fans on, extraction hood activated, gas primed, ignition, *click, click, click, boom*. The roar was reminiscent of the sound that Kevin McCallister's heating furnace makes in *Home Alone*. I can still hear it now. When it was eventually removed after the family business closed down, it had to be painstakingly cut from its home, the oven resisting at every opportunity. An end of an era.

Millions of loaves passed through that oven in the thirty-seven years it was in service, and by the end it was in a pitiful state, the hearth stones cracked and the steam hadn't been functional for years. Is there any greater indication that you are no longer a baker than seeing the mutilated corpse of your family oven in the back of a scrap merchant's pick-up truck? Another moment indelibly etched in my memory.

Value is transitory, crossing between things, people, tasks, anything we decide really. One day you're standing in front of an essential piece of bakery equipment: the next, its value is being weighed-in at the scrap yard. The value of bread grew as civilisations progressed, rose and fell. As our stock increased, so too did the value of our favourite food.

Each door that led from field to finished loaf became better fortified. There are things that sustain life which have

164 | BREAKING BREAD

no gatekeeper, air for instance or water from a stream. As such, historically these things have had no industry attached to them, although that has changed for water at least, huge companies controlling for so many of us our access to water and its purity.

The value of fresh air or water goes up as the quality goes down and for most of us, living in the West, we only appreciate them, take note of them, in a climate of decline or scarcity. With nearly everything else, as the quality depreciates, value is diminished. Bread's requirement for energy and equipment creates the seeds of a business. A hand clutching a baked loaf must be balanced with something of equal value for exchange or barter. While it would be impossible to recount the history of bread – and that's not the purpose of this book – I want to try to provide some context, to show how the value of bread has fluctuated through time. To do that I'm going to start with the original 'bread eaters'.

James C. Scott's book, *Against the Grain*, highlights the advantages of cereal production, and therefore bread, with relation to taxation. He argues that wheat and other cereals have distinct advantages that lend themselves to the financial mechanics of civilisations. Wheat has a single harvest that can be predicted, climate and nature allowing, of course. We see it growing, maturing, know when to harvest it, which enables those who profit from it to know exactly when to pick it up. Other rich sources of nutritional energy don't have that advantage – root vegetables, for example, are easily concealed underground and can be 'clamped' or stored in sand for months. Likewise, beans can be harvested over a long period of time and in small amounts which would make collecting a tax on them too much bother.

Ancient civilisations, such as the Egyptians, Greeks and especially the Romans, had tax structures in place, which largely helped fund their various missions and growing empires, and income from grains was important. The Roman model was to take control of land and introduce the infrastructure and materials to begin wheat production and processing. This could then be left with local peoples who benefitted from the increased yields associated with the improved farming techniques. For the most part, they compliantly paid the tax on harvests that could be collected in a short period of time. This model of turning land into a taxable resource worked wonders for the empire and gave them the surpluses they required to hand out free grain and bread to the citizens of Rome itself. This reliance on the fertility of the soil also explains the inevitable end of empires such as the Ancient Egyptian and Romans, for as they grew, more had to be grown to sustain their military and the peoples they governed. If history has taught us anything it is that as resources are put under pressure, they yield less, eventually, in worst case scenarios, becoming depleted. Here, as more was grown, the soil became tired, supplies whithered and income declined. Unrest ensued and the fabric of the very systems that made these empires great unravelled. If you can't feed your people, they revolt. If you can't feed populations, they die. It's the classic Malthusian conclusion – and one that's all too real for us. Ashes to ashes. Dust to dust.

The ancient Egyptians valued bread – likely similar to sourdough and made from an ancient wheat grain called 'emmer' – highly. So highly that they used it as a currency, paying for labour in loaves, and there was a time when a person's wealth was measured in how much bread they had. H. E. Jacob in his book, *Six Thousand Years of Bread*, tells us that 'the ovens throughout the land were virtual mints. Flour baked in an oven eventually became the coinage of the realm. For hundreds of years wages were paid in breads, the average peasant receiving three breads and two jugs of beer a day.'

166 | BREAKING BREAD

The grain dole, or *cura annonae*, as it was spoken of in Rome at the time, was an allocation of grain to every person in the city (and later too in Constantinople, modern-day Istanbul). Each citizen was entitled to what amounted to freedom from hunger or the concern about it. Initially they were responsible for processing grain, making the dough and baking it which, in turn, created industries for the millers and bakers – which they dutifully exploited to the point where bread was handed out baked instead.

This all was down to the third-century emperor Aurelian, famous for uniting the Roman Empire during his five-year reign, and the allowance was two loaves per day for members of the lower classes. It wasn't a blanket deal, some got free grain or bread, others would get below market price loaves and if you were important you were probably paying for all the subsidies. The Roman Empire can be viewed as a golden age, the gold in the fields, but in order to maintain economic supremacy, it was essential to create political stability. Philosopher Karl Marx called religion 'the opiate of the people', but it may well be that the original pacifier was our everyday loaf. With bellies replete, power was safe in the very hands of those who wished to exploit it – and this has been the case, again and again and again. Control production and you arguably control the world.

But how does this relate to now? I'm keen to dig a bit deeper into the costs of producing bread commercially, so I go and visit one of the best bakers I know, Daisy Terry, whom I've spoken about before, one of the founders and executive head baker at east London's Dusty Knuckle. When I ask her what she thinks of bread, she tells me of an illustration of a Pain de campagne, or 'country bread' in French – her vision a line drawing from the front of a half-remembered book cover. Chef Raymond Blanc describes Pain de campagne as a 'rustic equivalent of sourdough'.

I ask Daisy why traditionally made bread commands such a big ticket price. 'A loaf of sourdough will cost you literally what the flour will cost you, as far as materials go. When you start out baking sourdough and you cost it up, the ingredient costs are forty-three pence a loaf. You think you're going to be a millionaire. Little do you realise [until you do it] that everything else associated with baking a loaf of bread costs a fortune.' Elements such as the cost of labour, time, rent, business rates, taxes, energy, insurance, pension contributions, wastage – the list goes on and on – all these things contribute to the total expenditure.

Running a small bakery business is a challenge, as we've discussed. There are many people who have taken the practice of making bread at home and scaled it into a business, some very successfully. A once-treasured pastime can quickly become a prison, however, resulting in human and financial costs as labour laws are ignored, staff are working impossibly long hours with early starts for very little money. At each turn there are bills, taxes of all kinds, in addition to the personal costs, such as working to a different clock to family, missed school concerts and sports events and late night suppers with friends. Everything is paid in full by baker, business and loved ones.

I know this better than anyone. I'm the youngest of five, who, like the rest of my family, was brought up working in the bakery, but my way, my ideas veered away from those of my parents. I took a different route. When I came back into the family business in 2012, moving back to Suffolk, to help an ailing business, I was shocked to find that my parents had been keeping things going by not paying themselves, or, at the very least, paying themselves

168 | BREAKING BREAD

far too little. My seventy-year-old father was working seven days a week and taking home less than £500 a month. This will resonate with other small business owners reading this. As labour costs soar, even now as I write in 2024, I am reading social media posts from bakeries about price rises of 5–7 per cent. In few other industries are the public so critical of such hikes – industrialisation has meant cheap food is viewed as our right as modern citizens in the Western world. The irony is that the food producers who make the most money are the ones who make the cheapest and, arguably, least healthy of foods. And the costs must be accounted for somewhere – in this case, the NHS, our health service, having to foot the bill, which means we are footing the bill as a lot of the money that supports these services comes from taxation. Cheap food has its own costs. It is only really possible by discounting other personal and communal assets such as health, environment, natural resources.

It's incredibly hard to attribute costs to a single loaf when the cost of production fluctuates as much as it does with artisan bread. The product behaves differently depending on factors outside of the business owner's control such as temperature, humidity, equipment breakdowns, employee sickness or the quantity of bread produced. Daisy knows all this only too well. 'It's a very difficult thing to forecast,' she admits, 'unless you go robot mode. In which case you have a shit product but it's much easier to predict the amount of bread you'll get from a certain amount of inputs.' Meaning you sacrifice quality.

Daisy's energy bill alone is eye-watering, with a big chunk of it directed to the ovens, mixers and walk-in fridges that make up the principal tools of modern sourdough production. Dusty Knuckle bakery makes around 10,000 loaves a week and it's about the best bread you'll ever eat. The bread they make passes through skilled hands and the value in those hands, the love and dedication, rubs off on the dough and accrues with every stage, every touch. We see that in other similar artisan operations, such as Ben Glazer's pursuit of the perfect loaf.

Most sourdough bakers will mix, then cut the dough out by hand into tubs. These are left to ferment over three to four hours, the folds, or stretching of the dough during fermentation, completed by hand every forty to sixty minutes. The loaves are then scaled into certain weights, shaped again by hand and refrigerated for a period of time in 'bannetons', special dough baskets. The other widely used practice is to chill the dough as a bulk, then weigh, shape, proof ambiently and bake.

In either case, there is a reliance on energy both to keep the dough cold and to bake it. The labour cost is also massive, with people acting out all the mechanical aspects as well as using their senses to gauge the readiness of the dough. Given that people have been making bread for six thousand years, pre-industrialisation, chilled storage wouldn't have been an option and the process would have required an extremely long day and the labour costs would have been high. This is why you get lots of stories about bakers sleeping on flour sacks as dough rises. Daisy pays a fair wage to her team, using the London Living Wage as a guide rather than the minimum wage set by the UK government, but that's not always the case. She's one of the best bakers in the country, making high-quality bread and yet Daisy is not a millionaire. But she is dedicated and hardworking. In any other field she would most probably be earning the big bucks, so why not here? Where has all the value gone?

What may help is to look back at history. I mentioned the medieval Assize of Bread and Ale earlier, so let's look at that in

170 | BREAKING BREAD

more detail. It was the first such set of regulations ever prescribed, and although they date back to the thirteenth century, we still feel their impact today. The basic idea was to link the price of bread and beer to the price of grain. This was a way of protecting the farmer, miller, baker, brewer and consumer. The regulations set not just the price but the weight and measures. King John had previously sought to fix the price of bread to grain before his successor Henry III refined the law that was brought into effect in 1266. That law lasted around five hundred years, which as laws go is a pretty ripe old age. This is important for our story because it is within these restrictions that bakers sought to find alternative methods to differentiate themselves from competitors. With weights and prices fixed, the customer had to be enticed in other ways.

With bread being fixed to grain, the value was centred in the growing and farming. The added value of the process was limited and the aim of the baker was to reduce the time required to complete the breadmaking. When the price was fixed, a baker who spent too much time on a batch could quickly go out of business or be forever chained to the oven. Value could be achieved by reducing the running time of the breadmaking performance, cutting lines where possible, adding in visual effects to appease the audience and making sure any actors played as many parts as possible. One thing the bread could never ever be was underweight, that was a crime, literally, and one taken incredibly seriously. A penny loaf in any bakery would weigh the same at any time, but that weight would fluctuate. The size of the bread would shrink and inflate as a result of harvest yields and . . . well . . . inflation. It's also the reason there are so many literary references to penny loaves across decades, when we are used to prices increasing (mostly) and decreasing (hardly ever).

THE BREADLINE | 171

As a boy I would clean the weights and scales at the bakery on a Saturday morning. They were the old-style balance scales with a platform on one side and a scale pan on the other. The platform would be loaded with the required weights, all Imperial (ounces, pounds, stones), and dough balanced to match. It amazed me how quickly the bakers could do the weird maths required to divide three pounds and twelve ounces by two, with a rummage in the bread tin that held all the various sized metal pucks. Quick as a flash the scales would be loaded with a two-pound weight and a well-worn, four-ounce friend. In the case of my dad, and men like him, as I've already said they were the scale.

As I scrubbed all the denominations of brass weights it struck me as strange how they all had holes on the underside, filled with lead and stamped with a crown. They were used by the inspectors who would show up to check weights were accurate and if not they'd add a little lead. Bakers were strictly regulated, and anyone caught selling underweight bread would receive pretty severe punishments, such as fines and being placed in the stocks, clamped in timber while being bombarded with fermented fruit missiles. So nervous were bakers of not making the weights that they'd add an extra roll or loaf for every twelve sold. That's why a Baker's Dozen is thirteen. The extra loaf or piece was known as the 'vantage', as it was to the consumer's advantage. Buy twelve, get one free doesn't sound like much of a deal but it is. Possibly not as good as a Texas dozen, which is fifteen. I'm not entirely sure why, but then everything is bigger in Texas.

Thirteen comes up again in the Assize, as it is the cap placed on a baker's profit in net percentage terms. That's a pretty tight margin, so there wouldn't be much wiggle room for wastage or burnt loaves. Bakers were also prohibited from taking on roles

172 | BREAKING BREAD

in local government, either because they couldn't be trusted to uphold the laws that directly screwed them over or because they'd fall asleep in meetings. The bain of bakers around the world.

As bakers were tightly controlled – and, as the saying, goes 'strict parents make for sneaky children' – many found ways to circumnavigate what were seen by many as restrictions. By controlling the weight of a loaf, the perceived value came with volume. The bigger the loaf the better. The illusion of getting your money's worth sat side by side with the desire of the baker to use any trick in the book to get a bit more bounce for the ounce. I believe that this contributed to the rise of the very white, very soft, very glutinous bread that flooded bakers' shops after the advent of roller-milling in the 1800s. White bread was associated with the rich at this time, not because it was better (far from it) but because it was bigger and therefore softer. By sieving the flour or 'boulting' it, using a cloth to remove all the larger particles of bran, the extraction rate is lower which makes the flour, and subsequently the bread, more expensive. Now that we don't have such controls over the weight of bread, the rich eat brown sourdoughs for its increased health benefits while the poor still largely buy or are fed the white fluffy stuff filled with additives and superfluous ingredients. The white emoji loaf.

Breads were sold at fixed prices, such as a penny loaf or ha'penny loaf (half a penny). If the grain price was low these breads were big, if the price of wheat increased, because of scarcity, weather or a bad harvest, for example, the bread would shrink accordingly.

The windfall that came with the advent of cheap sliced white bread in the 1950s was akin to the discovery of oil in Oklahoma at the end of the nineteenth century. *We've hit it big boys! Stack 'em high and let 'em fly.* Bread in the post-Second World War world was so much cheaper but still priced at a profit more appetising than the handmade stuff, once the capital investment was repaid to the factory owners (I refuse to call them bakers). The public went weak at the knees with all this cloudlike bread, heaven sent, surely?

In the UK, during the 1990s, supermarkets engaged in a destructive price war that saw supermarket giant Tesco charging seven pence per loaf in 1999. That's a white, sliced 900g Tesco branded bread. To give some context, an average worker one hundred years earlier would have expected to spend 15 per cent of their wage on bread alone. Seven pence a loaf represented 0.2 per cent of the average weekly UK wage on the cusp of the Millennium. This was a universal bread dole but not directly from the government. It was a demonstration of how to direct and control buying power by the supermarkets.

Bread wasn't profitable at seven pence a loaf but the traders knew if they could get customers through the door they could make up the shortfall on more luxury goods. The flour alone would have cost around thirty pence per loaf if you bought it off the shelf. 'Loss leading', as it is termed, is the practice of discounting essential items below their market price to entice patrons to spend money. Bread was the sprat to catch a mackerel but it has had lasting effects on the public perception of value with regards to the everyday loaf.

The average consumer loved it, however. Never mind what was in it – it gave a feeling of stability and allowed spending to rise in other areas of the economy. But it was misleading. And of course, had a price. This chapter of cheap bread came slap bang in the middle of sixteen years of continuous national growth. And that all came crashing down in 2008, when the markets

174 | BREAKING BREAD

collapsed. Like an over-proofed loaf, the bubble burst and prices found their natural level – they went back up. By then however, many small bakery businesses had already gone bust, forced out of business by the artificially and catastrophically low pricing of big business. The few that were left were on their knees. The damage was done and when a consumer today gasps at the price of a loaf of bread that took an artisan three days to make with quality ingredients, regretfully, their expectations have been fed by this low price watermark.

But is it possible to make a loaf of bread that is both nutritionally rich and reasonably priced as an artisan baker? Let's dig into the numbers to find out. Let's make an organic sourdough bread, buying the best flour grown by local farmers, stoneground, with no chemical inputs. We pay about £2 a kilo which works out at £1.20 per loaf. That's just the flour. Already we are approaching supermarket prices for a loaf that's sliced and wrapped.

The process for making our bread takes two to four days, but that time is not all hands on and we can make more than just one loaf at a time. Labour in a bakery tends to be much higher than other manufacturing businesses, so we can allow 30 per cent of the material costs to help us along. That takes us to £1.56. We have to consider running costs which including fixed costs – rent, business rates – and all those other glorious unforeseen necessities. That adds another £1 to the loaf. So, we're now at £3.06 and counting.

Then, of course, there's the packaging. That'll be another 10 pence for a branded bag, taking us up to £3.16. Call me a capitalist, but for my efforts, I'd like to add a little profit margin – plus pay my bills and eat – 20 per cent seems more than fair as we're an artisan outfit. Ah, but I haven't allowed for all the capital expenditure, which includes repayments on mixers, ovens and a load of other odds and ends. This will be significant and all adds another 50 pence to our product.

So the minimum we could realistically sell that loaf for would be £4.29. At the present time, Daisy sells an 800g loaf for £4.20 at Dusty Knuckle. In comparison, an average sliced 800g loaf at the supermarket is £1.45. You can buy 'sourdough' at the supermarket and that will cost you £3.36 for the same weight, plus – spoiler alert – it isn't actually sourdough as we will discover in the next chapter, Flour Power.

So, that's a big difference, £2.75 between the price of Daisy's loaf and the factory made one, which if you tally it up over a year, assuming a weekly consumption of two loaves per three-person household, is £286. A huge hit to most people's budgets. I know that's a lot but when you see higher ticket prices on bread, it is often justified. In fact, I'd argue that for all the benefits and avoided harm, the handmade artisan bread is much better value for money. What you're paying for is food for a healthy body and mind.

Again though, we have to be careful because the trap has been laid. In order to take advantage of the better value afforded by artisan breads, we must have the extra money to pay for it, which many people don't. Food is cheaper when bought in bulk but having enough cash to buy large quantities of food is ironically the preserve of the wealthy. There must also be access to a lovely little artisan bakery which for many is just not the case. You must also have the time to go to the bakery during business hours which, again, many people don't. White sliced bread dominates the market because it meets the needs of the time rich, cash poor and also the time poor, cash rich. Whether on price or convenience, it's no mystery why 75–80 per cent of the UK market is commanded by big business, mass-produced bread.

The cornered market is the cash poor, time poor one, with citizens having neither the money to buy their way to healthy choices or the time to make them from raw materials. These are the people who shake their heads at middle-class politicians who can't fathom why people don't feed themselves from their gardens.

If you do have the time, you could take M. F. K. Fischer's advice at the beginning of this chapter and bake your own. It is true that you can create a truly superior loaf of bread with the finest ingredients and still beat the supermarket prices.

To do so has just three hurdles: the time, equipment and skill required to make traditional bread. Breadmaking machines have been incredibly popular over the last twenty years and seek to solve those problems yet require an investment in financial terms and in counterspace. Many are buried at the back of cupboards while their owners still stump up for the convenience of grabbing a packaged loaf along with their other groceries.

Historically, homebaking was the provenance of women in the domestic sphere. The starter dough that inoculates each batch of traditionally made bread is called a 'mother' and the way we treat homemade bread can be seen in this light. The expectation is always for a beautifully made loaf, made by our mothers or grandmothers, hot, fresh on the table each morning and yet we don't expect to pay for the labour. Mother must produce it out of her own deep reserves of love for us, and, in return, we keep her busy with a number of other domestic tasks for which she isn't paid. The bread made at home may have a lower material cost but the value is just as high, if not higher, in labour terms and also love.

As Fischer points out, baking can be turned into a pastime, a hobby, and as such goes from being a work task to a leisure activity. The value system then completely shifts and we are happy to pay for the pleasure of the time to make bread for the household. There is a big market for teaching bread classes, of which I am a part of as a teacher at Pump Street Workshop. People have an interest in relearning these forgotten skills, the ones their mothers and grandparents may have used on a daily basis and they're willing to pay for it, whether it's because it's a trend or they really do want to apply the skills they learn, to make changes to how they view, make and eat bread. Baker and food writer Dan Lepard told me many of the Brits in his classes enjoy them as an experience as much as an opportunity to learn new skills and put them into practice. In Japan, by contrast, his students are notable for their diligent note taking and concentration. What does that say about us?

I went to Devon in the southwest of England, to do a bake shift with Hylsten Bakery, a small wholesale operation making delicious sourdough, set up by Megan Nash and Kate Marton. The bakery is on what appears to be a converted Victorian industrial estate and is housed within one of the newer buildings. They supply local shops and businesses and are able to keep costs down as a result of their location, but breads still retail at around the £5 mark.

After finishing the bake with Oliver, the head baker, he took me to an adjacent unit to meet Andrew Gilhespy who runs the Fresh Flour Company, supplying flour, pasta, crackers, noodles and biscuits nationwide. Andrew also supplies Hylsten with some of the flour they use and for him, bread is more than a meal: it's a movement.

Andrew explained to me that he buys the very best grain he can, direct from farmers, always organic or regenerative.

178 | BREAKING BREAD

If he buys grain at £1 a kilo, he can sell it as flour to a baker for a maximum of £2 a kilo once milled. However, if he turns the flour into a finished product his margins go up massively. The organic grain can become pasta for £7 a kilo, biscuits for £14 a kilo and crackers for £18 a kilo. This kind of vertical integration makes a lot of financial sense: by bringing multiple aspects of production in-house the margins increase exponentially as you go from raw materials to finished goods. Nothing goes to waste, with any leftover bran being sold to local mushroom growers who use it as a very productive substrate for their fungi spores.

Early Hollywood studios employed the same theory, controlling the writing, filming and processing – and ending by showing films in their own cinemas which would only show their movies. The profits were better, but the downside was that the choice was limited and if a small town had only one cinema, then people would have to drive miles to watch a picture by another studio. Unsurprisingly, the practice was outlawed in 1948, too much control leading to cheaply made films that exploited their captive audiences. Yet Andrew uses that same system on a smaller scale to make great food that can realistically support his business and those who sell his products. 'If people need cheaper pasta and flour, the answer is to sell without packaging,' he explains. By doing away with the costs of packaging and the labour included he can offer a much better price. I'm reminded of the Jeffrey Lewis lyric, '*One quarter for the product, three quarters for the wrap.*'

Andrew wants to take on the middle ground between very expensive luxury goods and cheap mass-produced products. Ideally, he wants to set up a number of appropriately scaled businesses in different areas of the UK, working with local farmers and grain associations to create a sustainable infrastructure. A sort of satellite, franchise-esque model that could work, but, in reality, would the temptation to centralise production or find economies of scale be too much? Then there is always the chance that if it were to become too successful, the bigger companies would line up with appetising offers of a buyout. Having met Andrew however, I think the chances of him selling out are pretty close to zero. This means too much to him.

He has copied the model that big business uses to get a stranglehold on the market. A natural disrupter, he isn't afraid of stepping on toes to get his message across. 'Even some smaller bakeries that call themselves "artisan" are buying flour that comes from grain traded in Chicago,' he muses, 'and that grain could actually come from anywhere in the world. It's then roller-milled by big mills in the UK and packaged to appear artisanal.' This I know to be true, as I've visited many bakeries that advertise themselves as the real deal, only to find their flour stores are full of cheap flour that has been artificially boosted with added gluten and ascorbic acid.

Monopolies have long been feared when it comes to bread and milling. All the way back to the classical period, millers, bakers and brewers were kept separate to prevent them from exploiting the populace. During the industrial age, big millers and bakers became entwined through various mergers and acquisitions. W. B. Ward was an Irish immigrant to the United States who managed to seed a multigenerational skill for consuming bakeries. He eventually dropped his own name in favour of a brand from Philadelphia he had acquired, 'Wonder Bread'. It came to dominate the American market.

Likewise in the UK, mergers between millers gave rise to popular brands such as Mother's Pride, Kingsmill and Sunblest.

180 | BREAKING BREAD

Restrictions have curtailed this avalanche of mass-produced bread yet the domination has been long lasting. The suits triumphed, and the food security of most of the global population now rests in a handful of companies. It is this inequality that people like Andrew Gilhespy rally against, seeking to democratise the production of food and provide real, quality choice for consumers. 'The seeds are all owned by a few companies, the same with production and distribution.' By pointing this out, Andrew reminds me how fragile large empires can be, and how dangerous it is that a global population is so reliant on the fate of a few companies.

Company itself is a word that directly relates to bread, roughly translating to 'one who eats bread with you'. All these companies are so insular that they simply feed themselves, ever inflating to take up more and more of the market. As with rising bread, as it gets larger and larger, the glutinous membranes stretch and become thinner, the fermenting acids weaken the bonds and an over-proofed loaf will collapse at the touch of a feather. Top heavy and jelly-legged, our baking industry is following suit. We need smaller bakers to take a bigger share of the market to make it more robust. After all, none of the wonderful acts of humanity can take place on an empty stomach.

One of the questions that I want to dig down into is 'Why Bread?' Out of all the potential foodstuffs, what is it about bread that has brought it along for the ride of human development with so few changes? Those three basic ingredients I talked about at the beginning of this journey, used across nations, peoples, to create this essential foodstuff. I believe that it stems from its ability to provide a taxable income and to sustain not just the bodies of the people but furnish the economy with funds to develop other aspects of a fruitful society. It is the food of the people, that feeds the people and feeds our nation. Major countries even now protect the farming industry so vehemently with subsidies and incentives because they know that once the yields start dropping, the end is nigh. The issue we have now, just as civilisations have encountered before us, is that our soils are tired and so the economic support is fragile. Keeping the modern citizen stocked up with bread is of national, no, international importance. The crust we make, just as the crust we earn, is vital to our continued existence, and as the ongoing war in the Ukraine has shown, that can be at the hands of small bakers, not just big business.

7

Flour Power

The politics of bread

There's nothing more political than food.
– Anthony Bourdain, US chef and author

Politics is founded on the social contract. We, the people, hand over some of our rights to freedom in exchange for collective protection from starvation, war, persecution and criminal acts. Bread is a totem for freedom from hunger. In Anthony Bourdain's words: what's more political than food?

When we sit down to a restaurant meal and there is a basket of bread on the table, the symbolic gesture is this: 'You have bread. You are free from hunger. Now enjoy yourself.' That freedom is taken for granted by those who possess it, but many would kill for it. The power to feed is often greater than the power to suppress by force or contain through imprisonment. Without it, great civilisations have fallen.

In this chapter, I want to find out how much power bread has within a society. For thousands of years, it has been a principal foodstuff – the staff – in many political frameworks. A prisoner is entitled to bread and water, a tramp in 1920s' London was entitled to 'tea and two slices'. Bread is the entry level package for many a civilian, as the Romans showed. Sign up to society! Free bread!

Is bread the bait that masks the hook though? Is our political will muted by an abundance of bread? Is there really no such thing as a free lunch? In ancient Rome when they gave bread to the lower classes, what were they purchasing in exchange? Votes? Compliance? Has our social contract been hollowed out by industrialised food? A lot of questions to think about.

Juvenal, a Roman satirist writing in the third century, wrote: 'Already long ago, from when we sold our vote to no man, the People have abdicated our duties; for the People who once upon a time handed out military command, high civil office, legions — everything, now restrains itself and anxiously hopes for just two things: bread and circuses.' Circus here, alas, doesn't mean prowling tigers, the highwire and clowns doing tricks. Juvenal meant huge staged events such as the gladiatorial games, free to citizens.

When we blame politicians for the state of our nations, should we perhaps be a little more self-critical, though? Like the Romans before us, have we given too much power away for cheap bread and entertainment? Certainly, nothing seems to cause more anxiety than the price of bread going up, as it is representative of larger potential crises – inflation, war, depression. The price of bread in the UK is rising as I write – not helped by Brexit impacting on taxes, freedom of trade and supply networks, the pandemic, climate change, war, the elections on both sides of the Atlantic – so many things factor in. So what does this say about our current times? How much power does flour really have?

*

We can start in the late 1970s, at a turning point in British history. Just over thirty years after it was the darling of the international stage, Britannia, the empire, was long gone, even if we Brits were loath to realise it. The country was in crisis. The government was in financial free fall and the challenge was to keep bread in bellies. That was my parents' experience of the bread strike, when bread, or a lack of it, seemingly broke the nation, bringing it to its knees. All over the country, bedlam ensued, as people fought in the streets for the last crusts, leading newspapers such as the *Oxford Mail* to scream: 'Breadlam! The great loaf rush!'

My dad, Peter Wright, was not a member of the union which called a nationwide bakers' strike in September 1977. He wasn't a member of the union two years before and would still stand alone a year later. All over the UK, bread became hard to find. People across the country were frantically trying to come to terms with what it takes to make a loaf of bread, for the first time questioning where their bread came from. For many people bread exists in a vacuum; there is no story behind it, no context, because bakers like me, my dad, my granddad, make it while they are sleeping. It appears out of the ether onto shelves ready for them to buy. Unless the supply dries up.

It is only when the staples of life disappear that people realise how much they depend on them. The few bakeries that remained open in 1977 were snowed under. Peter went to work in the early hours of Monday 5 September and after the bread was baked, opened at 8.15 a.m. as usual to queues outside on the cold high street. The shop quickly filled with people as panic buying ensued, despite my father's pleas for people to be sensible. By mid-morning the shelves were empty. It is hard for any baker to leave a shop that

186 | BREAKING BREAD

has no bread in it, and for my dad, it was impossible. He fired up the ovens again.

Working for eighteen hours a day, it soon became clear that no other bakery in the area was supporting the townspeople. The ovens never went cold that week as the bread turnout became the sole purpose of the shop. The floors shook with the beating of the dough; the flour spilled down the stairs from the workshop, down onto the shop floor to be trampled out into the cold street, leaving white footprints from the shop to various corners of the town. The flour became precious as picket lines formed outside all the mills. One lorry managed to slip between strikers in Liverpool and made the long journey south, hellbent on getting our bakery as many sacks of flour as we needed. My mother would drive to the nearest mill in her Volvo estate every morning and fill up with as many sacks as she could. The load was covered over with linen blankets and she would sneak out the back gate. I can only imagine how frightened she must have been. But still my parents persevered.

By Friday, the bakery was serving over two thousand people per microsecond, or so it seemed to my dad. The telephone was rarely on the hook and the earpiece perpetually warm, with orders being called in at all hours of the day and night. Batches were barely mixed before they were tabbed out to hungry families. One new customer addressed himself to my mother, Christine, demanding preferential treatment because of a 'personal promise from the owner'. She didn't know him and the rest of the staff didn't recognise the man. She went upstairs to check with my father. He didn't know the man either. At any other time, the man's boldness might have earned him his bread. On that day, he went without.

The next man was treated with similar suspicion as he had brought his whole family to claim the two loaf ration. When questioned, it came out that he was a milkman with a conscience who was taking bread to elderly people in the remote villages of Suffolk. He was sent out of the shop immediately, as the other man had been, but went round the back to take whole bags of bread to the needy. The man, Wally Horne, even got his name in the paper.

The strike was called off on Saturday, when the bakery was reaching its straining point. The floors were raining flour. My father's hands were tougher than ever, his fingers fatigued and sore. His bruised arms would have been hung up for monuments if they hadn't been hard at work the very next day.

This moment changed the way Britain bought bread, it changed the high street and is the model that has created the food deserts that leave deprived communities without the option of healthy food. When the three big bakeries, Warburtons, Hovis and Allied Bakeries, along with the supermarkets, such as Tesco, Sainsbury's and the Co-Op, plunged the price of bread below the net profit line, they drowned the independent shops and many thousands of bakeries.

The period of time between the late seventies through to the Millennium was when a tactical move to control the market took place. Many people blame the factory-made bread but I blame the factory owners, the supermarket chiefs and the government. We lost more than just shops and our communities were gutted. We lost the countless small kindnesses that small businesses provide, from credit, to the sponsoring of a local football or cricket team, as my family did. Wally Hornes aren't given sacks of bread to deliver to the needy by supermarkets.

188 | BREAKING BREAD

There's a panel discussion from Thames TV in 1977 that you can still find on YouTube. It looks and sounds like a Monty Python sketch, but without a punchline. It discusses the bread strike of that year with Jackson Moore, the general secretary of the United Road Transport Union (URTU), an articulate, yet toadish man who is rounded upon by the other members. Ian MacLaurin, the managing director of Tesco, sits in his blue and white value striped shirt and the low image quality gives him dark, dead eyes. His speech is clipped as he slumps in his chair. Joan MacIntosh of the National Consumer Union would certainly be played by Eric Idle, too much of a caricature to be real – except she is. Lastly, there's Dick Branston, of V. G. Management, representing a number of minimarts, a white-haired weasel of a man, sporting thick rimmed glasses and a wiry moustache.

The argument centres around the price of bread that large supermarkets pay the big three bakeries. The supermarkets argue for complete freedom to negotiate the best possible deal and pass on the savings to their customers. The transport union's concerned because they feel this will drive prices up, resulting in fewer deliveries as bread consumption goes down and mass redundancies to balance the cut in deliveries required.

This is an example of the transport union getting the right answer with the wrong reasoning. Everyone in the bakery industry outside of the big plant operations should have taken to the streets, joined by shopkeepers and millers. The enforcement of a minimum discount was the last defence against industrial bakeries sweeping the market.

The unions for millers and bakers didn't object to this move, but URTU which represented the drivers of the delivery vehicles did. Jackson Moore, in his distinctive northern accent, raised the question: 'How can you reduce the price of bread when Mr [Roy] Hattersley and the industry accept that there is only one half penny of profit at the point of manufacture, without making the company go bankrupt or without escalating the price of bread?'

Moore argued that if the profit margin was so low at the point of manufacture and the wholesalers were to get more discount, they would have to raise the prices to account for this. As a result, there would be lower bread consumption, fewer deliveries and resulting redundancies. This would give too much power to the supermarkets, and small shops would go out of business, further reducing the requirement for deliveries.

Ian MacLaurin of Tesco made light work of allaying any fears, saying it was 'wild' and 'untrue' that bread prices would sink as low as 10 pence. Yet, as we've seen, in 1999, Tesco sold bread for 7 pence a loaf, which accounting for inflation, would have been 2.5 pence in 1977. He was thinking about the wave of customers that would flock to his stores for cheap bread, abandoning high street bakeries and independent shops, not the greater impact on the economy or on the population generally. Profit over everything.

Joan MacIntosh stated: 'The consumer has an interest in all shops. The individual consumer is not dictated entirely by the price of bread, where she can find cheap bread, she will go and get bread cheap, but she's not going to take an expensive bus journey or spend a great deal on petrol in order to buy a quantity of bread and buy all her shopping in the same shop.' Well, Joan, you were wrong.

Supermarkets and small-sized supermarkets dominate the commercial landscape today. The small independents are all but gone and people did go out of town to buy all their bread. What

190 | BREAKING BREAD

Jackson Moore failed to comprehend was that the supermarkets could and would sell bread at a loss. Bread was the bait to lure the shoppers away from the shops that had serviced them for decades, that had given them credit, sitting firmly at the centre of communities. Shops like my parents'. The transport union needn't have worried as there would be enough work for them with supermarkets springing up in abundance. For the small bakeries and shops, though, their fate was sealed.

The outgoing government was in crisis. The temptation to provide people with cheap bread and so give it a chance of holding onto power was enough to ignore the obvious monopolising of the bread market. In 1974, 24 per cent of the average worker's income was spent on food. This had plummeted to just over 10 per cent by 2019, principally through inflation and by industrialising every aspect of food manufacture.

It wasn't enough. In November 1978, Britain entered 'the winter of discontent', with mass strikes and the UK ground to a halt. While cheap bread can stabilise a government, it can't save one. The Conservative government, led by Margaret Thatcher, which followed, saw an acceleration of the slide into factory bread domination.

The English language has empowered the titles of 'Lord' and 'Lady' to the utmost extent possible. Followers of Christianity refer to 'our Lord Jesus Christ'; their prayer is the 'Lord's Prayer'. Within the political system the Lords sit in the highest house of parliament and The Lord Chief Justice is the big job in the judiciary. When we call someone 'my Lord', it is an act of deference. In the UK, the First Lord of the Treasury is another name for the

Prime Minister. The conclusion: to be a lord is to be powerful. And why, you may ask, is this important?

'Lord' comes from the Old English, *hlaford*, which literally means 'bread-warden', or 'the one who guards the bread'. 'Lady' has the same roots, *hlafdige*, or 'bread-kneader'. The power resides with those who make the bread and control the access to it. Interestingly, it's the latter that is afforded to the male and, within a patriarchal context, seen as the more powerful. The act of baking here is fundamentally a female act. Just as it is the male priest who hands out the Communion bread and provides access to the bread god, Jesus Christ.

The political power of bread is stitched into British society. When free from the prospect of starvation, the human spirit is at liberty to express itself. When the mind is fixed on the next meal, it is imprisoned. The greatest impact of poverty is not material but mental. The politician who can free the people from worries about bread will have a sturdy platform.

Considering bread is a symbol for so many powerful arms of society it seems unimaginable that we have chosen not to define it. I called upon Chris Young of the Real Bread Campaign to try to understand this better. In particular, I was interested in understanding the political power that large food manufacturers had over the very institutions that are responsible for guarding our bread.

'Bread, sourdough, freshly baked, artisan, heritage wheat, traditional – all of these terms which are often used to get people to part with their money, and often pay a premium, have no legal definitions,' Chris explains. If you take the word 'sourdough' and apply it to a product that is made by a fundamentally different process, it results in a substantively different product. 'We call that sourfaux.'

192 | BREAKING BREAD

I think that consumers should make their own decisions based on how they want to live their lives. My problem with the current situation is that people aren't given all the information or are being misled about the ingredients used to make their food. The beneficiaries are the big 'industrial dough manufacturers', as Chris Young terms them, not able to call them bakeries. By extension, political parties are included, those that receive donations from these organisations in exchange for lobbying power. Consumers and independent shops are the losers, however, both from a health and financial standpoint.

Initially, Chris continues, 'industrial dough fabricators were very sniffy about sourdough, they saw it as niche. Some craft bakeries, through their skill, built up – to use a marketing phrase – "brand value". Then the industrial companies thought, "there's money to be made in them there hills" – and they swooped in for a slice of the action.' And this illustrates the issue with not protecting the terms relating to bread such as 'craft', 'artisan' or 'sourdough'.

Sourdough baking requires skill, dedication and a commitment to following the process, as we've seen. The bakers often make many personal sacrifices to bake this way and by allowing large companies to appropriate their skill and sacrifice, it devalues them. At the same time their own products, which aren't dissimilar in many cases to the cheap convenience bread they produce, are overvalued.

Sourfaux products are often made with 'dry sourdough powder' which is a flavouring, not a leavening agent and these products still contain yeast as well as a host of additives. Trading standards officers and the Advertising Standards Authority have rebuffed many complaints that Chris Young has made over the years, astonishingly citing the fact that people can't possibly believe supermarket products are made by artisans for the very reason that they are purchasing them in a supermarket. It is also up to the consumer to realise the other terms used couldn't be true. 'People deserve to know, then make their choice,' Chris says. And, he's absolutely right.

It's hard to put into law protection that might upset your portfolio of donors, such as Warburton's which has contributed thousands to the UK Conservative Party, for example, £25,000 in one go after a Tory visit to the factory in 2010. If you believe there's no such thing as a free lunch, what were they after?

While making the very blatant choice to take advantage of quality loaded, yet unprotected terms to sell their products, many producers of ultra-processed bread choose not to declare everything that is in the loaf. By law, manufacturers do not need to declare 'processing aids' which usually take the form of enzymes and occasionally even recognisable ingredients such as white flour in a 'wholemeal' loaf.

After the bread strikes of the late seventies, independent stores and bakeries were decimated. They recovered by offering products such as sourdough, which industrial companies and supermarkets couldn't make, at an attractive margin. Now, back for a second bite of the cherry, these companies are stripping the value out of our bread culture and the government is standing by once again.

Our society is based on protecting the value of bread as it feeds into so many other aspects of society. Healthcare, farming, the environment, the economy to name a few – our broken bread system is symptomatic of a crooked relationship between business and politics. We have been failed by the lords and ladies. There is no such thing as an honest crust anymore.

194 | BREAKING BREAD

The Real Bread Campaign have put together what they call The Honest Crust Act proposal, focusing on defining commonly used bakery terms, full ingredient inclusion on labels (including processing aids) and the requirement to display ingredients for unpackaged bread products. Currently in-store bakery bread can be made off site, even in another country and if it's re-baked in-store then it can be displayed, unpackaged, with no full ingredient list. Chris calls these 'loaf tanning salons', the performance of freshly made bread but the reality is far from that.

When Joanna Blythman requested ingredient information from Marks & Spencer and Greggs for her book, *Swallow This: Serving Up the Food Industry's Darkest Secrets,* she was required to make applications to the customer services departments online. Both would only provide allergen information and headline macro-nutritional information such as the percentage of carbohydrate, protein, and so on. When these companies are challenged on such matters, the response is often that providing full information is not a legal requirement. Yet, they *could* volunteer the information and don't: that in itself speaks volumes. What do they have to hide? If their products were at all beneficial to the consumer, they'd have the information plastered over all the products, surely?

The legislation provides a loophole for smaller producers to easily sell their products at market stalls or in small shops. The bigger chains have jumped on this to create pantomime stores with the feel of an independent shop, replete with wicker baskets and 'bakers' with white jackets and hats. The truth is that this opportunity has been seized and is strangling the very businesses that are supposed to be benefiting from it. Yet, next time you visit an in-store bakery, ask for the ingredient list and see what happens.

'Successive governments have rejected the Honest Crust proposals,' Chris tells me, highlighting a review of the Bread and Flour Regulations in 2022 of which he sat on the advisory panel. 'The golden breadcrumb association had more of a say on the review than the Real Bread Campaign did,' he continues, 'and in the end the only major result was the adding of folic acid to the flour fortification list.'

Why doesn't bread receive the same access to protection as other food or drinks like fruit juice, butter, whisky, gin or jam? There are other factors at play apart from the donations of some big bread producers and ones that shed light on the power of the loaf within politics. If fruit juice contains even one per cent added water it must be called a 'juice drink', any adulteration restricts the use of the valuable word 'juice'. It is telling that Chris has to make the distinction between 'real' bread and everything else. Shouldn't all bread be 'real'? And if not, should it be called bread at all?

A 'KVI' is a key value indicator, one of a range of products that indicate to a shopper the value benefit of a particular store. Products get added and taken off the list all the time, but bread has always been on it. If bread is cheap then the perceived value of the store is 'good' and that supermarket will gain more of the market share. Ian MacLaurin knew this in 1977 when he eyed up getting better bread prices for Tesco's customers.

Bread is also a mainstay of the virtual shopping basket that helps determine inflation in the UK. On the website for the Office of National Statistics, it declares: 'Bread is thought to give the best coverage as a representative item because of its popularity amongst consumers.' This is from an article in 2024, 'Consumer Price Inflation Basket of Goods and Services'. The price of bread leads directly to how the cost of living is reported, So, if we find

196 | BREAKING BREAD

ourselves in a 'crisis' in that department, it wouldn't be politically prudent to do anything that might cause bread prices to rise.

The brutal reality is bread prices *are* rising. In January 2023, the price of a Warburton's loaf went up by 16 per cent compared to the previous year, with their own flour bill increasing by £118 million. Jonathan Warburton placed the blame firmly at Vladimir Putin's door, saying in *The Grocer*: 'Putin doing what he's doing in Eastern Europe, on the back of Covid is the major trigger. It has sent shockwaves through the food industry. It isn't my fault that bloody idiot went into Ukraine, quite frankly.'

This argument has been broadly accepted by the consumers, and if we can accept the rise in price of our bread being a result of a conflict on the far side of Europe, then why can't we accept honest ingredient declarations and more nutritious bread? What is the fear?

Well, let me have a go at working it out. If the government accepted The Honest Crust Act then bread manufacturers would need to label their products honestly. The value-added products that yield higher margins for them would no longer be marketable so the price of their standard range would have to increase to compensate. The label on the packaging would get longer with all the ingredients currently in the bread, some as the result of government regulation, having to be declared. Either consumers would buy less as a result, or they would demand clean label bread. Without the processing aids and additives, the bread would take longer to make – and be healthier as a result – yet this would drive up costs and reduce the output. There would not be enough smaller bakeries to pick up the slack as the industrial food system limits bread, intentionally or otherwise. There could also be a requirement for capital expenditure on equipment to handle the additive-free dough and once again costs would rise. The price of loaves would increase the cost of living and the incumbent government would be at risk of falling in the polls as a result. This is exactly the kind of policy that requires a stable majority, exactly the kind of policy that could destabilise any political advantage.

So, providing consumers with honest information about the food they eat is a risky political strategy. Andrew Whitley, the author of *Bread Matters*, and co-founder of the Real Bread Campaign we have met already, calculates that to meet the country's requirement for 12 million loaves a day, we would need 75,000 individual bakers. In reality, there could be a mixed solution with larger plant bakeries providing value in scale rather than by slashing costs and speeding up processes. Is there a government strong enough to take this challenge on, though?

Bread is a keystone food product and the impact of any major change sends ripples throughout society. It has the power to reshape communities and effect positive outcomes for millions of people. The current system has brought the price down, the value down, employment down, purchases down and wastage up. My message to a government faced with this situation is to be scared of what will happen if you don't act.

The 1906 UK election was fought primarily on a single issue, free-trade vs protectionism. There was a debate in parliament over the issue nicknamed 'Big loaf, Little Loaf'. It was so important that it had caused the Conservative Prime Minister Sir Arthur Balfour to resign the year before and ultimately resulted in one of the biggest landslide victories in British political history for the Liberals.

198 | BREAKING BREAD

On one side of the 'Big Loaf, Little Loaf' debate there was a group who wanted to make the British Empire its own trading bloc and charge tariffs on imports from outside of the empire. The issue split the Conservatives, and the Liberals sided with the free trade option but voters were scared a protectionist stance would see bread prices rise.

Fast forward to June 2016. The Referendum. The British people were given a similar choice between free trade with the European Union or protectionist measures influenced by racist and xenophobic notions relating to immigration. Leaving the EU or staying. Brexit, as it became known. The UK Independence Party, headed up at the time by the man who looks like an escaped Spitting Image puppet, Nigel Farage, knew the power of bread in the debate. One poster showed a white farmhouse loaf with the caption: 'Without the EU, food bills in every UK home would be £400 cheaper.' Nothing like threatening price rises or bread shortages to influence political outcomes, and throw in a bit of xenophobia and well . . .

I was working on the ovens in Woodbridge the night that the referendum results rolled in. Between baking batches of bread, I would check my phone for updates. Initially, the Remain vote looked strong but as the night went on, it became apparent that the people of the UK, once again scared about what might happen to their bread prices, had gone the protectionist route at every level. My father and his bakers had all voted to leave the EU, spouting misguided notions about keeping 'foreigners out of our country', protecting jobs and Britain. I knew then that we'd struggle to stay afloat as a business.

The fear now is that trade deals with the US could speed up the problems we have with our food system. When Mexico and Canada signed up to NAFTA (North American Free Trade Agreement) their waistlines increased with the revenue. Unfortunately, money won't stop you getting type 2 diabetes or prevent you from having a heart attack. Due to the UK legislation on fortification, many European flour suppliers have chosen to cut down their exports to us, thus driving prices up. I wasn't the only baker who feared the impact.

Jonathan Warburton complained that due to many of their lorry drivers returning to the EU, bread was hard to deliver. Far from saving households money, it has cost the UK a great deal. And not just in terms of bread. Even when we take into account the impacts on supply of Covid and the war in Ukraine, Britain is far worse off than other European countries also contending with those two bombshells.

Guarding our bread is nothing new, of course. We see an example of it in history. The Corn Laws that were in force between 1815 and 1846 sought to protect the rents that landlords obtained by keeping the price of wheat and bread high. A flood of cheap free trade wheat would have brought food prices down and tenants would no longer be able to afford the rents, which would have to come down as a result. The landlords were well placed, many of them sitting in government, to protect their own interests. Fast forward, some two hundred years and nothing has changed.

These nineteeth-century laws were coming into force just as the abolition of slavery came into force in Britain. In 1807, the slave trade was abolished and no new slaves could be bought or sold. It wasn't until some thirty years later that all slaves were freed by the British but only after the landowners had received handsome compensation packages for their loss of labour.

200 | BREAKING BREAD

The slavery system was replaced by indenture – essentially 'slavery lite' between 1837 and 1917. I know that's a lot of dates, but this is an important example of transitioning away from an ingrained system of food production, albeit one that involved great human cost and inhuman attitudes to equality and race.

The introduction of roller-mills came in during this time as human slaves were replaced by mechanical ones as the Industrial Revolution took force. When forced to adapt, industry responded. The shift away from the horrors of enslaving workforces to growing and processing foods paved the way for technological advances and economies of scale in production in Britain. And that caused a whole new set of horrors for citizens.

In many political systems, the agricultural areas are largely more conservative, and the urban areas more liberal. This can be seen as a facing-off between the breadmakers and the bread eaters. Peter Kropotkin, in *The Conquest of Bread*, advocates intensive agricultural policies that would flood society with cheap food. It's a rally cry for industry to take from the soil to feed the people. Yet at what cost?

Stalin followed this move in his first Five-Year Plan, of 1928–33, calling for the collectivisation of agriculture and development and expansion of heavy industry, and as a result, denuding the soils of vital nutrients and causing horrendous famines. Often we only need to look to the past to forecast what will happen in the future. History will tell. This tension between keeping the value in the land and distributing its fruits to the people will only become more strained as global populations increase, just as Malthus predicted. The political strategy for producing enough food for the masses must be reassessed – producing a sustainable food system for the planet a much more viable option. And yet this seems as impossible now as abolishing slavery would have seemed to a plantation owner in 1814, highly immoral as it was.

The upshot of all of this is there must be a balance between guarding our soil, our crops, our bread and sharing the bounty with the people who work the land and in bakeries. The extremes don't work well: history has shown us this time and time again. Bread, more than any other food, is enriched by the sharing of it. The power of bread, of flour, can be used in such a combination of ways that it can be a defining feature of a nation. Bread is not just food, it is the measure of a healthy economy, a healthy people.

Access to bread is essential, but so too is the protection we give to it. The land must be managed, not exploited or exhausted; the problems arising from this history shows. Prices must be kept steady and affordable for the people in order for governments and the population themselves to survive. This political balancing act needs also to account for the health, physical and mental, of the people and the impact on them that artificially cheap bread has. When Juvenal said that citizens are anxious about bread, he was right. We should be.

8

Bloody Bread

The costs of conquest

When eating becomes a matter of life or death, and each
new bite is a celebration, you may discover that none of
the other stuff was quite as important as sitting and
breaking bread together.

Bee Wilson, *First Bite: How We Learn To Eat* (2015)

I delayed starting university. While my friends were going off to study or travelling, I stayed home. My father needed me. He was recovering from his first hip surgery so I was needed at the bakery. Dad didn't trust his bakers, a hunch that proved to be well-founded years later, when he had his second operation. I wasn't there when they visited him that time, while bedridden, to extort ridiculously high wages, knowing Dad's only other option was to close the bakery.

During the first stint, the bakers did everything they could to make me feel unwelcome, even though many had known me since childhood, but it was different as I was now in charge of men predominantly some decades older than me. When my father had recovered enough to return to work, I decided enough

204 | BREAKING BREAD

was enough and went to teach eight-year old Italian kids how to speak English in Portogruaro, in northeast Italy at first, but later Belluno and Viterbo. I did this while making bread and pizza, strongarmed into doing so by the bambinos when they found I'd been a baker. It is amazing how much vocab you can squeeze into a baking session, and the buy-in you get from the kids knowing you can withhold a freshly baked pizza bap if they don't learn is second to none. I soon earned the title 'Baker Dave'. It seemed I couldn't outrun my past, no matter how hard I tried.

Every two weeks, I was shunted onto a new place, only learning my next destination when I was given an envelope containing train tickets. My next placement was in the small town of Ronciglione, a medieval town in the heart of Tuscia, which sits about an hour north of Rome. It was an ancient barnacle, stubbornly hitched to a slope. I was driven into town by my host family, none of whom spoke any English and from this moment on I would have to rely on the words I had accidentally picked up from listening to small children discuss bread production in a Venetian monastery.

As the car turned into a rustic looking courtyard, I was led up steps of a beautiful building to an apartment that was lavishly furnished. My hopes soared – was this where I was going to live? Yet, when it came time to show me to my room, I was led outside again, down the steps, into a windowless basement room. It was a rat palace, straight out of a horror movie set, complete with creepy religious trinkets and a bed that smelled like a broken fridge.

I woke up at around five in the morning the next day to the sound of mechanics in the adjacent space – impact drivers, pneumatic wrenches and loud Italian banter. The two spaces were linked by a door that I found to be unlocked, and more concerning, unlockable. As I opened it my eyes met with one of the mechanics in the next room and I swiftly returned the door to its latch. Unsettled, in a strange place, with very little Italian under my belt, I decided to get dressed and go for a walk and get the lie of the land. Like that first nightshift in Suffolk where my awkward teenage body was struggling to fit into the costume of an adult world, my uncomfortable English self was trying to fit into an international world.

The stone of the little settlement was familiar, giving off a scent like the cooling hearth of an oven, musty with a little funk but still oddly appealing. The sky was a light blue and the dawn chorus of birds discussing their dreams flooded every street and alleyway. After months of recognising mornings as the end of the day, it was a pleasurable change for me to witness the beginning of one.

As I strolled about, my nose twitched as I caught the familiar notes of a bakery, not the bread, but the bakery itself. The slightly acrid smell of burnt flour and fat, along with sweeter elements that reminded me of home. It made me feel homesick. My nose led me forwards, and I was soon looking in at the unlit window display of a bakery, one that I knew from home would not be open to the public for another hour at least. Suddenly it didn't matter that I was in a strange place in a strange land. Making bread is a language in itself and it's one I was familiar with.

I heard a radio and the percussion of trays and tins from the side street. My curiosity led me to the back door where the fluorescent strip lights laid out a welcoming carpet next to the rattly old concertina door. It was just like the one at home, sheets of galvanised metal held together with loose rivets and a maker's badge that could have been fifty years old. The same concrete steps down into a space built by someone who lacked a set square.

When I used to work on a Friday night in Woodbridge, during my time there, small town drunkards would stumble to our back door, at chucking out time, tongues tied in knots by the liquid bread they had imbibed. They wanted the solid stuff to soak up the alcohol, before they attempted their jelly-legged walk home. I would hand them rolls straight from the oven and pick through the grubby pennies they held out to me, eyes bleary, hands often shaking. This, often wordless, sealed with a thumbs-up as they staggered away. So, despite my severely limited Italian, I knew that it was possible, in theory, to get some fresh bread from this situation.

There was just one baker inside, with his back to me, a threadbare white T-shirt covering his back, apron strings hitched over some ample love handles. He was plunging his fingers into a tray of dough that had a veneer of olive oil, the light green oil sinking into the impressions he made. In the words of my baker friend, Daisy Terry, it was like 'watching a cat play the piano'.

I could tell he was aware of my presence, but he ignored me for a while, concentrating on his task. Dough finished, he unloaded sheets of baked Pizza Romana from the oven, closed the dampers, reset timers and loaded fresh batches. I watched in silence, familiar with this story. A baker's work is a series of soliloquies, they must not be interrupted, but between scenes there may be time for a cigarette at the stage door or a sip of cold coffee.

He turned and an old man's face looked back at me. It was a shock. For a moment, he could easily have been my dad, or my grandad standing there, and I was struck with such a wave of homesickness it was almost debilitating. I managed to stutter out the few Italian words I had been arranging in my head to make sense while waiting, wanting desperately to communicate that I was in The Club, that I was a baker, too.

He managed to sort through my verbal shrapnel, staring at my hands for confirmation. After a while, he seemed satisfied. I gestured my appreciation of his floury den and it became clear that I wouldn't be able to say the things I wanted to, but that, perhaps, we didn't really need to. I understood his world, I'd grown up in it, and he was due on stage any moment.

The old baker cut a slice of fresh pizza from a large rectangular sheet on the side, wrapped it in a piece of twice-used baking paper and pushed it into my hand and me out of the door in one smooth move. Backing away I mimed offering him some recompense for the bread, but he waved me away with his hand, with all the theatrical benevolence of an emperor. I felt special. Accepted.

As I walked back to my room, sinking my teeth into the bread, my lips soaking up the warm olive oil, I thought about the ancient Romans and how they had influenced my life, in taking wheat to my birth country, to all the other countries around the world that they'd conquered. Had they transported a gift or laid a curse? In that moment, as I finished the delicious, fragrant *pizza al taglio*, it felt very much like a gift.

Bread is a language, one that transcends borders. It is the food of the colonised and the colonisers, new variants brought to countries, taken from them, often through conflict and war. It's a subject that interests me, one I want to explore further. And I decide to begin delving into the relationship between bread, war and colonisation by speaking to an expert on the subject. Professor Martin Bricknell specialises in conflict, health and military medicine in the War Studies department of King's College London. He has thirty-four years' experience in the UK defence medical services, and as a former surgeon general of the UK armed services, he has completed tours in Afghanistan, Iraq and the Balkans.

208 | BREAKING BREAD

Professor Bricknell's research focuses on the relationship between the military and civilian populations, and our conversation soon turned to examples of military strategy influencing civilian life, such as the impact of the National Loaf, introduced in Britain during the Second World War. But more on that later.

With the colonies of the British Empire supplying many of the raw materials the 'Motherland' required, Britain itself became a processing and taxation hub that enabled it to grow rich from the spoils of these countries. Equally it was exposed to great costs during the First and Second World Wars, its supply routes targeted. In both conflicts, the Germans homed in on these chains of vital necessities, including food, to try and starve the Tommies into surrender. Ships carrying grain from Canada and the US were torpedoed, as they crossed the Atlantic, and pressure, consequently, mounted on the domestic supply chain. Every boat that made it through the German blockade was treasured. As such, the country could not afford to waste domestic flour by milling it into white flour that would have seen only 70 per cent of the grain ending up in the bellies of soldiers and civilians.

The government introduced a series of measures to make sure bread reached domestic and military audiences, designed to protect and control what people ate. In May 1917, the Ministry of Food brought in the Bread Order to ensure that most loaves were made from the imported grain. They had to be wholemeal, with a minimum initial extraction rate of 81 per cent which increased the following year to 92 per cent. It also became illegal to sell bread that was less than twelve hours old, with the logic that people would eat less bread if it was stale. Naturally these measures were despised by the local population, many of whom lived on little more than bread, jam, tea and sugar. Hefty fines and even prison sentences were handed out to those bold enough to buy 'new bread' and when the laws were repealed after the war ended, there was a collective sigh of relief.

Restrictions on bread were reinforced during the Second World War, leading to the introduction of the 'National Loaf' by the Federation of Bakers in 1942, to combat the wastage caused by the refining process to produce white flour. Unsurprisingly, these new measures did not sit well with local residents. From 1942 to 1956, there were only four recipes that could be used to make bread, enshrined in law. These wholemeal flour-based loaves were fortified with added calcium and vitamins and although the main objective was to stretch the flour as far as possible by reducing the wastefulness of white flour, they helped to significantly improve the overall health of the nation – particularly reducing obesity 'due to rationing', according to the professor.

My grandparents started their bakery during this time, opening in 1946, although their special focus was cakes rather than bread. Rationing was still in force but there were ways around it if you didn't mind a little clandestine family time. My grandad would drive the bakery van to the docks with my infant father in the passenger seat, using him as an excuse if he was stopped by police. This charade of father and son excursions to the Ipswich waterfront allowed the bakery to operate using blackmarket raw materials. By all accounts it was the only way to stay in business through these tough years. This reminds me of the stories of my mother driving through pickets to get flour from the same docks in Ipswich, during the Bread Strike, decades later (see page 182).

It really is no wonder that the introduction of Chorleywood bread, five years after rationing ended, caused the market in

210 | BREAKING BREAD

white fluffy, fibreless bread to explode. Invented by a group of UK scientists at Chorleywood Lodge, just outside west London, tasked with creating a new kind of bread, one that could be produced en masse and was tasty and cheap, they developed the Chorleywood Bread Process (CBP). The CBP revolutionised bread in Britain, changing tastes for decades, and its influence didn't just stop there, spreading across the globe.

By increasing yeast, fat and water ratios, adding in oxidising agents (that were later banned and replaced by ascorbic acid) and employing high-speed mixers to give the dough an intense working over, a sack of wheat could be turned into a packaged, sliced loaf in less than four hours. A nation whose loaves were restricted for a good part of the first fifty years of the twentieth century suddenly gorged itself on those previously forbidden loaves. While in reality, people may have been better off healthwise with the unappetising, stale and mealy bread they'd been eating, as dictated by law, they dreamt of soft, fluffy, plentiful loaves.

The fear and anxiety of food shortages was washed away with this new process that didn't rely on imported wheat, was cheap, convenient and plentiful. And yet whether we realised it or not, we suffocated in this cotton wool bread, and it's one that we exported to our former colonies and to many other countries around the world, with profound impact. By 2009, around fourth-fifths of the bread made in Britain, India, New Zealand and Australia was made using CBP, along with another thirty other nations globally. Can you imagine that many people eating this kind of bread? So, the war being fought in many developed and developing nations today is a war on obesity rather than on hunger, and white, ultra-processed bread is a major contributor to the body count. Our legacy. We should be so proud. Colonisation and globalisation has much to answer for.

Yet, in the climate of the Cold War, the Chorleywood bread was a national defence against supply lines being targeted. It served a purpose. With the constant threat of a nuclear armageddon during those years, I'm not surprised that little attention was paid to the long-term effects of eating this super soft bread.

Bricknell says that this 'denial of food is a weapon of war', adding 'access to sources of bread becomes a really important part of sustaining a campaign'. I'm curious what he thinks of when he hears the word 'bread'. Is it like mine or one of the other people I've spoken to. Interestingly his loaf is flavoured from an in-store bakery or one encased in plastic, that convenient bread for making a quick sandwich. His bread is the easiest way of delivering the carbohydrates locked up in wheat to troops or civilians, with its dried-out cousin, the biscuit, especially important.

Anyone with some seeds can grow wheat – a crop that, as we've discussed, has one predictable harvest a year and can be taxed by simply showing up at the right time, all things being equal. The wheat must then be milled, another cut can be taken, before its finally baked in a specialist oven (if you want a decent loaf) and yet more revenue can be extracted. It's the argument that James. C. Scott uses in his book, *Against the Grain*, to explain why other grains have not been as successful. Beans and pulses have an extended, drip-fed harvest, hard to predict, and roots that lie underground are impossible to quantify and spoil quickly once harvested. But wheat, rice and maize can all be counted, divided and are well-suited to taxation.

One of the principal benefits of colonisation is food production, the ancient Romans and Egyptians got that. According to most

212 | BREAKING BREAD

accounts, wheat farming dates back to Mesopotamia (modern-day Iraq) around 12,000 years ago. The name 'Mesopotamia' itself means 'between two rivers' – the Euphrates and the Tigris. Iraq produced four million tonnes of wheat in 2023. The global production in that year was 791 million tonnes, with China, India and Russia accounting for 41 per cent of global wheat production. In short, with 219 million hectares being given over to wheat in 2022, wheat has colonised more of the earth than any other grain. It is that important.

Bread is one of the products of conquest. The basic ancient Roman model was to fight your neighbours into submission, send in the farmers or gift land to your faithful soldiers, use the conquered population that remained as free labour, install the structure to turn wheat into bread – if it didn't already exist – and then tax them to build funds to buy more weapons and soldiers.

I imagine breadmaking in the past, and its associated industries, as an augmented reality, laid over a newly conquered land, the people allowed in many other ways to continue as they had been, with their own traditions and customs, if they swore allegiance to the emperor, grew wheat, made bread and paid their taxes.

Bread that was made outside this restricted model was seen as subversive and attempts to control it come up at various points in history. The quern stone that was a human-powered milling machine consisting of two stones, was employed in ancient Egypt to mill wheat into flour, the effects of which can be seen on excavated skeletons from the region. The remains show specific injuries to knees and the kind of RSI (repetitive strain injuries) that would yield a bumper payout in a modern employment tribunal.

With subsequent innovations provided by the ancient Greeks, in the form of animal-driven mills, and the Romans, in the form of water mills, these quern stones began to represent an unwanted opportunity for people to make their own flour – and, if they rejected the chamber ovens first developed by the Egyptians, then they could make flatbreads on the fire.

Once bread was controlled by the state, the population was also under its control. Manipulation by subsidy or starvation is a tactic used as much in the modern day as it was in ancient Rome or in more recent wars, such as the one in Ukraine, as we shall see. In Rome, grain and then bread itself, were given to parts of the population to cement political stability at the heart of the empire. They also used siege starvation tactics to devastating effect.

When the enslaved Hebrews fled Egypt under the guidance of Moses, they took with them hard flatbreads known now as Matzoh. It has been suggested that the unfermented nature of these breads was a rejection of the Egyptian culture of leavened bread, as well as the need to flee quickly during what is now marked as the festival of Passover.

In the same region, separated by millennia, we can see bread being used in the same way, as a symbol of defiance against aggression. When Israel invaded Gaza in 2023, many news agencies, including the BBC and the *New York Times* ran with images of bread being handed out to civilians from the back of vans. I find it compelling that when we look for a visual aid to suffering, so often we use the scarcity of bread to communicate it for us. Whether in ancient Egypt, modern-day Palestine or the Sudan, it is bread more than any other food commodity that provides hope of survival. It's why we so often see food supply places targeted in conflicts.

In April 2024, a car of the non-profit organisation World Central Kitchen (WCK) was hit by Israeli forces on its way to deliver food aid. Seven aid workers were killed in the missile

214 | BREAKING BREAD

attack on the vehicle, which had its logo clearly visible on the roof. CEO of WCK Erin Gore stated that it was unforgivable: 'This is not only an attack against WCK, this is an attack on humanitarian organisations showing up in the most dire of situations where food is being used as a weapon of war.' In military speak, this is an example of 'disrupting supply lines', arguably another term for 'siege warfare' or 'forced famine'. Beat them down by starving them.

In Ukraine – known as 'the breadbasket of Europe', they continue to grow wheat despite the devastation, their land littered with Russian mines, making bread in the fiercest of conditions. Breadmaking is once again being used as a defiant act by local people, and even when forced from businesses and homes, Ukrainians are continuing to produce bread. It is a lifeforce for many.

I spoke to baker-in-exile Kateryna Kalyuzhna, originally from Kakhovka in the Kherson region of southern Ukraine. A region famous for its rich, black soil, known as the 'chernozem' which produces high yields with few inputs due to its high fertility, it has been fought over for centuries and, since 2022, much of it has been in the hands of Russian occupiers. Kateryna had to leave her home, bakery and way of life behind. She travelled to Lviv in the West, where she is now working in a small local bakery. In the tradition of journeying bakers throughout time, her most valuable cargo was also her lightest – experience and knowledge. She has been uprooted, displaced, and, as we talk, I can sense the pain behind her words, her longing for home, for this all to be a bad dream. The nightmare is real, however, and she is doing her best to survive.

When I asked Kateryna about 'bread' and what it meant to her, she went back to her childhood. It's a hot and sunny July day in the Ukrainian south and she is at her grandparents' house and her granny, also a Kateryna, has just made some borscht. Table set, she begins slicing a two-kilo loaf of freshly baked, golden wheat bread. Still slightly warm, with an incredibly crunchy crust, its fragrance is released. For Kateryna this is obviously a meaningful memory, more so as this is a memory of a homeland that she's been forced from. For me, this is a scene of utter delight. I can feel the sun warming my cheeks as Kateryna recalls this meal, imagine the steam rising from the crumb, illuminated by shafts of light. A simple meal of soup and bread, elevated to riches. The two most desired colours of all humanity, the imperial purple of the borscht and gilt crust of the bread. And yet, this must be a bitter–sweet memory for Kateryna.

Bread is sacred in Ukraine, and morale is boosted significantly when bread is given, for example, to soldiers on the front line who may not have seen a loaf for weeks at a time. Ukrainian is full of proverbs but for me '*Bread is the head of everything*' seems to sum up the relationship between the nation and its staple good perfectly. In the same way that cereal derives from the Roman god Ceres (meaning 'to nourish'), in the Ukrainian tongue the words 'to live' (zhyty) and 'rye' (zhyto) have the same root.

The history of bread and conflict in Ukraine is heavily loaded, especially with the various examples of Russian aggression over the centuries. Kateryna describes the lasting effects of what she describes as 'the many Soviet artificial famines' typified by the 'Holodomors' that took place early in the twentieth century. Holodomor translates as 'death by hunger' from Ukrainian and although there have been multiple examples of this kind of attack, the worst occurred in 1932–3, resulting in an estimated 3.5–5 million Ukrainian deaths. The industrialisation of agriculture during Stalin's first Five-Year Plan is cited as a contributing

216 | BREAKING BREAD

factor, although poor harvests were also affected by the weather and other agricultural policies, such as depleting the soil through intensive farming practices. These policies were aimed at crushing Ukrainian nationalism and controlling the people.

Kateryna tells me that her great-grandmother, Daria, who survived deportation and famine, used to sleep on a 'big chest full of sliced dry bread'. She says, 'She kept it for the worst times when the communists would return to expropriate all bread again.' The fear of going without bread and the resulting safety of having a treasure chest of bread as a defence against occupation is a stark manifestation of the trauma of the Holodomors.

Kateryna's aunts, who were in their teens when famine struck, ate everything, including fruit, cakes and puddings with a slice of fresh wheat bread. When she asked them why they did this, they replied that they could not get enough of it, adding, 'In our childhood we used to suffer without bread.'

The Soviet famines of 1921–3, 1932–3 and 1946–7 are among the worst examples in modern history of where bread has been used as a weapon of war, to control and subjugate the masses. Here, it was intended as a way to suppress the Ukrainian Liberation Movement. A century later, we are seeing history repeat itself with Putin mimicking Stalin's tactics. Kateryna tells me that the Russians are attacking port facilities on the Black Sea, bombing Ukrainian grain stores and commandeering grain supplies in occupied territories.

'Ukrainians are once again experiencing the absence of bread and talk about it with tears in their eyes.' More to the point, people are starving.

I have lived a life surrounded by bread, and the thought of it being withheld so that I or those I love might starve seems incomprehensible. Yet, that's what is happening now in the world in so many places, people facing food insecurity exacerbated and caused by conflicts. Gaza and Sudan led the charge in 2023. In the latter more than 18 million Sudanese, roughly a third of the country, faced food crisis.

There's an image etched by both Sathnam Sanghera and Lizzie Collingham, in their respective books *Empireworld* and *Hungry Empire*, in which they describe a method of executing West Indian slaves by chaining them up with a loaf of bread just out of reach, so that they starved in the sun, the bread taunting them. A simultaneous denial of life, freedom and humanity.

In modern times, a positive is that some global organisations are actively trying to combat food insecurity caused by conflict. In 2024, for example, a joint initiative of the African Development Bank (AfDB) and United Nations World Food Programme (WFP) saw a 70 per cent increase in wheat production across five Sudanese states. In real terms that's 645,000 metric tons of wheat for the year, or 22 per cent of Sudan's total wheat consumption needs. Its success has been largely attributed to distributing climate-adapted wheat seeds to some 170,000 smallhold farmers. This proves that if we are committed, we can help solve food insecurity issues, particularly those caused by conflict and population displacement and that helping small farmers is a successful way to do this. Such a seemingly simple solution to a massive, heartbreaking global problem.

And what of the West? What have we learnt from war? The post-war period in the twentieth century was typified by the industrialisation of food and especially bread. When food

218 | BREAKING BREAD

became abundant to the point of excess, the memory of war and continuing fear of starvation fuelled companies and consumers alike to demand ever more. We built our own international chest of dry bread to sleep on and took bread at every opportunity, devouring every crumb with the thought that it might not last. I'm too young to remember those feelings, but my grandma, who was born in 1912, used to pile up plates of sandwiches for me – white bread with thick ham and butter so thick you could have created a milk-fat Mount Rushmore in it. She wasn't satisfied until they had all been eaten. No easy task.

Kateryna remembers only too well the occupation of her country in 2022: 'Those terrible days full of endless rage, stress, pain and sorrow'. Her own town of Kakhovka was besieged and they were cut-off from the rest of Ukraine with no food supply, reliant only on the resources that were left, which were quickly running out.

'On the third day of the Russian occupation, our people and local bakeries found themselves without yeast and flour,' she tells me. 'As a sourdough baker, I offered my help to a local bakery in a nursing home where there was some flour but no yeast. Every morning, I delivered two enormous bowls of sourdough levain [starter] that I made at night. We managed to make 250–300 loaves a day. We worked hard for two weeks or so, then flour and yeast appeared in the shops again and my assistance wasn't needed anymore. As I left the bakery, Larysa, a fellow baker said to me "you know this war has united us, making us much stronger!"'

The Ukrainian flag is blue over yellow. I've been told that the blue represents the sky and the yellow signifies the wheat that grows across the fertile land. A nation so proud of its grain and bread that it's on their flag. Running out of grain and bread has brought many armies grinding to a halt and Ukraine's natural treasure of wheat has left me wondering whether they would have been better off without the chernozem, the black gold. Would their food supplies have been left untargeted?

My knowledge of Ukrainian breads, of which there are many, from dark ryes to white wheaten pillows, comes from working with Bake for Ukraine, which I first encountered when I was head baker at Pump Street Bakery in Suffolk. We were making *pampushky*, a deliciously soft tear and share style loaf based on Ukrainian food writer Olia Hercules's recipe, the sales going to the Red Cross humanitarian appeal. We wanted to show support and also, by doing this, we were helping to keep an important part of Ukrainian culture alive, one that the Russians seem to want to eradicate. Bread. Our protest.

I spoke to Felicity Spector about bread and conflict. She was working with Bake for Ukraine, which helps get native bakeries impacted by the conflict back on their feet. A celebrated food writer and journalist, Felicity has covered some seminal moments in recent history, such as the 1989 Velvet Revolution in Prague and the inauguration of President Obama in the US. When we Zoomed, she was in Odessa, about to travel to Kiev, and then eastwards to deliver bread to the frontline. Russia has repeatedly denied targeting civilians in the war but every day in the month that I spoke to Felicity, it hit civilian areas, resulting in many deaths. Despite this, Felicity was disarmingly relaxed and upbeat when we spoke and at times I had to remind myself of the danger she faced as she fought to get bread to the people who needed it most.

When I ask Felicity about her associations of bread, like Kateryna, she is taken back to her childhood. 'My late father used to make himself a cheese sandwich every night at twelve o'clock,'

220 | BREAKING BREAD

she recalls. So often when I've asked people to think of bread, their mind seems to replace that word with 'family' or 'home'. For so many of us, this is a place of safety and security.

There are few places on earth so connected to bread production as Ukraine and Felicity recalls she first became involved in her fundraising and charity work after seeing a post by Dan Lepard on Instagram about a Kiev bakery called Bakehouse, part of a bigger company called Good Wine. 'The warehouse was hit by a rocket and the whole thing went up, everything had burnt. I've since been there – it's completely destroyed.' Felicity managed to use her contacts to secure four van loads of baking equipment to get them back up and running: they were at the time a key supplier to the Ukrainian military so crucial to the war effort.

Bake for Ukraine asked if Felicity could help some of the smaller bakeries affected and she's been fundraising for their projects ever since, which includes getting equipment to the frontline and the deployment of a mobile bakery. Their website is emboldened with the message '*Bread means life for Ukrainians*' and the mobile bakery is a roadshow of hope for the people who fear a return to Soviet rule. Originally built for the Swiss Army, it was purchased, renovated and fitted out with a wood-fired oven, generators and mixers. The oven can run on gas although care must be taken not to produce too much heat as the drones that are sent to bomb targets are often fitted with thermal-seeking technology.

Maintaining autonomy over food production is a powerful symbol of defiance and provides many with the resolve to carry on fighting, especially as bread is often emblematic of culture. Felicity recounts an experience that a Rabbi had with a Jewish soldier upon seeing *challah* for the first time in many weeks, after a diet consisting almost entirely of porridge, his joy, the bread was nourishment for the body and soul. A kindness in a hostile world.

Mobile bakeries have been deployed to feed troops since the late nineteenth century and played a pivotal part in the aftermath of the Second World War. As Allied forces gained back previously Nazi-held territories, they fed the people as well as the soldiers that had been left starving by the crumbling enemy war machine.

In Peter Frankopan's book, *The Silk Roads*, he argues that it was the Nazis' requirement for wheat that led to the invasion of Ukraine and Russia in June 1941, timed to secure that year's wheat harvest to supply food to their forces that were, to use Bilbo Baggins' words, 'stretched, like butter scraped over too much bread'. Their eye was drawn from the shores of Britain to the East, in a move that reshaped the entire conflict.

The scorched earth tactics of the Russians left fields of charred ground for the invaders to inhabit and by the winter of that year, 1941, the US had joined the conflict. It's interesting to think that had the Germans not needed grain so desperately, they would almost certainly have invaded Britain and the story of the twentieth century may have been very different. My grandparents, parents, own story may have been different. Would I even be a baker? Would I have the legacy passed down to me? Grain and the demand for it during a world war changed the course of my family's history. I think about Ukraine and its bloody history and the place that grain and bread, arguably, have in that.

Ukrainian food writer Olia Hercules believes her country's relationship with grain and bread has shaped the nation's identity and also made it a target because of its bounty of resources. When I ask Olia to conjure up an image of bread, she is taken back to the 1990s, eating a chunk of sour crusty *palyanitsya,* accompanied by

222 | BREAKING BREAD

a cold glass of raw milk in her native town of Kakhovka. It's the antithesis of the Soviet 'brick bread that you could kill someone with', she adds.

Olia tells me how it was the Russian Empire that first planted wheat in the chernozem, which stretched from Romania all the way across southern Ukraine. Olia, who loves bread, is conflicted about this use of land. 'It's a double-edged sword,' she admits. '[T]he more I look into it there's the steppe that used to be an upside-down forest, because of all the deep roots of wild grasses. The Soviets came and just ploughed it all up, just put all these fields in. I can't wrap my head around it yet, because [bread is] something that I love and miss and can't live without but on the other hand makes me feel . . . oh! . . . What about the soil? The eco systems?'

In 2019, 57 per cent of Ukrainian land was used for farming, growing 4 per cent of the global wheat output and even larger amounts of maize and 30 per cent of all the sunflower oil. The naturally fertile soil requires low amounts of fertilisers, making the land more ecologically beneficial, when compared to farming on land that is less inherently fertile and requires higher doses of chemical inputs. With the rising costs of agricultural chemicals, it also makes it much more economically productive, leading some EU countries to fear the possible impact that the cheap wheat Ukraine can supply could have on the market. This was evidenced by Poland discarding two grain shipments in a protectionist measure to avoid flooding its domestic market with cheaper grain, much to the agony of a country fighting for its survival.

Once a conquered population becomes dependent on bread they are more readily controlled, pacified by the supply of a staple food. To combat this Peter Kropotkin, in *The Conquest of Bread*, advocates unleashing all the weapons of modern agriculture on the land to free people from food insecurity. The West arguably did this during the Cold War, as seen by the megalithic food system created by the US and Western Europe (under the Marshall Plan) created during these years. Yet the cost of this blanket of nutrition is that food culture tends to become more homogenous, flattened by this generic flooding of a market by a dominant product, in this case bread. The regional identities are swallowed up by national interest and we arrive at a point where we can talk about a Standard American Diet, for example, to describe the general eating habits of millions of people. Think McDonald's' globalisation of fast food.

In Ukraine, there are still regional breads, as I discovered when I was working with Olia's recipe to raise money for those suffering, and they have played a part in the war outside the direct nourishment they provide. While many Ukrainians can typically speak Russian as well as native speakers, Russians struggle with the Ukrainian language – in the same way that a Welsh speaker has no trouble speaking English but very few English speakers can speak Welsh.

The bread that Olia described has become a *shibboleth*, a word that threshes the true Ukrainians from Russia pretenders. It comes from Hebrew and means 'ear of corn' and has been used to weed out 'enemies' who may be able to disguise themselves outwardly but are often betrayed by their tongue. Reportedly in the 1381 Peasants' Revolt in England, the mercenary Dutch were often found out when they were asked to say 'bread' or 'cheese' and if they responded with an accent, they were executed. And so, it continues. Today, 'the Russians can't twist their tongues around the word [*palyanitsya*]', Olia tells me. And that's significant. Such is the national pride in that humble loaf, that it appeared on a 2013 national postage stamp and is the name of their new cruise missile unveiled in 2024.

224 | BREAKING BREAD

It's clear to me from speaking to Olia, Kateryna and Felicity that the Ukrainian spirit is strong and the memory of the Holodomors and events in recent history are enough to keep the passion for fighting alive. And yet, in many ways nothing changes. We don't learn from history. We repeat ourselves – the colonisers to the colonised, the invaders to those defending their turf: bread is still being used to manipulate masses, to control how people behave. It has been used against Ukraine in the past and in this conflict again. And what we're seeing is people coming together to keep bread on the table. Not just Ukrainians but people from other nations too. And the bread is good, as Felicity Spector can testify: 'Some of the best bread I've ever tasted has been Ukrainian bread.'

Yet there is a human cost to all this, people putting their lives on the line to make sure supplies are kept going. Olia's father is working at grassroots level to make sure that the farmers can continue to grow wheat safely. He has designed a remote-controlled minesweeper that has been fashioned using a tractor to make sure the fields are safe to farm once more. And wheat is a vital export for the country: the more grown, the stronger the country becomes. Yet Russia won't stop using the control of agriculture as a weapon against it and with the breakdown of the grain deal that saw over 30 million tonnes having to be exported via Black Sea channels, Ukraine is becoming increasingly more creative in the way it exports its most valued commodity.

The world is littered with countries and cultures which have had their foodstuffs and diets, including bread, subsumed by colonisation, conflict and war, and we Brits have had a lot to do with that questionable legacy. As can be seen in New Zealand, bread was introduced into Maori culture yet wheat was very much seen as a food of the coloniser. A friend and colleague, Matthew Burgess is of Maori–British heritage and is founder of food consultancy business Kaiwhenua, which means 'food' in Maori. He describes his food as a mix of 'old colonial recipes and southern Pacific soul' and told me that the Maori diet before the introduction of bread was mainly made up of small birds, several varieties of potato, coconut, fruits, edible leaves and plants that required no extensive processing. Knowing that the European settlers valued wheat, it was grown for trade and the refined dough products were coveted. There are examples of the Maori boiling wheat in lye water, in the same way that Mesoamericans did with maize and cooking the grains as a kind of pottage rather than consuming it as what we would think of as bread.

Matt thinks the strong spiritual culture of the Maori protected them against bread colonisation. 'They believed that in the real world and spiritual world everything was sacred, so there was a superstitious wariness when it came to new foods.' Even in 2020, only 2 per cent of New Zealand's land mass was given over to arable farming. In the UK, which is of comparable size, 25 per cent of the total land mass is farmed for arable crops. New Zealand may have a much smaller population but its agricultural output in areas such as dairy and livestock is massive.

Bread's relationship to colonisation and conflict is one of exploitation and fear. Grain being a way for dominating nations to extract the marrow of the earth, to bleed it dry which, in the case of the Roman Empire led to dwindling harvests and an ever-greater need for fresh lands to exploit – all of which became unsustainable in the end due to over-farming.

226 | BREAKING BREAD

The giving of bread to placate, or restricting it to dehumanise or punish populations, has been a common power play throughout time. Bread fuels life: it is hope and freedom from hunger for many nations. And looking at history, one could argue that a society hooked on bread is more easily manipulated. Certainly, if we look at Ukraine, Gaza or Sudan, should we be questioning our relationship to bread, not just how it is made but our supply lines too? In so many cases, targeting the fields in which grains are grown by placing landmines in them, or blowing up ships or roads, making it impossible for vital ingredients to reach the populations or armies that need them most, has won wars. So should we be looking at alternative methods to feed our populations? Perhaps, in a world that is fracturing, we should consider our diet as our first line of defence.

9

Our Daily Bread

What the gods want

*... he was ripped, Jesus. I don't think he gets enough
credit for the shape he was in. Anytime I'm in Mass
and I just kind of daydream, it always strikes me when
you see Jesus on the cross, he had a six-pack. He never
touched the bread at that wedding. No way did he put
starchy carbs in that wee welterweight frame of his.*

Kevin Bridges *The Overdue Catch Up* (2023)

While working as head baker at Pump Street Bakery, I would
make *pastel de nata*, those buttery, flaky custard bombs that
originate from Portugal, which evaporate in your mouth and leave
a whisper of lemon and cinnamon behind to remind you that, yes,
you really did eat something so delicious. I had the enviable task of
cutting one each day to test if the custard was set perfectly. My
knife would crack through the crisp pastry, and as I gently nudged
the halves apart I'd see, almost every time, the sheen of a smooth
silky custard. I'm not sure I was contractually obliged to eat it
afterwards, but, hey, it couldn't be sold on, so it would have been
sacrilege to discard it. In 2012, I went to Belém, a district of

228 | BREAKING BREAD

Lisbon, from where this lovely morsel originates. A morsel with religious connections, like a lot of the breads around the world.

My friend Tony, who worked at ST. JOHN BREAD AND WINE in London at the time, took me to the pastry shop *Fábrica de Pastéis de Belém*, a relatively unassuming café bakery considering it's the birthplace of one of the most wonderful pastries ever created. As we walked in, I could see the bakers behind a glass wall, a table of seated women were chatting away, while pressing pastry into moulds at a pace I've never been able to match. Others were making custard, laminating pastry and dancing the dance to bake the hundreds and hundreds of pastries necessary every eight or nine minutes. We joined the queue at the counter and Tony paid for a box. I felt the heat through the cardboard as we walked away to a nearby park. We sat on the grass and scattered cinnamon and icing sugar onto the fresh pastries from little sachets. The aroma... the taste... it melted like a Communion wafer on my tongue – I've never actually had one but my dad used to buy huge sheets of rice paper for making macaroons and I've eaten enough of that stuff to know it melts. I asked about the history and Tony pointed to the monastery, icing sugar coating his moustache, 'The monks invented them.'

I knew God had to have something to do with creating something so divine.

The story goes that in the eighteenth century, the monks of the Jerónimos Monastery in Belém used a lot of egg whites for starching their clothes and needed a way to use up all the surplus yolks, so they baked. A lot. With the colonial bounty of sugar and cinnamon from Portuguese colonies, they created the tarts we know today, so delicious that they could trade them when revenues were needed to pay off bills. They sold the recipe to the sugar refinery when the monastery was dissolved. The memory of this got me thinking about the links between religion and baking. How pervasive are they? How important might they be in giving power to bread?

I caught up with Zara Mohammed, the secretary general of The Muslim Council of Britain to chat about this. The first woman to hold that position, Zara is also the first Scottish leader and the youngest person to become secretary general when she was elected in 2021. A smasher of glass ceilings, most certainly, Zara met with me to break bread and discuss the impact this seemingly simple food has had on Islam.

Islam is the youngest of the three Abrahamic religions, with Christianity the middle child and Judaism the oldest. The portrayal of the faith is complex, particularly in our post-9/11 world, and often conveyed as very conservative, which is at odds with the charmingly open person who shares her experience of bread with me. Commenting on this, Zara tells me, 'In some ways I'm part of reframing the narrative on who Muslims are. Showing that we are really diverse,' she tells me. 'Fifty per cent of Muslims are under twenty-five; it's a very young, dynamic and vibrant community. I'm a link between the older generation and the new.'

When Zara contemplates what bread means to her, she describes a scene rather than a particular loaf or product, a family dinner at Ramadan. 'Generally speaking, bread isn't something I think about, but when I do it conjures up an *iftar*, when we're breaking the fast because typically that's when we carb-up a little bit. When I'm talking about bread, I'm not talking about Warburton's or Hovis, I'm thinking about more traditional breads from our cultural backgrounds. Chapatis, naans, pitta breads – for me it's breaking the fast . . . it's an act of worship in a communal setting.'

230 | BREAKING BREAD

This idea of bread being a frame for a communal act strikes a chord. I start thinking about the bread rolls that so often begin a meal. The bread is a bridge into conversation – conversation between diners but also between the establishment and its guests. In this way, bread's unassuming simplicity is its greatest strength. It is inclusive and has the power to disarm, to relax and help showcase more elaborate dishes. 'Bread is the starting food. Everyone can start at bread,' Zara adds, confirming exactly what I've been thinking.

'With Muslims all over the world there is a tradition of bread, not because it's a holy food but because it's a staple food for all communities,' Zara explains. 'Bread, well food, in general, is seen as an immense blessing. We don't waste it and we give thanks for it. Not just bread – that's all food.'

I can see that bread's significance comes from its ability to be shared. Infinitely divisible, it presents itself as the ultimate communal food. Most of the examples of bread that Zara gives me are round flatbreads, so a piece taken from the edge is the same as a piece taken from the centre. Zara continues 'There's a tradition of flatbreads – chapatis, roti, parathas…bread is unpretentious. An even playing field. Everyone can take a piece.' These breads require no expensive technology to bake; they can be made wherever there is fire and represent the most accessible and democratic end of the bready scale. They are made to share and there is pretty little wastage.

The reverence for not wasting any bread reminds me of my grandad's recipe book, filled with ideas for using up old bread so that it didn't go to waste. Things like bread pudding, treacle tart and Christmas puds. Equally at Pump Street, where I now lead their workshop programme, they save every scrap of sourdough so that it can be crumbed and toasted to go into their exquisite craft chocolate bars – sourdough and sea salt has always been a bestseller. I have heard of bakeries soaking old bread and adding it back into new dough. It used to be frowned upon and often done in secret but now bakeries advertise the fact as proof of their commitment to reducing food waste. It's a resurrection that the bread god would appreciate at least.

I ask Zara if she feels that bread has a part to play in the future of major faiths and the relationships between them. It's a big question that she answers with simple grace. 'Bread is universal. When you invite people for a meal, it humanises.' She recounts something that happened in York where Far Right protesters were demonstrating outside a mosque. 'They were invited in for a cup of tea. I don't know if there was any bread involved, but it diffused the situation.' I like to think bread did play a part in this. What might that say for the world we live in, as I type, with Far Right rioting everywhere. The power of bread is immense in scenarios like this, eating the same food, 'breaking bread' with your foe as well as with your ally, it provides a setting at which to talk. When we need our religious leaders to come together, or any leaders for that matter, I say, give them bread and see what follows. Simplistic perhaps but history might say, it's worked before.

The ancient Egyptians paid a great deal of attention to their bread and it was highly valued. They were most likely the first civilisation to consider it a staple food. Even after life, they were concerned about finding the 'grain of the dead', which was a field of wheat in the sky. They would bury their dead with enough bread to sustain them on their quest for the everlasting bread of heaven, a particular spell from *The Book of the Dead* provided to the deceased, should an enemy challenge their right to it.

232 | BREAKING BREAD

> *I am a man who has bread in Heliopolis*
> *My bread is in Heaven with the Sun God*
> *My bread is on earth with Keb*
> *The bark of evening and of Morning*
> *Bring me the bread that is my meat*
> *From the house of the Sun God.*

As long as they had these words, no cruel spirit could deny them their loaf.

In the Roman tradition, the sun god was Mithras whose birthday was Christmas Day. The sun god became the son of God. The guardian of bread in heaven became the bread god, Jesus Christ. Much like my grandfather's approach, nothing has gone to waste when it comes to theology, everything is reused and recycled. Gods reborn and resurrected.

The breads of Egypt were the first recorded leavened loaves, made with sourdough or *barm* from the brewer, baked in specialist bread ovens. The cold fire of fermentation was coupled with the hot fire of the oven chamber to create a body of bread. And it was precisely this kind of bread that the Hebrews rejected when they left Egypt, freed from their enslavement by Moses. On the eve of Passover, it is still customary to sweep every crumb of leavened bread into a pile and burn it. When the mono-god swept over the land of Egypt in the last plague, he looked for the lamb's blood painted on the doors of the Jews. Perhaps he was also looking for those households that ate leavened bread, the Egyptian 'bread eaters'. The eating of Matzoh is also customary during the seven-day Passover festival, and the dough must be mixed and baked within eighteen minutes. After that time, it becomes *'chametz'* or leavened, inoculated with yeasts. The break between leavened bread and flatbread was complete.

In ancient Greece, Demeter was worshipped as the goddess of the harvest, grains and agriculture. She was the giver of bread and food, with the unruly Dionysus given the realm of fermentation. The Greeks imported some of their grain from Egypt and it must have come loaded with a reverence for bread, yet their agricultural systems were better suited to pasture and herding rather than ploughing and sowing.

During the Persian Wars of the seventh century BCE, the value of wheat and by extension bread as tools of national security were cemented. Demeter was believed to have swung a plough through the enemy army, dropping them into the ground, and after such a display who would argue that wheat was to be worshipped? The goddess of agriculture developed a cult following and fast became a favourite among humans.

Demeter controlled the growing seasons. Her daughter, Persephone, was abducted and taken to the Underworld by Hades, who ruled there. Demeter, in despair, grieving the loss of her daughter, forgot to tend to the harvest and so famine ensued. Zeus intervened, commanding Hades release his daughter, but she had eaten a pomegranate seed and couldn't be fully integrated back into the world, so, according to myth, spends a third of the year in the Underworld, when the fields are barren, and two-thirds back where she belongs. When Persephone is with Demeter, the fields yield the food that the people so desperately long for, including the grain to make bread.

The cult of Demeter was transferred to the Romans through Ceres, who essentially represented the same interests as the Greek goddess, and the affection grew through the Roman Empire along

234 | BREAKING BREAD

with all the wheat fields. Egypt became part of the Roman Empire in 30 BCE – famously after Octavian's (Emperor Augustus's) defeat of Marc Anthony and Cleopatra – and was an incredibly valuable agricultural territory, the grain that flowed into Rome seen as a bounty bestowed by Ceres on the people.

The Romans took over the mantle of both the Egyptians and Greeks as the pre-eminent 'bread eaters', with agriculture central to achieving their aims for complete domination of every parcel of land they laid eyes on. The goddess Ceres's stock rose as the importance of the very things she oversaw increased, and although this was still very much a polytheistic society, some gods were seen as more equal than others.

My first school was a Catholic girls' school in Ipswich. Yes, you heard me. An interesting choice from my parents as I was neither Catholic nor, as is probably evident by now, a girl. I can only surmise that they wanted their son educated at a school with a philosophy for loving bread as much as they did. That, and the fact my four older sisters also went there. Boys were considered to be genderless until the age of seven at the school, which seems incredibly progressive now, in retrospect. We were regaled many, many times with the story of Jesus, how the Romans were the bad guys and then later adopted Christianity themselves. How Jesus was Jewish but entirely separate from the Jewish faith, which for a child let alone adult can be quite difficult to comprehend, and yet my focus was all the bread chat as my pre-gendered mind had spotted an opportunity to take advantage of my intimate knowledge of bread-related matters. I had an inside track.

Jesus' love of bread set him apart from his Jewish brethren. They perhaps saw this as being a bit too Egyptian for them, leavened bread had a cultural weight to it and it symbolised the oppression from which the Jews had escaped. The real issue seems to have been when Jesus started saying that he was, in fact, bread. If that wasn't enough, by suggesting that followers could eat bread in remembrance of him it became a bit too close to cannibalism for many Jews, and they rejected him. Jesus became a free agent, and while his appreciation for bread may have lost him support up until his death, he was remade in the eyes of those who had previously persecuted him.

The lower classes of Roman civilisation quite liked this new spirituality, with all the equality stuff coupled with a love of bread. Jesus can be seen as a spin-off of Ceres, a standalone figure to follow. A champion of the working fellow, a miracle worker, open to all the marginal characters in society and most importantly – the deliverer of bread. I'm being simplistic here but I'm focusing in on the bread aspect of this. The Roman model of taking lands and planting themselves into the fabric of the conquered society by initiating a grain-based society was a deliberate act of subjugation. Grain-based economies are very stratified as a rule, and it's usually the lower elements of society, the dispossessed and more powerless people, who work the fields. I believe the Roman elite saw an opportunity to use Christianity to further the aims of Empire. By adopting Christianity, they could take the thread of Keb, Demeter and Ceres and Jesus would be the new bread god. The new religion would need tweaking but Roman administrators were up to the task.

The dominant religion of Christianity gave a voice to the workers and enslaved, it also celebrated suffering on Earth for the *Bread of Heaven,* as the eighteenth-century Welsh hymnwriter and farmer William Williams put it.

Bread itself has been personified to a large extent, the words we use to describe certain things put in human context. The top

236 | BREAKING BREAD

crust is known as a 'crown', as in crown of a head, and when buying industrial ovens, the height is referred to as 'high crown' or 'low crown'. The bottom crust is a 'sole'. The end crusts are 'heels', all of which justify the fact that the middle of the loaf should be the 'body'. Bread being a person isn't as strange as a person wanting to be bread, though, it seems. Or perhaps the human labels we use have their origins with Jesus?

The Eucharist is the transubstantiation of red wine and bread into the real-life blood and body of Jesus. Well, according to Roman Catholics. The indecision around this spiritual snack contributed to the split between the Roman Catholics and the Orthodox Catholics in 1054, as West and East went in different theological directions. The detail was whether leavened or unleavened bread should be used, with the Eastern Orthodox branch opting for the risen host and the Western Roman faction preferring a wafer-thin representation.

Later the various Protestant denominations characterised themselves by having a direct relationship with God that wasn't mediated (and some would say exploited) by the clergy. The act of turning a hunk of bread into a hunk of godly flesh does seem quite mystical, and the sacrament isn't the transformed body itself but a representational wafer . . . made of rice. The practice can be seen as a sort of inverted sacrifice. So taking Holy Communion today is a complex exercise, a representation of a representation of the body of Christ.

Other major religions see bread as part of life, but are much less focused on it as a whole. It isn't singled out for worship in the same way as it is within Christianity. I went to some Buddhist temples in Vietnam and saw countless comestible offerings at the feet of statues; sweets, fruit, potato chips and all manner of instant ramen packets – but rarely bread.

In the opening pages of the 1970 *The Tassajara Bread Book* by Edward Espe Brown, he says: 'Bread makes itself, by your kindness, with your help, with imagination running through you, with dough under hand, you are breadmaking itself.' This vision of bread as autonomous is quite removed from the Christian idea of bread – perhaps not surprising as Brown is a Zen Buddhist. Here, it is the action of making bread that is humanised. The universal human, not a specific spiritual icon. It's a wonderful thing to be celebrated but only in the context of everything else. No one wants to eat Buddah.

Bread is a pillar of civilisation that major religions have had to accommodate. Some have excluded some breads for some of the time, but I couldn't find any that totally rejected bread. Bread seems to provide strong symbolism for many faiths, the cyclical nature of it. Loaves are born from 'mother' doughs; they represent life and once eaten they give vitality. When a person dies, they are recycled into the soil. When we die, we're 'toast'. I walk through a cemetery with my dog sometimes and often think the shape of headstones look like slices of farmhouse bread.

Once we have become dirt, the wheat feeds on the soil and grows. The wheat is then sacrificed with the harvest and put through the torment of threshing and milling. Eventually that lifeforce is born again into bread. This is the wheel of life, we see in almost every faith – Hinduism, Buddhism, Christianity, Judaism, Islam. Themes of sacrifice, rebirth, resurrection and charity are all bound up in a loaf. I believe our food systems need to recover this cyclical nature, in as many different variations as we can muster.

238 | BREAKING BREAD

There is a set of shelves in a church near to where I live that is meant to provide bread for the poor on a Sunday. A local man by the name of John Sayer put some land in trust, the rents of which were to be used to fill the shelves on the Sabbath 'forever'. Fittingly these lands were in the village of Bredfield. Another man, George Carlow, set out a bread dole in his will, to be distributed from his tomb, to the needy of Woodbridge. The custom of charity taking the form of bread is an old one and I wonder how bread has been used to convert otherwise agnostic, yet hungry, parishioners.

In George Orwell's influential *Down and Out in Paris and London*, written in the early 1930s, he spends time with the poorest of poor and visits many Christian-led charitable institutions which give bread and tea to the needy.

> *We ranged ourselves in the gallery pews and were given our tea; it was a one-pound jam-jar of tea each, with six slices of bread and margarine. As soon as tea was over, a dozen tramps who had stationed themselves near the door bolted to avoid the service; the rest stayed, less from gratitude than lacking the cheek to go. The organ let out a few preliminary hoots and the service began. And instantly, as though at a signal, the tramps began to misbehave in the most outrageous way. One would not have thought such scenes possible in a church.*

Here, Orwell shows the reluctance of these people to attend the religious service, seen as the trade-off for the free or discounted bread and tea. Charity though necessary, is despised. It's the bread that's the sustenance, not the religion. And yet how would Jesus feel about that?

How would he see the big bread factories of today? Making adulterated bread that brings disease rather than life to the 'bread eaters'. I'd argue that we could see a repeat of The Cleansing of the Temple, where he threw out the money changers and merchants. If we ever needed a Second Coming, surely it's now?

I don't know if there was a concerted effort by the Roman Empire to adopt the religion of Christianity and tie it closely to bread. I do know from the evidence that this happened. Bread is such an influential force that it could also be imagined as a parasite that attaches itself to whichever dominant human structure it can. It flowed through ancient Egypt, to ancient Greece, then on to ancient Rome and embedded itself into the roots of the Catholic Church. With the diversification of the bread religion that is Christianity, and its spread through the creation on empire, it has stabilised the place that bread has in the world. It's one of the most successful partnerships in human history.

There are many kinds of religious breads. Ones that are made at specific times to mark times of the year. Some also mark significant moments such as marriages and bread has been part of sacrificial offerings. Equally other foodstuffs have gained this kind of importance, such as cakes, honey, milk, eggs and lamb.

There are examples of bread being linked to death too. There's the Mexican '*pan de muerto*' or 'bread of the dead' to be eaten at the graveside of a loved one and in Maori tradition, a '*Rēwena*', a transliteration of the term 'leaven' or 'bug', is a sweetened sourdough potato bread that is crumbled over the hands to counteract the taboo of visiting the grave of a family member or friend.

240 | BREAKING BREAD

There are a group of breads that symbolise baby Jesus in the womb or swaddling clothes. These include the German stollen, *rosca de reyes* in Spain or the similar *galette de rois* in France. Stollen uses marzipan to represent the Christ child, whereas the other two bake figurines into the cake–breads.

Easter traditions too have a selection of breads, such as the Italian *colomba di pasqua* which I bake every year for Pump Street Bakery. Similar to a panettone, which is a Christmas bread originating in Milan, it is thought to symbolise an ecclesiastical hat. The 'dove of peace' version is studded with candied orange peel and topped with a glaze scattered with almonds.

Easter is the time when celebration breads really come into their own – *paska, kulich, cozonac, pasca, babka, kalach, pinca, tsoureki and paasstol* are among the many, and then there's my personal favourite, the quintessentially British hot cross bun. Sweet, spiced, fruit buns, decorated with a cross and glazed.

Once buttered and served with a cup of strong tea, hot cross buns are majestic. As a child I would anxiously watch them toasting under the grill, their sugariness making them liable to burn if left unattended. Their origins are thought to lie in the Anglo-Saxon celebration of the coming bounty of spring and summer but the canny addition of a cross brought them under the auspices of the Catholic Church.

In Clarissa Dickson Wright's book *A History of English Food* she tells of how Catholic breads were mostly given crosses and the Eucharist breads were stamped. After the Reformation and evolution of the Protestant Church of England under Henry VIII, the crosses had to go but the ones on the buns made on Good Friday and handed out to the poor could remain. I am often asked why these buns have crosses on them, but it's more a case that they didn't have the crosses taken off them.

Other breads like Matzoh, as I've mentioned, mark the festival of Passover, and I would argue constitute one of the original sandwiches. Hillel the Elder ate a sandwich of soft Matzoh, roasted lamb and bitter herbs around the time Jesus was performing his own bread miracles. Yes, I did just refer to the sandwich as a bread miracle.

Our fascination with bread miracles might have something to do with our ceaseless efforts to produce massive amounts of bread in no time at all. When Jesus performed the miracle of multiplying five barley loaves and two fish to feed five thousand people (with leftovers), it wasn't a white sliced loaf, but rather a metaphor. Yet, perhaps our commitment to buying industrialised bread, churned out by the million, is in some way related to this dream of never-ending bread. At what cost though?

I am fascinated with the ways in which bread has been knitted into our spiritual lives. For something that can seem so simple – three humble ingredients at its essence – it has been elevated to the heavens. A food of the poor and sacrament of the highest priest, a foodstuff that Jesus himself claimed to be in John 6:35. Yet its importance is more than that. On a practical level, bread brings people together, allows warring factions to sit side by side and break bread. It is this congregating of people that is the first step not just in the practice of worship, but in breaking down barriers.

A few free slices can muster a churchful of reluctant vagabonds, as in George Orwell's example. It can help break the fast during Ramadan in a shared meal, as Zara told me, or remind us of Jesus' life and teachings in the Orthodox Christian faith. Whichever

242 | BREAKING BREAD

religion it plays a part in, it is important. Bread is a central and important food, a staple of life, and yet so much more than that, as we see time and time again.

Matthew's testament tells us that Jesus said: '*Man shall not live by bread alone, but by every word that proceedeth out of the mouth of God.*' This statement doesn't cheapen bread's importance but magnifies it. Jesus is saying I know bread is the thing you think is the most important, just don't forget about faith, too.

Bread may not be godly or religiously significant on its own, but it gathers the crowd. And once together, breaking bread together, sharing it, bread provides the opportunity for us to discuss how we might live our lives. Freed from hunger, our minds can wander into the spiritual desert to find those things that give meaning to birth, life and death, a path that we can follow to create better worlds, whatever bread we hold in our hands, whichever god we hold in our hearts.

10

Breaking Bread

A once ropey baker looks to the future

It is said that mourning, by its gradual labour, slowly erases pain; I could not, I cannot believe this; because for me, Time eliminates the emotion of loss (I do not weep), that is all. For the rest, everything has remained motionless.

– Roland Barthes, *Camera Lucida: Reflections on Photography* (1980)

There is a photograph that haunts me. I'm on my haunches with my two-year old son and seven-year old step-daughter beside me, halfway through cleaning a mixer for the final time. Forced smiles fill the frame as my wife captures the moment. Like clowns at a funeral, it all seems incongruous. In fairness, Wilfred looks genuinely happy, which is all the more heartbreaking.

I'd been trying to keep the bakery open since returning to the business nine years before, in 2012. I had overseen its slow death and felt ultimately responsible for its closure after seventy-five years in my family, although so many factors had, in reality, led to its demise. But I was left with the feeling of failure, and now, with

244 | BREAKING BREAD

crippling debts the hard work of three generations had been lost, it seemed. The question was: what did the future hold?

The intensity of the situation ripped through the family and left relationships in tatters. Bonds that I had assumed unconditional, revealed themselves to be dependent on the bakery. It was bread that had held us together and now that that was gone, we had no reason to be united. We were adrift.

We had enjoyed some success, but I had been swimming against the tide for the last years. My vision was for a bakery making 'real bread' like my father had told me was important when I was a child and infatuated with the business. Slow fermented loaves with flavour and heart. And yet I'd been told at every turn that it wouldn't work by the bakers I'd inherited, the ones my parents were insistent I kept on but whose priorities, it turned out, were at odds with my family's.

While I was making Bakewell Tarts for *Vogue* and tapping into Harrods with my supplier card in London, Dad and Mum had stepped back from the bakery in Suffolk. I found out later their trusted bakers had been taking kickbacks from the representatives of the industrial bakery sector, filling the dry stores with bread mixes, tubs of readymade icing and bags of what they called 'gunpowder' – the mix of dough conditioning additives that are so derided by Chris Young and the Real Bread Campaign.

The shop staff were suspicious of the additive-free bread I made, buying white-sliced batches from the store instead of taking any of my loaves home at the end of the day. We had been employing some of these people for years and my parents insisted they must stay, despite their public defamation of the new products we made and sold. My sister, Lindsay, and I entered competitions to attempt to convince our colleagues that we might be onto something.

However, taking home World Bread Awards, Great Taste Awards, a prize for Britain's Best Baker and even the trophy on a television bakery competition wasn't enough. I had failed to deliver the message home, and my ageing parents didn't want to rock the boat. So, we didn't swim but sank. Every other bakery I've worked at has been a success, but this one, the one that mattered most, it went down in a ball of flames.

I painstakingly reproduced all the synthetic products with proper ingredients so that the customers could continue to buy the loaves they loved. These new versions cost more to make and took more time. It would have been an embarrassment to admit how far our standards had slipped so my parents kept the prices the same. We tried to save money where possible, family members even working for less than minimum wage in an attempt to balance the books. In hindsight, it was obvious where we were heading, that what was there was already broken, well beyond saving.

I was the only baker on that night the photo was taken; as the wheels came off, the others had peeled away. My little family were there beside me, and for them the outcome was probably for the best. My kids would grow up with a dad who could be around and take them to school and I would be a presence in their lives, not a shadow. At the time, though, it was hard to see past the obvious failure I felt. It was my hands that had to pull the last loaves of bread from the oven and my face in the local paper explaining why it had all come crashing down.

If I hadn't needed the money, I'm not sure I'd have ever have set foot inside another bakery again. My confidence and heart were fractured by what had happened. Even though so many factors had played into the end of the family business, I couldn't help but feel I'd failed, losing not just all I had, but everything the family had built up since my grandparents made the journey south from Northumberland, in 1946. But, there were bills to pay and my own little family to sustain, so I took a job at a bakery nearby. It was the best decision ever. And I owe so much to Chris and Joanna Brennan at Pump Street Bakery for taking a punt on me. No doubt, many had cautioned them about me, about my failures, but they decided to see for themselves if I had any talent.

There are certain strains of bacteria that cause something called 'ropiness' in bread, the result is that the crust remains intact, but the crumb turns to soup, something I've referenced before. You only realise something is wrong when you cut a loaf open, and it oozes out all over the bread board. This was more common before the industrialisation of bread and for a long time was unheard of – but it is returning as contemporary bakers reject the additives that keep it at bay. I was a ropey baker. My crust was holding up, but inside I was a mess. Bread had broken me. Slowly, I regained my confidence at Pump Street, as I realised the bakers respected me and listened to me. That I had something to contribute. I began to believe once more that there was a future for bread, and for me in it. In 2022, I was a very small part of a brilliant team that won the *Observer Food Monthly* Best Producer Award. For me, that was huge: we had won; I hadn't ruined it for everyone else. Perhaps now I could believe what my loved ones had told me: I wasn't completely to blame for the disintegration of the family business, after all?

This is what got me thinking about all the ways in which bread is broken. We should have succeeded for many reasons, and yet we didn't. Part of that was because the game was rigged from the start. For my family's bread to move forward, we had to examine its past, follow the crumbs as far back as we could. The old paths had something to tell us. And I realised that relates to everything, not just my family. We must look back in order to move forward.

So, where do we go from here? Where do I go from here? After examining bread's influence, the many ways it has shaped our world and the people in it, what are the next steps? I have no doubt that the current system is broken. I know that from personal experience, but my journey to this point, the people I've spoken with, the research I've done, has endorsed that. It's too narrow, too flabby and over-extended. This system has birthed a global population that is now hard to handle. There has to be another way of feeding over eight billion people, surely? But what? How? Huge questions.

In Belgium, there is a library that could hold some of the answers. It doesn't hold books, but cultures. Sourdough cultures. Every library has a librarian and here it is Karl De Smedt, The Sourdough Librarian, as he's known. A friendly man, the passion he has for bread evident, as it is in all the people I've spoken to, over the course of this journey, Karl is well-groomed, with stylish glasses and a neat salt-and-pepper beard. He reminds me a bit of a Schnauzer, in the best possible way.

When I ask Karl to comment on what 'bread' is, what it means to him, his answer comes immediately. 'To me, bread is one of the most amazing human inventions. It's such a complex thing to bring water and flour to life. When you make sourdough bread, where you have living organisms, lactic acid bacteria that take care of the digestion – you make one of the most amazing foods ever produced by humans in all of history.' *One of the most amazing foods ever produced by humans.* So true.

248 | BREAKING BREAD

'If there's no bread on the table – something is missing,' he continues with the air of a priest hammering home the theme of his sermon. 'You can have all sorts of different things on the table, wine, cheeses, meats – but if you have no bread, these things don't combine. Not really. Bread brings everything together.'

This is a light bulb moment. I've spent a lot of time considering exactly that, how bread connects people, but Karl shows how it can also bring other foods together. The sandwich in this sense becomes a meeting place for ingredients. Bread can be a synapse between foods, just as it can between people, bringing combinations that shouldn't work together and sometimes creating something bigger, better than the sum of just themselves. These three pure ingredients that lie at bread's heart have so much to answer for, so much potential.

Karl works for Puratos, one of the biggest industrial food companies in the world. At its hundred-year anniversary, the company had turned-over two billion euros. I mention this because when I chatted to Karl, it felt like I was talking to a representative of an artisan movement rather than someone involved in a billion-euro business.

The company message is simple: 'The future of bread lies in its past.' Not the recent past either, Karl explains. He is looking back hundreds of years, before we took, what he believes, is a collective wrong turn onto the path that has led us to a dead end. 'I know what the problem is,' he tells me. 'We were trained to make the maximum amount of bread in the minimum amount of time. The introduction of commercial yeast began the white-washing of the baker's mind.' But what does he mean by that?

Commercial yeast isn't in itself a bad thing, yet Karl sees it as representing a desire to speed-up a process that needs time to achieve its nutritional potential, something we're in agreement with. More bread in less time has come at the expense of both quality and health, as we've seen throughout this book. I'm reminded of Upton Sinclair's 1905 novel, *The Jungle*, in which the meat-packing industry speeds up the line, resulting in workers getting worn out and products becoming unsafe and adulterated. Karl compares the baking industry as a whole to those of wine, cheese, beer and coffee, stating: 'In the bakery industry we are thirty to fifty years behind.'

He explains how those other industries have managed to continue maintaining their ability to communicate quality to their customers. The baker, however, is 'a ghost', working at night, never seeing another soul. In the morning, when our customers come into a shop, we are too tired to explain why our breads are worth the extra effort and the extra expense required, a fact I know too well from my own experiences.

It also tallies with what food writer and baker Dan Lepard told me about his time working at Baker and Spice in London. He wanted to leave before the customers arrived. He was tired and couldn't face the questions, the requests or minor complaints when he had sacrificed a night's sleep to furnish the bakery shelves with warm bread. I have felt that, too. How can a customer understand the effort we put into making these loaves? Why should they believe the mumblings of a baker, all bloodshot eyes and drunk with fatigue? Bakers at the end of night shifts are not good ambassadors for our own bread. Believe me. Compare this to a crisp-looking sommelier or barista, fresh from a good sleep, able to discuss the terroir, mouthfeel and flavour notes of wines or coffee with passion. When bread went against the clock and production was measured in numbers rather than quality, the

250 | BREAKING BREAD

game changed for us. It's not the same. It should be but it's a different playing field. But does it have to be? There are bakers who I've met who are changing things.

Karl opened The Sourdough Library in 2013 and holds hundreds of cultures from all over the world. 'Each starter might share 80 per cent of the same characteristics,' he explains. 'It will produce CO_2, it will acidify your dough, but it's the other 20 per cent where each sourdough is different. This is what intrigues me.' He has high aims, hoping to understand the elements of these microbial soups to an extent where it will have a universal effect on the bread we eat.

'By doing this research, I believe we will be capable of making the best bread ever produced in human history. Not just in flavour but digestibility too.' The unflinching conviction in Karl's words is evident. 'Using DNA technology we can select the best micro-organisms for breadmaking.' The age of super-starters may be just around the corner.

I wonder if the people who developed commercial yeast at the end of the nineteenth century shared these very same aims, selecting yeast strains that would lift bakers from their toil, that might allow the decrepit figures who made bread some respite by speeding up the process? Yet in doing so, in all the progress we have made, good intentions may have led to the degradation of the bread itself, and by extension, how bakers live and work. So, how is Karl's mission going to be any different?

Imagine a grain-to-loaf bread machine that apes the bean-to-cup coffee makers. A hopper of single origin grain, precisely milled and made into a dough and baked, all while the owner of such a contraption sleeps. There could be a section that holds a sourdough starter at the optimum temperature. We'd probably have to sacrifice half our kitchen counter space and a few months wages but we'd surely be the envy of bread eaters everywhere?

'The main function of The Sourdough Library is to preserve the biodiversity of bread,' Karl states firmly. 'We know that biodiversity is important for the future.' This is a powerful statement coming from a representative of an industrial giant such as Puratos. But if industrial forces begin to target the quality market, this, surely, will push craft bakeries further into the margins? Karl disagrees. 'Artisan bakers have not paid enough attention to their bread,' he says simply.

I agree with him where, in some instances, small bakeries have become satellites of the chem-bread industry – attempting to compete with factories on price, and producing bread that is an imitation of a supermarket loaf.

'Artisans have three main advantages over the industrial bakeries,' Karl states. 'Freshness, Customer Interaction and flexibility. Artisans must leverage these to stay in competition with industry. Not price. On price, they will never compete.' But does that matter, when people are already paying for the much higher price for smaller batch, better quality, more sustainably produced artisan loaves? It's just that not all people can afford to do that.

Karl isn't fussed who or what makes his bread as long as the quality is exceptional. It could be a machine, a robot or a human. 'In the future, [the] industry will be able to make fully artisan bread.' In other words, if the artisans want to stay relevant, then quality will be at the forefront. There are many excellent bakeries out there, but we need more and we need to shift the focus of how consumers see bread.

For Karl, 'artisan' is certainly a quality indicator and this is perhaps where our views differ. When I look at an artisan or

252 | BREAKING BREAD

craft loaf of bread I'm buying, even if the bread is being made by a machine I want a sense of the person who operates it. I want to see beyond the end product to the individual behind. But does everyone? Perhaps I'm in a minority.

Karl finishes by saying, 'The bakers of the world, big, small or medium, should find a way to make people aware that bread isn't just a stomach filler, but is something that can be a pleasure to eat. It can be nutritional. You can feed a family on good bread for five pounds. How much meat can you buy for [the equivalent]? Not enough to feed a family.' And yet, that makes it all the more important that the bread we make, bake and eat is made from the very best and purest of ingredients. And this goes back to what bakers like Ben Glazer (see page 151) are trying to do.

It's clear that Karl De Smedt wants to have an impact on bread generally and his attention to the nutritional quality of the loaves he makes and eats is a big shift. Industry has up to now been concerned with the volume of bread, both in numbers and airiness, its softness and image. None of those aims has served the people eating that bread. The ideal of seeking quality and nutrition may yet reinstate bread to its place as the 'King of the Table', but only if we advocate for transparency about what goes into it.

The simple truth is that bread needs a relaunch. Sales are going down steadily, as more people eye the bakery aisle with suspicion. Here there can be only one solution. Whoever makes our bread, whether this is supermarket, in-store or craft bakery, should provide information on every ingredient that has been used in the process. Including the processing aids and enzymes that governments, such as our own, deem unnecessary to disclose to the very people who consume it.

Bakery environments need to become more enticing for anyone who wants to work in them. The changes are taking place, and, with the bakery sector seeing a big increase in diversity, it is clear to me that there is a strong link between that diversification and the increase in quality. Many head bakers of the best bakeries in the world are women, a fact that wouldn't have been the norm twenty years ago – certainly not in the UK. My father was threatened by his all white, all male, all English team that if he hired any women or 'foreigners', God forbid, they would all walk out in protest. In retrospect, he missed out on some great opportunities. The world is full of bakers of all descriptions, all genders, races, sexualities and we can all learn from each other, as the changes being made in our industry by companies like Wildfarmed show.

We are also seeing more home bakers as the costs involved in making bread continue to soar. Consumers' access to great bread may well come from their own hands. The skills needed to make good bread at home were once universal, not just a matter of necessity but recipes shared from generation to generation, often through our mothers and grandmothers over the kitchen table. In some cases they have skipped a couple of generations or are being lost through conflicts and forced migration. We need to share that knowledge though, or it will be forgotten.

When I catch up with Martha De Lacey, a former journalist turned 'bread dork' (her words) who teaches people to make sourdough in her London home, I ask her my usual question, what comes to mind when 'bread' is mentioned? 'A hot piece of toast, covered in butter,' she replies immediately, the sounds of her baby happily gurgling away coming through the monitor. (It reminds me of the time I took my own little girl to one of Martha's supper clubs, and left her sleeping in a bedroom with a monitor on the table, next to my napkin. She didn't sleep for long, awoken by the delicious smells and spent the duration of supper on my knee, face covered in food!) As a fellow lover of toast though, Martha's description has my full backing. She fleshes out the picture further: 'I have always been obsessed with toast which is why I got into bread. I imagine a slice of toasted sourdough with cartoonish steam coming off the top. I've loved toast ever since I was a child.'

I've spoken to many people while researching this book and asked them all to tell me what they think about when they hear the word 'bread', the loaf they imagine. I confess that when I started doing it, I wasn't entirely sure why, it was more a comfort thing, I guess, to see if my loaf matched anyone else's. But as I've listened to more and more stories, I've noticed how revealing they are, how what's told to me is often a way of placing people. For many, that question has taken them back to childhood, to home, a feeling of safety, a loving place. I've been asking for a picture of bread and in return I've been getting a window into how people see goodness, nourishment, their loved ones, nostalgia, family. The notion of bread, the meaning of it to so many of us, that's important.

If we want to change eating habits then we must concentrate on these childhood experiences, the power they have lasts a lifetime and beyond, influencing future generations. The Japanese government knows this and invests heavily in healthy school meals that are mandatory. They are one of the only economically developed nations that doesn't have a problem with higher rates of obesity. Dan Giusti, former head chef at the world's best restaurant, Noma, recognises this too. He has set up Brigaid in the US, with the aim of getting more skilled chefs into institutional kitchens.

While Noma catered for an elite food audience, Dan's charity, Brigaid, targets the most vulnerable, initially school children but now the elderly and people in the prison system, through outreach programmes. His team of professional chefs uses their culinary skills to help institutional services shine. They make the bread, the pizza dough and the focaccia, passing vital knowledge and healthy products on. We need a Brigaid in every country, cementing healthy food as our national love language. Imagine the impact.

I ask Martha how bread in our home kitchens differs from bakery-bought loaves. 'The bread you make at home...can be experimental. It can also fail more easily and be more surprising, but you love it because you made it yourself – even if it isn't very good.'

It's a magical process to take a clay of flour, water and salt and turn it into delicious bread – or toast, if you're Martha. She is hooked on the buzz that comes her way when students fall in love with breadmaking. 'It's completely mad.'

Most of Martha's students are women and I am curious to see why she thinks that is. 'I think men want to learn from a "baker" in a "bakery". They don't necessarily want to go to a girl's house and make bread in her kitchen.' Martha goes onto explain some differences she has seen in the gender of her students, 'In my class, I always joke that men are really obsessed with hydration and holes. Of course, if you use really white roller-milled flour you can get loads of water into it. It doesn't make you a better baker,' she finishes wryly.

I agree. When I've taught in the past, my large male body seems to act as a green light for them to regale me with their baking exploits and the high hydration doughs they have mastered. This is the kind of peacocking you can see splashed all

256 | BREAKING BREAD

over social media but many of the really amazing bakers I know opt for a closer, more nutritious crumb. If your holes are so big that you end up with a table covered in jam, then your bread isn't doing its job.

There are a few exceptions. A baguette should have a chewy, creamy crumb with an open texture and gets away with it because the bottom crust acts as a barrier to keep everything in place. The same goes for one of the 1980s' finest innovations, ciabatta, which was made by Italians who viewed the baguette with jealousy but couldn't bring themselves to adopt it. The focaccia is perhaps the finest example of an open-crumbed success story, the oily crust wrapping everything up while also acting as a hand moisturiser. The Genovese answer to a Cornish pasty.

'Bakeries probably weren't calm, nice places to work historically – they were loud, rough and aggressive,' Martha tells me. My own experience backs her statement up, thinking back to my teenage time working in my father's bakery, the machismo, sexism and racism. I've been in many bakeries that are like male locker rooms. Bawdy, working men's clubs that shield themselves from integrating into the rest of society by emphasising the hard work, the long hours and sacrifice. Martha thinks that women are taking over the commercial baking sphere, moving from the private to public spheres, and trade seems to be booming as a result.

I ask if she thinks that artisan bread is going out of fashion. 'Judging by the number of sourdough bakeries that spring up every week, I don't think the interest in artisan bread is waning. I think people are more obsessed with bread than ever.' And Martha points out that even when people can't eat wheat, they still want bread. They haven't rejected this historic foodstuff, just a specific form of it.

As international and domestic events paint a gloomy scene, Martha again thinks this will reinforce the power that bread has over us. She muses that 'bread is the first thing people turn to in a crisis because it feels safe. If you can bake your own bread, you have control over something – and if you can master it, you feel powerful in a turbulent world.' And I've seen that in different forms, during the making of this book, through the people I've met, the conversations I've had, the research I've done into the subject – bread is life for so many people, the heart and soul of cultures, religions, for many their very survival.

No generation has ever been as informed about their food, where it comes from, what's in it, as we are. The question is, what do we do with that information? The boomers grew up in a glut of ultra-processed food that was a fix for the fear of food shortages. Today the fear that most of us have in the Western world is that of an excess of food, calorie-rich, nutritionally devoid and ultra-processed.

The breadline has long been seen as a marker of financial and other security, but perhaps we need to think of it more simply, as a nutritional line. We have the best bakers that have ever lived, baking now. We can demand more of our bread and the farmers, millers and bakers will be only too happy to show off their skills. The currency of bread has become devalued, and we must do more to protect it. It should be forbidden to sell a loaf of bread for less than it costs to make. That would stop big business selling cheaper, lower-grade products and also prevent them from pushing smaller independents out of the marketplace, which has happened time and time again. When bread is used as a value indicator for consumers, its price should be based on solid foundations. The volatile markets we live with today are built on the quicksand of loss leading.

258 | BREAKING BREAD

Artisans must share their knowledge with industry to maximise the impact that bread can have. Nutritionally beneficial bread shouldn't be the preserve of the elite – good bread is a human right. The artisans and industry will come together, I believe, to create a solution for the pappy bread-like imitation we have put up with until now. The media often don't help by driving a wedge between them, as a 2024 article in the British newspaper the *Guardian* showed, when it referred to 'bread wars' between sourdough and Chorleywood processes. 'Pick a side,' it seemed to say, serving only to ruffle feathers.

The ways of making bread should not define social classes, and by serving up sourdough as a hoity-toity bread, it acts only to detract from the additive-infested loaves that line our supermarkets. We should be protecting our baking terms better too. If we buy a sourdough loaf we should get a sourdough loaf. If we are the proud bread eaters we profess to be, then let's demand an honest crust.

Governments will often tell citizens to make healthy choices yet flatly refuse to make ingredient information available to those same citizens, as previously discussed. We are collectively spending billions of dollars globally on medication for 'preventable' diseases. These diseases are often preventable only if consumers have access to the truth about their food. I don't mind what kind of bread you eat, but I think you have a right to make that choice based on having all the facts. That's 'choice'.

Bread has shaped the world we inhabit. It's been used in many controlling and aggressive ways, but these dark shadows have solutions. Countries with many smaller bakeries are more robust than those with fewer huge operations. If I were going to fight a war with the UK, I would target bread factories like those

BREAKING BREAD | 259

of Warburton's and Hovis straight away, knowing that it would send the country into a panic. We need more bakeries and they are opening, but they need support – and, let's be frank, they deserve it.

Whichever way you slice it, running a small business is hard work and bakeries are some of the toughest in that category, as I know from personal experience. If consumers change their habits and wholesale customers don't all demand their bread at seven in the morning, then small bakeries can support communities' lives without costing the baker their own. So, if you see a small bakery in your neighbourhood, buy something every now and then – they are good things to have around, often doing far more than just feeding people.

Religion can divide us but so many of the major ones share a love of bread, we can at least agree on that. Bread is representative of so much good and can be something to celebrate. We are so often given a window into a religion through its food and bread can help us understand each other, our values and stories. Whether challah, Matzoh, panettone, hoe cakes, johnny cakes, injera, chapatis or tortillas – every bread has a story to share. We should break bread together more often and eat more consciously so that we nourish our souls, and those of the people around us, as well as our bodies.

I set out at the beginning of this book to understand bread better and to look at my own relationship with this foodstuff that has defined my life and that of my family's, causing much joy and much strife. I wanted to understand the power that bread has not just over me, but over the world. How bread has shaped it, shaped us and how we can shape bread in turn to help our futures.

I don't believe my personal failings were a result of wanting to make nutritious bread, which was an aim for me starting out.

260 | BREAKING BREAD

They were, in part, due to the environment in which this bread was being made and my inability to change it. I wasn't strong enough to steer my family's history in a new direction, or possibly recognise that when I tried to do that, it was already too late. But that doesn't mean it's too late for bread, that the way we make it, the ingredients we use, the methods, are all doomed. Far from it. The people I've encountered and journey I've been on in this book show that there is a positive need and want for bread to be better and, by extension, for us to have more healthy, more sustainable futures.

This has been a book about bread and bakeries, but so much of it is true of the other foods we eat. If bread can get out of shape, then it can happen to any of our staples. If bread can turn its fortunes around, then it can provide an example to the whole food system. It is a keystone food. We will be judged by future generations as to what happens next, our decisions or lack of them impacting not just on our own systems, own bodies, but the very planet we live in, if we have a planet. So, what do we do? There isn't one answer.

Everything in a bakery is a cycle, a continuous wheel of birth, life, death and resurrection. No one day can stand alone, no one generation can live apart from the previous or next. From the ashes will come green shoots of life, and the bread we have broken will be made again, fresh, anew. Yesterday's dough is today's bread and tomorrow's toast. Our lives will go on, one way or another, with bread in our bellies. I believe that.

Acknowledgements

This all started with Rich Myers. The man behind the wheel of Get Baked posted on Instagram about his own journey and the struggles he had with getting a bakery business to work. Rich's personal account touched me at a time when I was feeling particularly defeated; perhaps mine too was a story worth telling? I had Rich's book *Get Baked* (mainly so I could have a go at making his world famous chocolate cake Bertha - née Bruce) and noticed it was published by White Lion Publishing. I liked this because it reminded me of the pub in Ufford, Suffolk that hosts a great fireworks show every November.

I sent a DM on April 10th to White Lion Publishing with very little information, just that I had an idea for a book. Jessica Axe responded on 4th May and asked me to send her the idea which I duly did. Even to get to this point was a minor miracle but when I sent the proposal for a nonfiction narrative book about bread this fell outside of Jessica's domain, so she sent it on to colleagues at Aurum. She didn't need to do that and it would have been perfectly acceptable to give me a swift 'thanks but no thanks' and

262 | BREAKING BREAD

move on. It somehow made it in front of Richard Green and after a few calls we had the bones of the book you are now holding. Turns out he had been wanting to publish a book like this for a while but hadn't found the right food. Bread always brings people together it seems.

I'd like to thank everyone at Quarto but especially those who have been so kind and generous to me. Richard and his team at Aurum have helped build this book and it's been a pleasure to see them work. Nothing of any significance in this world is the result of one individual and publishing is a team sport. Richard Green, Charlotte Frost, Phoebe Bath and Liz Somers have all been a joy to work with and without them none of these pages would exist. My copyeditor on this book, Aruna Vasudevan, has played a huge part in shaping this story and I'd like to thank her for the way she challenged me to dig deeper into my experience so that it might enrich the book. Lisa Maltby did such a wonderful job on the cover so special thanks to her too.

I didn't have an agent when I began the process of getting the book off the ground but Claudia Young at Greene & Heaton has provided me with invaluable support through the process. I hope we go on to work together for many more books to come.

I have to thank all the people who contributed to this book, all the bakers, millers, farmers, doctors and professors. If you are one of those who gave up your time to speak with me, know that I am so grateful. Most of you are featured in the book but some aren't and yet everybody helped me create this story of bread. Special thanks go to Oliver Hornsey-Pennell who opened his home and his contact book to me – one day I'll send you some chocolate I promise.

ACKNOWLEDGEMENTS | 263

Josh Jones is the best. His magazines are better. Without his encouragement I wouldn't have had the confidence to start this book. He let me write articles for *Sandwich Magazine* and gave me the nudge I needed to spread my bready wings. I have also to thank Christian Stevenson and Chris Taylor who have both been so supportive and encouraging. Christian and Chris helped me by collaborating on our book *Backyard Baking* and if anyone gets credit for seeing a writer in me it is these two. I'll always remember reading chapters of this book to you in a tent at Big Feastival to get you off to sleep.

I must give a special thank you to Jo and Chris Brennan at Pump Street Bakery, but also to everyone there and at Pump Street Chocolate too. During a tough time for me I was able to rebuild myself and it was due in no small part to the support and trust I was given. Together we have created Pump Street Workshop where we can share all our collective knowledge with the public.

I have some wonderful friends and many of them have helped me with this book: Nik, Clara, Doug, Tim and Jack – you are my treasure trove. Special thanks to the last two on that list, Jack Cooke who is a wonderful writer has helped me to find my voice and shared his experience so generously. Then there's Tim, I can't think of any time you haven't been there for me. You have pushed me and nurtured a creativity in me that has brought purpose to my days. I can never repay that.

And my own story is also the story of my family. Without my grandparents, parents and sisters I would have no story to tell. Special thanks go to my Mum, Christine for always being my fiercest champion and filling our home full of books. Thanks to Lindsay too for reading me those books and Sophie for encouraging me to perform and play.

264 | BREAKING BREAD

One teacher in particular needs some recognition, my high school English teacher Mrs Hudson who took the time to notice the love I have for words. Thank you for giving me permission to explore that passion.

My principal inspiration is my own little family, especially Billie who has supported me through some trying times. Thank you for buying me a computer (that works) so I could follow my dream. You are the kindest person I know and I hope I can make you proud, if not by writing this book then in some other way. My children, 'The Rats', three people who stretch me and for whom I have bottomless love and pride. When I thought of the daunting task of putting down seventy-thousand words it was my children who spurred me on – how could I tell them to go after their dreams if I wouldn't go after my own? Lastly I must thank Nina (Nines, Ninells, Scruffle-face), our dog. She provided me with the structure I needed to get the book written with her clockwork desire for walks and food.